– A True Story –

Most
Dangerous

Sherwood Kent

Published by:
Trine Day LLC
PO Box 577
Walterville, OR 97489
1-800-556-2012
www.TrineDay.com
publisher@TrineDay.net

Library of Congress Control Number: 2015948425

Kent, Sherwood.
Most Dangerous—1st ed.
p. cm.

Epud (ISBN-13) 978-1-63424-041-3
Mobi (ISBN-13) 978-1-63424-042-0
Print (ISBN-13) 978-1-63424-040-6
1. John F. Kennedy Assassination. 2. Psychological warfare -- United States
-- History -- 21st century. 3. Occultism -- Political aspects -- United States. 4.
Secret societies -- United States. 5. Conspiracies -- United States. 6. Political
corruption -- United States. I. Kent, Sherwood. II. Title

FIRST EDITION
10 9 8 7 6 5 4 3 2 1

Printed in the USA
Distribution to the Trade by:
Independent Publishers Group (IPG)
814 North Franklin Street
Chicago, Illinois 60610
312.337.0747
www.ipgbook.com

ONCE UPON A TIME

The conscious and intelligent manipulation of the organized habits and opinions of the masses is an important element in democratic society. Those who manipulate this unseen mechanism of society constitute an invisible government which is the true ruling power of our country.... We are governed, our minds are molded, our tastes formed, our ideas suggested, largely by men we have never heard of. This is a logical result of the way in which our democratic society is organized. Vast numbers of human beings must cooperate in this manner if they are to live together as a smoothly functioning society.... In almost every act of our daily lives, whether in the sphere of politics or business, in our social conduct or our ethical thinking, we are dominated by the relatively small number of persons ... who understand the mental processes and social patterns of the masses. It is they who pull the wires which control the public mind.

– Edward L. Bernays, *Propaganda*

Edible substances evoke the secretion of thick, concentrated saliva. Why? The answer, obviously, is that this enables the mass of food to pass smoothly through the tube leading from the mouth into the stomach.

– Ivan Pavlov

Most men, after a little freedom, have preferred authority with the consoling assurances and the economy of effort it brings.

Walter Lippmann

Hollywood is a place where they pay you $50,000 for a kiss and 50¢ for your soul.

Marilyn Monroe

Youthful idylls, cut bare by flim-flam shenanigans partnered with the constant meme-drama-drone of apocalypse and jubilee, are seemingly cut short. Out of the ashes ... a new covert slavery is being birthed.

We now live in much different world than we were born into.

Where it stops ... nobody knows?

This book, *Most Dangerous*, is a tale of aftereffects – from the writing of Kent Bain's book, *The Most Dangerous Book in the World,* to the consequences of years of psychological abuse directed at the American people.

From sales techniques to sophisticated political control, the American population has been and is being subjected to massive amounts of propaganda and psychological manipulation – meme warfare.

What is a meme? According to the *Urban Dictionary*: [1] An idea, belief or belief system, or pattern of behavior that spreads throughout a culture either vertically by cultural inheritance (as by parents to children) or horizontally by cultural acquisition (as by peers, information media, and entertainment media). [2] A pervasive thought or thought pattern that replicates itself via cultural means; a parasitic code, a virus of the mind especially contagious to children and the impressionable. [3] The fundamental unit of information, analogous to the gene in emerging evolutionary theory of culture.

Sherwood Kent examines the arena using images, words and humor in this commentary about today's pressure-cooker bombastics that overwhelm us with cultural effrontery emblazoned across our shared consciousness daily.

A sly attempt to foist upon us a contrived reality based not upon mutual liberties and freedoms, but through the deliberate and conscious manipulation of personhood – thralldom. As Goethe, stated: "The best slave is the one who thinks he is free."

Time is a-coming, time when we must make choices, to kneel in fealty to the corporate masters, genuflecting on cue in our assigned roles … or do we stand up? Be human beings with the courage and understanding that what we accomplish is: Mankind's future.

Many excuses are used to do nothing, to disengage from our responsibilities. But as Krishna in the *Bhagavad Gita* says, "Shake off this base faint-heartedness and arise, O scorcher of enemies!" And as Christ scourged the moneychangers in the temple decrying it, "A den of thieves."

Now is the time for all good men and women to come to the aid of their country!

So please take our slaughtered president's words below to heart, and understand … *you* can make a difference. The future is yet to be made!

Things do not happen. Things are made to happen.
                                                           – John F. Kennedy

Onward to the Utmost of Futures,
Peace,
Kris Millegan
Publisher
TrineDay
August 18, 2015

TABLE OF CONTENTS

PART ONE

AND SO IT BEGINS

Prologue by **Peter Levenda,** author of *Sinister Forces*

The Most Dangerous Book in the World

9/11 as Mass Ritual

INCLUDES EXTRA BOOK: *The Next 9/11? — A Work of Predictive Fiction*

S.K. Bain

CHAPTER 1

HITTING HOME

September 30, 2013: Blue Mountain, Mississippi

11:10 P.M. – William's mother, Amy, kneels on the con-crete floor of the garage, cradling her 16-year-old son's head and broad shoulders in her arms as his taught torso stretches out in front of her. He is having a grand mal sei-zure, his first, and as his 220-pound frame jerks violently and he gasps desperately for air, his father, Kent, can only watch in horror.

Amy works in mental health and has seen patients having grand mal seizures; Kent had never seen one in real life, and, even if he had, it wouldn't have prepared him for the sight of his only son writhing helplessly on the ground.

"Can we get him in the car?" Kent implored his ex-wife, knowing that it might take an ambulance some time to reach them in their small, rural northeast Mississippi community. The seizure hadn't begun as a full-blown grand mal, and they'd been trying to get William to the car when he'd gone completely rigid and began convulsing.

"No," answered Amy in a reassuringly calm voice, "call 911."

"Are you sure?" Kent replied with growing desperation.

At that moment, William, who had been struggling for air, suddenly ceased breathing altogether. *My God*, Kent thought, was he watching his son die? After what seemed like minutes, Will jerked and drew one short breath, then another. He began gasping in air, slowly relaxed and started breathing again—not normally, but at least he was breathing.

Kent ran into the house and dialed 911. As he paced anxiously back and forth at the end of their street waiting for the ambulance, he could only wonder what had just happened. Resting in his mother's arms, Will was breathing, but completely motionless and unresponsive.

When the paramedics finally arrived, Will was somewhat alert, but had an alarmingly uncomprehending stare in his eyes and resisted the rescue workers as they attempted to take his vital signs and establish an I.V. He couldn't speak and reacted like a frightened animal.

Having barely gotten over the specter of his son seemingly dying before his eyes only minutes earlier, Kent was now faced with the very real possibility that his son might have some type of brain damage due to lack of oxygen or the seizure itself.

As the ambulance drove off with Amy sitting beside her son in the back, Kent hurried inside to grab the car keys. He made sure not to follow the ambulance too closely, and as he drove, the freshly imprinted image of his son taking what could have been his last breath replayed in a continuous loop in Kent's mind.

This was Will's first grand mal, his third seizure altogether. The two previous episodes, though frightening, had been far less severe. The first had happened on the evening of September 11, 2013, just a few weeks earlier.

As he drove into the darkness, Kent had the awful realization that he might well know why all this had happened—and it had everything to do with the date of William's first seizure.

11:55 P.M. – By the time the ambulance arrived at the emergency room ten minutes away in Ripley, William had already become more alert and coherent. After Kent completed registration and walked into the examining room, he was filled with relief to see that familiar spark in Will's eyes and hear his voice. William didn't remember much of the last hour, but, *Thank God*, he was back.

Kent and Amy made the decision to have their son transported by ambulance to Le Bonheur Children's Hospital in Memphis. Tippah County, Mississippi, only has two ambulances, and one was tied up with a patient delivery in Jackson, so the other was unavailable to transport William. Le Bonheur dispatched one of their ambulances, but it was more than a two-hour drive each way.

They arrived in Memphis just in time to hit the early side of rush hour. When they finally pulled up to the Le Bonheur E.R. doors, a wave of relief washed over Kent. William was now at one of the finest children's hospitals in America. Although William had undergone previous tests at the North Mississippi Medical Center in Tupelo, Kent knew that his

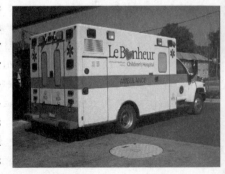

son would be under the care of some of the best pediatric specialists in the nation.

William had shown no prior signs of a seizure disorder. Neither the previous CAT scan done in Tupelo nor the one at Le Bonheur showed any sign of brain injury, but the Le Bonheur EEG did show brain activity consistent with epilepsy. William was officially diagnosed with this condition and immediately started on anti-seizure medication.

For the first night in weeks, Kent was able to relax and get some sleep, even with the regular interruptions of the nurses as they checked on William. All three of Will's seizures had been nocturnal, and Kent had heard every little bump in the night since the first episode.

Kent reflected that he hadn't slept so lightly or been so sensitive to noises in the night since William was an infant. But now he was just thankful; thankful that William was alive and receiving the best medical attention available.

the weekly Standard

SEPTEMBER 18, 1995 $2.95

PERMANENT OFFENSE

The Theolog
CHARLES KRAUTHAMME

The Strateg
FRED BARNE

The Speakership
DAVID McCLINTIC

The Shortcomings
DAVID FRUM

FIRST
ISSUE

DAVID BROOKS: HAVING MORAL SEX?

WILLIAM KRISTOL: PRESIDENT POWELL?

ANDREW FERGUSON: ARE DEMS CRAZY?

CHAPTER 2

PAYBACK IS A BITCH

WASHINGTON, DC

Kent Bain had worked as art director for the *Weekly Standard* magazine in Washington, DC, from the inception of the publication in the fall of 1995 until the spring of 2001.

The magazine was owned by the News Corporation, the Chairman and CEO of which was media mogul Rupert Murdoch, who Kent met his first day on the job when Murdoch stopped by to wish the staff well.

The *Weekly Standard* had been started by a trio of Washington political insiders: William Kristol, Editor; Fred Barnes, Executive Editor; and John Podhoretz, Deputy Editor.

The son of the "godfather of neo-conservativism," the late Irving Kristol, William served as Chief of Staff to former Vice-President Dan Quayle (*The New Republic* magazine dubbed Kristol "Dan Quayle's brain").

Kristol has been a regular panelist on ABC's *This Week*, *Fox News Sunday* and *Special Report with Bret Baier*, as well as a columnist for *Time* magazine and *The New York Times*. Kristol is also associated with a number of prominent conservative think tanks, including the *Project for the New American Century*, which he co-founded in 1997.

Political commentator Fred Barnes was a regular panelist on *The McLaughlin Group* for a decade and co-host of *The Beltway Boys* on the Fox News Channel. A widely recognized television personality, Barnes has made cameo appearances in several Hollywood films, including *Independence Day*.

7

John Podhoretz is the son of another famous neo-conservative, Norman Podhoretz, who was a protégé of Lionel Trilling and Editor-in-Chief of *Commentary* magazine for 35 years. John served as a speechwriter to former Presidents Ronald Reagan and George H.W. Bush, and has appeared as a political commentator on Fox News, CNN's *Reliable Sources* and *The McLaughlin Group*.

He has worked at *Time*, the *Washington Times* and *U.S. News & World Report*, and has a regular column at the *New York Post*. Podhoretz wrote the book *Hell of a Ride*, which offered an unfavorable assessment of Bush Sr.'s administration; was a consultant for the popular television series *The West Wing*; and, in 1986, became a five-time champion on *Jeopardy!*

AN ALL-STAR CAST

The editors of the *Weekly Standard* also assembled a roster of conservative heavy hitters including Tucker Carlson and David Brooks, who helped the magazine become a ubiquitous presence inside the Beltway.

Tucker Carlson is co-founder and editor-in-chief of *The Daily Caller* and a former host on CNN's *Crossfire*. Known for wearing a bow tie during much of his career, Carlson was once asked by *The Daily Show*'s Jon Stewart, "How old are you?" "Thirty five," Tucker answered. "And you wear a bow tie," Stewart retorted.

Carlson did eventually give up wearing bow ties a couple of years after that exchange, saying that he'd found that "If you wear a bow tie, it's like a middle finger around your neck; you're just inviting scorn and ridicule ... the number of people screaming the F-word at me ... it wore me down after a while so I gave in and became conventional."

In 2006, Carlson decided he'd give his public image another boost and agreed to be a contestant on *Dancing with the Stars*. He was expeditiously voted off the show, stating afterwards that teaching him to dance was "like Einstein teaching addition to a slow child." When asked why he accepted ABC's invitation to perform, Tucker offered the following: "I'm not defending it as the smartest choice…"

David Brooks is a columnist for the *New York Times* and a commentator on the *PBS NewsHour*. He has worked for the *Washington Times, The Wall Street Journal, Newsweek, The Atlantic Monthly* and has also been a commentator on National Public Radio.

Brooks, not your typical conservative by any stretch of the imagination, has frequently expressed admiration for Barack Obama, even before he became president. *The New Republic* ran a profile of Brooks in August 2009, which describes his first encounter with Obama in the spring of '05:

> Usually when I talk to senators, while they may know a policy area better than me, they generally don't know political philosophy better than me. I got the sense he knew *both* better than me. […] I remember distinctly an image of—we were sitting on his couches, and I was looking at his pant leg and his perfectly creased pant, and I'm thinking, a) he's going to be president and b) he'll be a very good president.

With his enthusiasm running high, Brooks penned a column in the *New York Times* entitled "Run, Barack, Run" two days after Obama's second autobiography, *The Audacity of Hope*, hit bookstore shelves, in which he urged Obama to seek the presidency.

DIFFICULT ADJUSTMENT

A number of other conservative luminaries worked for and contributed to the *Weekly Standard*, including Pulitzer-Prize-winning syndicated

columnist Charles Krauthammer. Kent was always interested to see whose familiar face from the news circuit or Capitol Hill would show up at the weekly editorial meetings. It also never ceased to impress him how far-reaching the influence of the *Standard* was, and in how many different venues its writers and editors appeared. It seemed as if he couldn't turn on the radio or television, day or night, without seeing or hearing one of his colleagues.

The magazine went to press on Friday evenings, and the staff would work late getting the book ready to send to the printer. Kent would interact with the editors throughout the week, Fridays in particular, and he never quite got accustomed to seeing his bosses around the office, then sitting down in the break room to eat supper and watch Fox News— where he'd routinely see Bill Kristol, Fred Barnes or both—and then encounter them walking back into the office half an hour later.

He also never really felt comfortable sitting around at home in his skivvies on Sunday mornings and hearing Bill Kristol's voice and/or seeing his face on the Sunday news shows. Damn unnerving, he always thought, like the nightmares where you find yourself in your underwear in the middle of a classroom.

NIGHTS AT THE ROUNDTABLE

The office building in which the Weekly Standard was located sat three blocks from the White House and just around the corner from ABC News. The American Enterprise Institute, a prominent conservative think tank, was in the same building, and the Philanthropy Roundtable moved its offices right next door to the Standard a couple of years after the magazine started.

As it turned out, Kent was given the opportunity to art direct for Philanthropy magazine, published by the Roundtable, which he did for a couple of years. It was a bi-monthly publication, so he was able to effectively handle the additional workload.

During the time that Kent worked for Philanthropy, the Roundtable was under the leadership of John P. Walters, who went on to be appointed by President George W. Bush as the Director of the White House Office of National Drug Control Policy, or, as the position is more commonly referred to, the "Drug Czar."

"A NEW PEARL HARBOR"

Like the Philanthropy Roundtable, the aforementioned Project for the New American Century (PNAC) that William Kristol co-founded also had its office on the same floor as the *Standard*. In fact, it was co-located with the magazine's offices and shared a workroom with the publication.

Although now defunct, PNAC promoted American global leadership and advocated for "a Reaganite policy of military strength and moral clarity," maintaining that, "American leadership is both good for America and for the world."

In June of 1997, PNAC released a "Statement of Principles," which began:

> As the 20th century draws to a close, the United States stands as the world's pre-eminent power. Having led the West to victory in the Cold War, America faces an opportunity and a challenge: Does the United States have the vision to build upon the achievements of past decades? Does the United States have the resolve to shape a new century favorable to American principles and interests?

Signatories to the Statement of Principles included future Vice-President Dick Cheney, future Secretary of Defense Donald Rumsfeld, future Deputy Secretary of Defense Paul Wolfowitz and a number of others who would go on to hold key positions in the Bush administration, as well as influential businessmen, politicians and thinkers such as William J. Bennett, Jeb Bush, Steve Forbes, Norman Podhoretz and others.

In September 2000, PNAC published a 90-page report entitled *Rebuilding America's Defenses: Strategies, Forces and Resources for a New Century*, which stated that, "America should seek to preserve and extend its position of global leadership by maintaining the

preeminence of U.S. military forces." Section V of the report, "Creating Tomorrow's Dominant Force," included the following now-infamous sentence:

> Further, the process of transformation, even if it brings revolutionary change, is likely to be a long one, absent some catastrophic and catalyzing event—like a new Pearl Harbor.

Following 9/11, various left-leaning mainstream social critics stopped short of accusing PNAC members of complicity in the attacks, but argued that they capitalized on the event as an opportunity to enact long-desired plans. Conspiracy theorists, however, felt no such compunction and asserted that the "new Pearl Harbor" quote was absolute proof of everything from simple foreknowledge to total orchestration of the attacks themselves.

USS ARIZONA (BB-39)

PAYBACK?

If there was any truth to such assertions, it would certainly seem that Kent had been in the right place at the right time to have gained insider knowledge—and answering the question of whether he did or did not do so could well lie at the heart of what happened to his son, William.

On September 11, 2012, TrineDay had released *The Most Dangerous Book in the World: 9/11 as Mass Ritual*, written by S.K. Bain—Kent Bain. Exactly one year later, on September 11, 2013, William suffered his first-ever seizure, with zero prior signs of epilepsy.

DIRE CONSEQUENCES

When Kent had written his book exposing the occult underpinnings of, and the psychological warfare tactics employed during and after, the attacks of 9/11, he'd had very real concerns that he or his family might become targets of retaliation. Now, it looked as if his fears had been realized.

The idea that his son was suffering because of something he had done was difficult enough for Kent to contend with. The notion that worse might lie ahead was more worrisome still. *What the hell have I done?* Kent thought to himself.

NOT THE FIRST

The precise timing of Will's initial seizure wasn't the first piece of evidence that Kent had in fact attracted the attention of the true perpetrators of the September 11th attacks. A series of events earlier in 2013 had put him on edge and given him good reason to believe that he'd made himself an "object of interest" to some of the most powerful psychopaths on the planet.

These events had not been minor hints, obscure clues—they were newsmakers, some *headline* news stories, some unfolding at his doorstep.

PART TWO

TWELVE DAYS OF TERROR

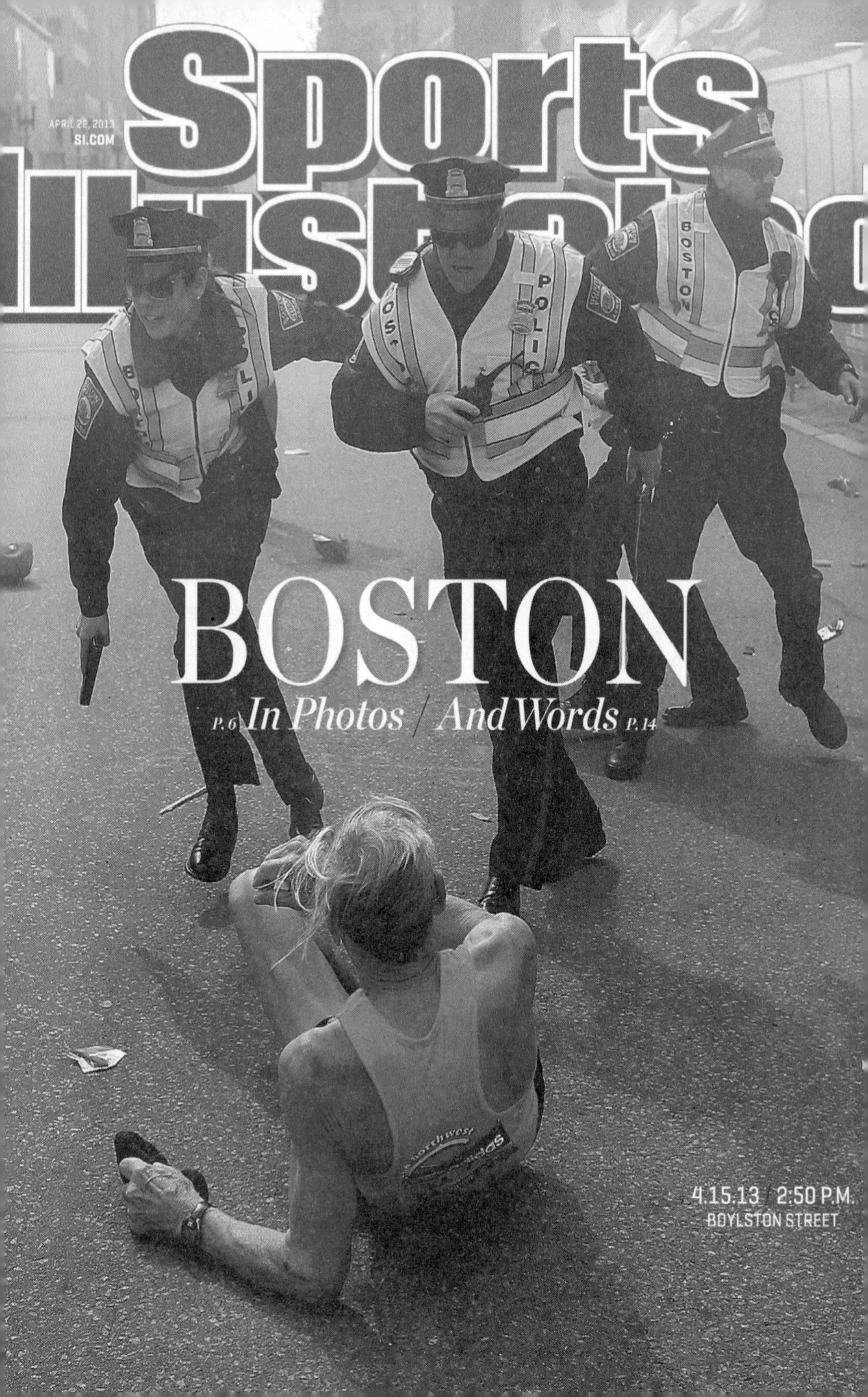

Sports Illustrated

APRIL 22, 2013
SI.COM

BOSTON
P. 6 In Photos / And Words P. 14

4.15.13   2:50 P.M.
BOYLSTON STREET

Chapter 3

The Boston Massacre, Part II

Monday, April 15, 2013: Boston, Massachusetts

Twin explosions, later determined to be the result of homemade bombs, injure dozens at the finish line of the 117th Boston Marathon. Debris and body parts are strewn everywhere as rescue workers rush to treat the wounded.

In the midst of the frenzied media coverage of the event comes word of another incident: a fire at the John F. Kennedy Memorial Library, only miles away. Was the blaze somehow related to the bombings? Authorities didn't know, but there was a sense that Boston was a city under siege.

The Big 5-0

As Kent digested the news, two things occurred to him: 1.) Boston, the Brookline community specifically, was JFK's birthplace; and, 2.) 2013 was the 50th anniversary of his assassination.

It was Patriot's Day in Boston, Tax Day for the nation, and here in the birthplace of President Kennedy, in the fiftieth year following his killing, his Presidential Library is ablaze and two bombs have gone off at the finish line of one of the biggest annual sporting events in the country.

This suggested that the fire and the bombings were perhaps connected, and that the unfolding events might not be what they at first appeared. But what sort of terrorist group would mark the anniversary of a presidential assassination in such a fashion?

At that moment, there was no evidence that the explosions were the work of terrorists, domestic or foreign, but such evidence would quickly emerge from the carnage. Investigators found fragments of the devices—pressure cookers loaded with an assortment of deadly projectiles.

The bombings were the result of terrorism, all right, and the hunt was on. Law enforcement authorities took the unprecedented step of releasing stills and video footage of the primary suspects in hopes of identifying and locating them as rapidly as possible. It was *America's Most Wanted* on speed.

No Link?

The Tsarnaev brothers were quickly identified as the prime suspects, and subsequently one was killed and the other apprehended. Authorities found no link between the fire and the bombings, and determined that they were

Deep Roots

Below this drawing of the Green Dragon Tavern, the artist wrote these words: "Where we met to Plan the Consignment of a few Shiploads of Tea, Dec 16, 1773."

John F. (Honey Fitz) Fitzgerald, the maternal grandfather of John F. Kennedy, was mayor of Boston from 1906 to 1908 and 1910 to 1914. For a time, the Fitzgeralds lived near the former site of the Green Dragon Tavern, which was home to the Lodge of St. Andrew's, the first "Ancient" Lodge in Boston, formed in 1752. After the Lodge purchased the building in 1764, they rented out the space to a number of groups, including the Sons of Liberty.

Both Paul Revere and John Hancock belonged to St. Andrew's, and the Boston Tea Party was purportedly planned here. Some historians have called the Green Dragon Tavern "the headquarters of the American Revolution."

On the night of the Boston Tea Party, men with painted faces calling themselves "Mohawks" met at the Green Dragon Tavern, an event immortalized in the song, "Rally Mohawks" sung by the North End Caucus:

Rally, Mohawks – bring out your axes!
And tell King George we'll pay no taxes on his foreign tea!
His threats are vain – and vain to think
To force our girls and wives to drink
His vile Bohea!
[the tea of the East India Company]
Then rally boys, and hasten on
To meet our Chiefs at the Green Dragon.
Our Warren's there, and bold Revere,
With hands to do and words to cheer

For Liberty and Laws!
Our country's "Braves" and firm defenders
Shall ne'er be left by true North-Enders,

Fighting Freedom's cause!
Then rally boys and hasten on
to meet our Chiefs at the Green Dragon.

unrelated events. But Kent strongly suspected that the two incidents *were* related, and that there was far more to the story than the mainstream media had uncovered, or ever would.

The day of the bombing, he knew it was highly probable that, over time, many odd details and peculiar circumstances surrounding the brother's lives and alleged involvement in the crime would come to light—such as prior interactions with law enforcement, the FBI, in particular, which in fact turned out to be the case.

If this event fit the mold of many other such incidents he'd studied, there would be a predictable pattern to subsequent developments in the case. And, boy, was this ever true.

MASTERS OF ILLUSION

*T*he Most Dangerous Book in the World dissected the attacks of 9/11 and revealed them to be not simply acts of terrorism, but of *false-flag* ter-

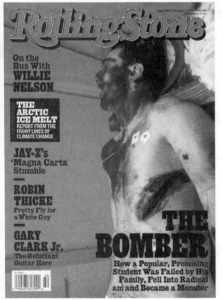

rorism, staged terror. There were real terrorists involved (and/or individuals portraying radical jihadists), real buildings were destroyed and real people died. But the plot underlying these acts of terror was far more sophisticated and complicated than most people ever imagined.

A range of powerful interlocking interests, for their own purposes, staged the events of 9/11—they didn't just "allow them to happen," they *made* them happen. And this wasn't the first such instance of staged terror. As Kent discovered during the research for his book, American history is filled with acts of false-flag terrorism, in which influential

Issue 1188 >> August 1, 2013 >> $4.9⁹
rollingstone.com

Rolling Stone

On the Bus With WILLIE NELSON

THE ARCTIC ICE MELT
REPORT FROM THE FRONT LINES OF CLIMATE CHANGE

JAY-Z's Magna Carta' Stumble

ROBIN THICKE
Pretty Fly for a White Guy

GARY CLARK Jr.
The Reluctant Guitar Hero

THE BOMBER

How a Popular, Promising Student Was Failed by His Family, Fell Into Radical Islam and Became a Monster

parties manipulate the levers of government, its security and military apparatuses in particular, to further their own agendas—and it would be a gross understatement to say that these agendas *never* align with the best interests of our nation or the majority of its people.

The unseen manipulators are master illusionists. They can do whatever they want, wherever they want, whenever they want. They have practically unlimited resources and unlimited power. As little as Kent or anyone else wanted to believe that this could be true, the evidence he'd seen in instance after instance proved this beyond a reasonable doubt.

Kent knew what to look for, knew the tell-tale signs of a staged terror event, and they were littered all over the place in Boston like so many body parts at the finish line … but that was only the beginning.

A photo-illustration created for Kent's interview on an internet radio program.

KURT RUSSELL KEVIN COSTNER
3000 MILES TO GRACELAND

CRIME IS KING

CHAPTER 4:

A FAULKNERIAN FEUD

Tuesday, April 16, 2013: Washington, D.C. and Tupelo, Mississippi

The day following the Boston Bombings, in an eerie parallel to the anthrax letters sent following 9/11, news outlets reported that letters containing the poison ricin had been mailed to President Obama, U.S. Senator Roger Wicker (R-MS) and a local judge in Tupelo, Mississippi.

The letters to Obama and Wicker had been intercepted at offsite federal mail sorting facilities, a precaution instituted following the anthrax scare in 2001. Eighty-year-old Justice Court Judge Sadie Holland, however, according to her son, State Representative Steve Holland, not only received and opened her letter, but, upon seeing the powdery substance inside, gave it the old smell test—not exactly wise protocol in the current environment, but fortunately the judge was unharmed.

HOMETOWN OF THE KING

Judge Holland works at the Lee County Justice Center in Tupelo, Mississippi, where Senator Roger Wicker lives and has his main district office. Tupelo is also where Kent's office is located, but the community is best known as the birthplace of the King of Rock'n'Roll, Elvis Presley.

23

The original suspect in the ricin case was Kevin Curtis, an Elvis impersonator whose brother also happens to be an Elvis impersonator. In fact, the duo is listed in the *Guinness Book of World Records* as the world's only fraternal Elvis-impersonator act.

Both brothers are gifted impersonators, and Senator Wicker had hired Kevin Curtis about a decade prior to perform at a party he was giving for a soon-to-be-married couple.

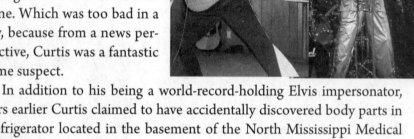

There was just one small catch in the case against Curtis, however: investigators found absolutely no evidence linking him to the crimes. None. Which was too bad in a way, because from a news perspective, Curtis was a fantastic prime suspect.

In addition to his being a world-record-holding Elvis impersonator, years earlier Curtis claimed to have accidentally discovered body parts in a refrigerator located in the basement of the North Mississippi Medical Center in Tupelo where he worked as a janitor, and further claimed that he was fired as a result.

Curtis wrote a manuscript for a book, entitled *Missing Pieces*, which he unsuccessfully attempted to have published, centered upon his contention that the facility was engaged in illegal trafficking of human body parts as part of an international criminal enterprise. Curtis even sent letters to then-U.S. Congressman Roger Wicker and Senators Thad Cochran and Trent Lott seeking their assistance with his attempt to expose the alleged plot.

Although no one took his claims seriously, Curtis subsequently suffered a series of personal misfortunes, all of which he attributed to an organized effort to shut him up. "I'm on the hidden front lines of a secret war," Curtis claimed. "My brothers fear me. My sister hates me. I have lost most of my friends. They burned down my home, killed my dogs, my cat, my rabbit."

His car also exploded. He was fired from a series of jobs and his wife eventually left him, taking their kids with her. Preoccupation with the case turned to obsession, precipitating a steep personal and professional decline and resulting in his becoming a full-time unpaid conspiracy theorist (an occupation Kent was somewhat familiar with). In addition, Curtis racked up twenty-two arrests in the relatively short span of thirteen years.

I Approved This Message

Upon Curtis' release from jail in April 2013, however, the story only got better, richer, more Faulkneresque.

Finding no incriminating evidence against him, investigators had asked Curtis if anyone he could think of might want to frame him. The letters had contained certain phrases Curtis was well known for using, "I am KC and I approved this message," in particular. This and other seemingly self-incriminating clues had led law enforcement to Curtis in the first place, but there was a total lack of material evidence that he'd been involved with producing the ricin or mailing the letters.

Forget Elvis! Wayne Newton impersonator now eyed by authorities for mailing letter tainted with ricin to Obama

James Everett Dutschke, 41, was denied bond Monday on a charge of making and possessing a biological weapon.

BY STEPHEN REX BROWN / NEW YORK DAILY NEWS / Tuesday, April 30, 2013, 1:11 AM

Curtis had an immediate answer for authorities: Everett Dutschke, a local rival, fellow martial artist (both Kevin and Everett were, like Elvis, black belts), and, according to news reports, so help me God, a Wayne Newton impersonator. The two had been in an ongoing feud for years.

Illustration by David Sandlin

Newsmakers

The Elvis Impersonator, the Karate Instructor, a Fridge Full of Severed Heads, and the Plot 2 Kill the Presiden

CHAPTER 5

IT JUST KEEPS GETTING BETTER

In truth, the Curtis-Dutschke affair was so chock-full of fat, juicy morsels that the media damn near choked on it as reporters from far and wide descended upon Tupelo like a bunch of turkey buzzards, voraciously consuming the particulars and attempting to out-humor one another.

The most insightful, and by far the funniest, coverage of the events came in the October 2013 issue of *GQ* magazine, in a somewhat belated 8,000+ word piece by Wells Tower entitled, "The Elvis Impersonator, the Karate Instructor, a Fridge Full of Severed Heads, and the Plot 2 Kill the President."

The lead-in for the article read, "Remember that crazy story about the dude in Mississippi who mailed ricin to Obama and then tried to frame some other dude in Mississippi for the crime? Well, as Wells Tower discovered when he traveled to Tupelo and started poking around, the story is a thousand times crazier than you thought." And, if anything, this teaser *undersold* the hilariously bizarre revelations to follow:

> Spend a week or two in Tupelo, Mississippi, and you begin to wonder if the air down here perhaps contains an element that causes dreams to ignite and burn hotter and stranger than elsewhere in the world. What are the dreams that catch fire in this town? They are dreams of rock 'n' roll; of valor, metamorphosis, and ruination; sex and betrayal; of the government and shadowy forces; of the grand dream, American. The ether here is surely spiked with something. How else do we explain the dream of the poor hillbilly born in a shotgun shack in east Tupelo, who

invented rock 'n' roll and changed the world and died on the toilet at the age of 42? How else to understand a man like Kevin Curtis, one of northeastern Mississippi's preeminent Elvis impersonators, whose life was nearly ruined by the sight of a severed head on a refrigerator shelf? How else to make sense of the story you are about to hear, the tale of Mr. Curtis and Everett Dutschke, two men who might have shared a lovely friendship but instead had a weird feud that ended in the attempted poisoning of the president of the United States?

Theirs' is a story of human dismemberment and righteous causes, of martial arts and murder intrigues, sexual perversity, political conviction, and resentments dearly held. What lies behind Mr. Curtis and Mr. Dutschke's spectacular collision? A lot of odd and complicated things. But in the simplest sense, perhaps it's that these gentlemen simply had too many dreams in common, and in their particular America, there are only so many dreams to go around.

The feud makes history in the third week of April 2013. Spring has broken brightly, gently, but Kevin Curtis is lately being haunted by dark fancies and dreams. Kevin is sure someone is watching him. For the past few days, every time he looks in his rearview, he sees some guy in sunglasses tailing him in a Crown Victoria or an SUV. And is it just Kevin, or is that the chuddering of chopper blades high in the air above his home?

Curtis, 46, lives alone with his dog, Moo Cow, a Holstein-spotted Chihuahua–Jack Russell mix. Tonight, Wednesday, April 17, he and the dog are due at Kevin's ex-wife Laura's house for dinner with the kids. Out on his street, something weird is in the air. Kevin's neighbors are the kind of people who tend to hide out in their houses, but tonight they're out on their lawns, "pacing like ants." He waves at a few of them, and they look at him queerly, like maybe they want to wave back but they're afraid something bad might happen if they do.

With Moo Cow riding on his lap, Kevin slows his white Ford Escape to check his mailbox when all of a sudden—skreeeeeek! A whole fleet of cars and SUVs—maybe twenty, twenty-five—comes swarming in around him at eighty miles an hour. A frightening parade of G-men pours out of the cars. FBI, Homeland Security, local cops, Secret Service, Capitol Police. Rifles, pistols, machine guns, all of them aimed at Kevin Curtis and his dog. Kevin swivels in his seat. He figures a serial killer or somebody must be lamming it down the street behind him.

"Freeze! Do not move! Do not resist! We will shoot you!" an offi-cer screams at Kevin.

Kevin is confused. "Me?"

"Shut up! Get out of the car and get on the ground!"

Holding Moo Cow in his arms, Kevin steps from his vehicle into a thicket of loaded guns.

He does not immediately get on the ground. "I've got my little dog, Moo Cow," he explains to the G-men.

"Drop the dog! Drop the dog!"

"Can I just take her back inside and secure her?"

"Definitely not!"

He drops Moo Cow in the driver's seat.

The agents cuff Kevin's hands, shackle his feet, and latch his wrists to his waist.

"Am I being arrested?"

"Don't ask questions. We'll ask the questions."

"What about my dog?"

Some guy with a machine gun goes to Kevin's car, opens the door, and tries to take hold of the lapdog. Moo Cow spooks. She growls at the machine-gun guy, leaps, and hauls ass down the street.

"My dog! What about Moo Cow!" Kevin yells.

A hulking officer with arms like bowling pins smirks at Kevin through dark glasses. "Your dog will be fine," he says.

This is not Kevin's first tussle with law enforcement. He knows when he is being played false by men in uniform.

"Sir, can you please take off your sunglasses so I can see your eyes?" Kevin asks the officer.

"Excuse me?"

"I want to see your eyes when you tell me she'll be fine," Kevin says, "because I don't think you give a damn about Moo Cow."

With Moo Cow still on the loose, Kevin Curtis is hustled into a van bound for the Lafayette County jail in Oxford, where he will be held on suspicion of sending letters tainted with the poi-son ricin to a local judge, a Mississippi senator, and Barack H. Obama.

On the ninety-mile ride to the jail, Curtis begs to know what he is supposed to have done. The G-men will not tell him. They do not say a word about ricin or Obama. They offer up no clue as to why an army descended on his neighborhood.

In Oxford, Kevin spends three hours chained to a chair in an empty interrogation room before anyone so much as speaks to him. After a time, he is in need of the commode. "Three agents walk me to a restroom, open the stall, and they say, 'I know it's uncomfortable, but we have to watch you have a bowel movement.' I say, 'You gonna wipe me, too?'"

Wells relates further details of Curtis' maddening ordeal with authorities before he was finally released, and then continues:

He grins habitually, cheeks bonhomously bunching beneath a pair of lively blue eyes. He is grinning even as he unspools the most baroquely strange tale I have ever heard directly from a human mouth.

If we had the time, I would tell you of Kevin's early life as a child prodigy on the Elvis-impersonation circuit, of how his mother, Elois, drove him to Memphis to have an Elvis suit made by Elvis's official suitmaker and a belt made by Elvis's official beltmaker and took out a bank loan to cover the $3,825 bill. I would tell you of how Elois briefly met the King after a performance at the Louisiana Hayride in 1954, and how decades later, in his years of decline, Elvis would call her up from time to time, she says, to pray with her over the phone.

Although one wishes time had permitted him to elaborate, Wells moves on to a range of related topics, at one point offering the following observation concerning the feud between Curtis and Dutscke:

... perhaps Tupelo was just too small a town for two conspiracy-minded, snappy-dressing, nunchuck-swinging rock 'n' roll men to coexist in harmony.

Tower then recounts his visit with Rep. Steve Holland—the son of Judge Sadie Holland, with whom he runs a funeral home—who invited him down to his place of business one early summer morning to help him put a nightgown on a corpse. Concerning the experience Tower writes, "The dead woman's hand feels about like the undefrosted wing of a Perdue roaster but smoother and denser to the touch."

Holland arranges the gown about the body's collarbone and gives a nod of tempered satisfaction. "I think she looks rather angelic in this little apparatus. But I think I'm gonna aggrandize her just a bit."

With a couple of fistfuls of loose cotton tucked just so, he amplifies the departed's bust. Her lips are slightly parted. He seals them with a clear adhesive, applied with a tiny steel spade. "This is nothing but airplane glue," he explains. "You can pull a damn eighteen-wheeler with this shit."

Tower continues,

Holland Funeral Directors stands due west of downtown Tupelo in a metal building that formerly contained "the largest nightclub and beer joint in the state of Mississippi." In 2006, Holland bought it, "put brick on the front, hung some shit [ornamental pediments and moldings] on it, and now I'm doing 300 funerals a year."

Holland has been in the mortuary business for four decades. Due to a lately discovered allergy to formaldehyde that nearly took his life, he no longer embalms bodies unless he's in a "hazmat suit." His hairdressing talents he considers to be inadequate, so this morning we loiter in the coffin showroom while the coiffeurist treats the deceased to her final styling.

The caskets are as opulent and beautiful as a fleet of limousines. The top-tier models sell for upwards of $5,000, but Holland begins his sales pitch to prospective clients with a humble gray container in a far corner of the room. "I bring 'em to this little $995 jobbie right here. I say, 'Okay, this will get you from point A to point B. Now, water and worms will get in there, and if you read the Scripture it says "Ashes to ashes and dust to dust," and that's what this is really all about. What you are buying is $995 worth of dignity to keep

me from tying a rope to your heels and pulling you into the hole, which would accomplish the same thing.' Then they'll come buy this shit over here." Holland indicates a box that retails for $3,495. "And ka-ching-ka-ching-ka-ching. Forty years I been doing this.

It's f*cked! I mean, the [funeral] services are incredible. I love the services, but all this merchandising-pagan-ass-crazy-certified-lunatic-damn bullshit—it's so f*cked. God bless America!"

The reporter goes on to discuss Everett Dutschke's profound dislike of Holland, stating:

Not long after Dutschke and Curtis's unfriendly introduction in 2006, Dutschke mounted a campaign for state House district sixteen, against long-term Democratic incumbent Steve Holland. By all accounts, Dutschke's PR strategy was little more than a public display of bitter, empty vitriol—its rhetoric revolving around comparisons of Steve Holland to Boss Hogg from the Dukes of Hazzard and suggestions that the 9/11 hijackers were Holland's friends. Why Dutschke loathed Steve Holland so hotly is not clear.

"I had never stood eyeball to eyeball or dick to dick with the man, but for some reason he just hated the hell out of me," says Holland, a gloriously profane and paradoxically genteel man of 58. "He called me everything from gay to communist. Everything but a child of God. I mean, he had no campaign or agenda except to cut my nuts out.... But you got to get your ass up early and go to bed late to beat my ass. I've held this seat for thirty years. I can absolutely make love to a bull moose on the steps of the Lee County courthouse and garner more than 5 percent of the vote."

* * *

"I had never stood eyeball to eyeball or dick to dick with the man, but for some reason he just hated the hell out of me."

* * *

As it turns out, Kevin Curtis didn't care much for Holland either, but in his case at least we have some idea why:

Because Holland runs a funeral home … Curtis suspects that Holland has an important if unspecified role in the body-parts conspiracy.
Kevin Curtis's loudly bruited suspicions about Holland's purported ties to the North Mississippi Medical Center's organ-harvesting ring

have not hurt his business, though he allows that he has had to deal with "people saying, 'Are you stealing our bodies and selling parts?' And I said, 'Are you f*cking crazy?' " Holland points out that to sell body parts would cut against his interests. If he were to butcher and trade bodies rather than simply burying or incinerating them, "you sons of bitches wouldn't be coming to see me for $8,000 a funeral."

To quote Rep. Holland, "… all this merchandising-pagan-ass-cra-zy-certified-lunatic-damn bullshit—it's so f*cked. God bless America!"

SUSPICIOUS MINDS

After a whirlwind comedy tour of Tupelo, Mississippi, Tower begins to wind down:

> On Tuesday, April 23, Kevin Curtis was released from jail. And in the course of a couple of hours, he underwent a transformation from public enemy number one to an unlikely sort of hero, a man falsely accused and wrongly imprisoned by the blundering feds. The following day, he boarded a plane to New York for a media spree, and his name was soon on the lips of "all the news people, from Piers Morgan to Wolf Blitzer to Jon Stewart."

Tower also observes that Curtis became "the sacrificial innocent in an Internet-age cautionary tale about how a man's life was nearly destroyed on no more evidence than a few choice glean-ings from his Facebook page."

The author then provides a sympathetic vignette, giving the reader a glimpse of the creative genius that is so often the flip-side of lunacy (or near-lunacy):

Kevin Curtis has brought along his guitar. Out in the parking lot, he props a leg against the running board of his Ford and plucks out the opening arpeggios to "Suspicious Minds," one of his favorites from the King's Vegas oeuvre. Hearing Kevin Curtis sing, it's not hard to imagine how a lesser talent like Everett Dutschke might come to envy him. Curtis has a voice, a pro-caliber voice, sonorous, superbly tuned. His rendition of the Elvis song transcends mere mimicry. He retools the melody with his own distinctive virtuosity, spinning out fancy little trills and runs at the end of the lines. ... *We can't build our dreams on suspicious minds...* One hears persuasive grief in his voice when he breaks it Elvis-style. It's good enough to call to attention the small hairs on your arms. It's good enough that a grown man feels not the least bit awkward being serenaded by another man in a parking lot in Mississippi with midnight coming on. It's good enough that one is moved and sad-dened to know that it's real, the gift that Kevin has sacrificed on the altar of his cause.

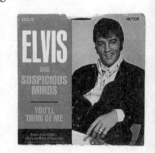

DRUG THROUGH THE MUD

Speaking of suspicious minds, in reading the article, Kent couldn't help but notice that Kevin Curtis ever-so-neatly fit the profile of so many patsies and pawns who unwittingly find themselves enmeshed in situations and scenarios such as this one (not that there's ever been one *quite* like it)—an individual with a history of mental illness, which always provides the perfect cover story for anything they do, willingly or otherwise.

As Tower reported, soon after the story hit the headlines,

> Kevin's brother, Jack, releases a statement referencing "Kevin's lengthy history of mental illness" and pleading for the public's understanding. "He may be better off in the custody of the federal government," says Jim Waide, an attorney who once represented Kevin.

Now, this is by no stretch of the imagination to imply that every person with a mental problem is the victim of a conspiracy, serving as a programmed puppet acting against their will to carry out some ill deed or another. However, it is very frequently the case that the reverse is true—that in practically every instance where some serious false-flag shit goes down, there's almost always a known nutcase on hand to immediately lay the blame upon.

Jack's public statement about Kevin's purported mental illness is something Kevin will not soon forgive. "To have your own brother saying to the world, 'Kevin's crazy, he's bipolar.' Do you have any idea how much that hurt?"

"In hindsight," Jack Curtis says, "the statement was a mistake, but it was made with good intentions," the idea being to lay the foundation of an insanity defense if Kevin were to find himself charged, rightly or wrongly, with the ricin plot. Kevin rejects this view. "They tried to institutionalize me. The doctor said I was fine. I've been on medication, and the only time in my life I've felt like putting a gun in my mouth and pulling the trigger was when they had me on those drugs."

Staged terror and psychotropic drugs—they go together like peanut butter and banana (sandwiches, fried, one of Elvis' favorites).

I Approve This Cell

Given everything that Kevin Curtis was put through at the hands of Everett Dutschke, one couldn't blame him for taking pleasure in the subsequent trials and tribulations of his arch rival and would-be frame-up artist, or, for instance, in "the thought of Dutschke languishing in the federal jail in Oxford where Kevin himself was wrongly held," as the *GQ* article noted.

Curtis claims that one of his former jailers, with whom he became Facebook friends, told him that Dutschke is awaiting trial in the very same cell where Kevin spent his week in custody. It is especially delicious to Kevin Curtis when he imagines what Dutschke must have felt, his first day behind bars, when he glanced at the wall beside the stainless-steel toilet and read the Magic Markered graffito the prior tenant had written there: "I am KC and I approve this cell."

Payback's a bitch, ain't it, Everett?

* * *

"… you got to get your ass up early and go to bed late to beat my ass. … I can absolutely make love to a bull moose on the steps of the Lee County courthouse and garner more than 5 percent of the vote."

– Mississippi State Representative Steve Holland

"RIVETING." —*Washington Post Book Review*

FIRE ON THE
MOUNTAIN

THE TRUE STORY OF THE SOUTH CANYON FIRE

JOHN N. MACLEAN

CHAPTER 6

UP IN FLAMES

K ent worked in Tupelo with the Mississippi Hills National Heritage Area, which he helped estab-lish. Kent organized an impressive group of over 50 local, state and federal Founding Partners to support the initiative, and then-U.S. Representative Roger Wicker (R), along with Senator Thad Cochran (R), had been in-strumental in securing Congressional approval for the Na-tional Heritage Area, one of only 49 in the country.

mississippihills
National Heritage Area

Kent's mother also lived in Tupelo, where she'd moved after her apart-ment in the Smoky Mountains burned to the ground in the spring of 2012. Investigators discovered that the fire had started in the unit directly above hers. The blaze rapidly engulfed the entire building, and due to unfortunately high winds, spread to other apartment buildings and eventually set the entire side of the mountain on fire.

She'd lost everything, barely getting out in time, with the proverbial clothes on her back and her dog, Sidney. Her car, parked nearby, had been to-taled as well, its tires melted to the ground.

At the time, Kent had chalked it up to co-incidence and bad luck, but the incident *had* occurred on the very day that he'd signed the contract to write his first book. Now, he wasn't so sure it was just misfortune, and with his book out for a little over eight months, and another major false-flag event apparent-ly unfolding at least in part at his doorstep, Kent was begin-ning to get a little nervous.

SCHWARZENEGGER

SAM WORTHINGTON · JOE MANGANIELLO · TERENCE HOWARD · JOSH HOLLOWAY

TEN MEN. TEN MILLION. ZERO TRUST.

SABOTAGE

FROM THE MAKERS OF *TRAINING DAY* & *END OF WATCH*

JANUARY 2014

CHAPTER 7

GONE WEST

Wednesday, April 17, 2013: West, Texas

A mere two days after the Boston Bombings, and the day after the news of the ricin letters hit international headlines ...

The plume from the massive explosion looked like the mushroom cloud from a nuclear detonation, rising hundreds of feet into the sky. Damage from the blast at the fertilizer plant in the small community of West, Texas—located only about 10 miles from Waco, site of the 1993 Branch Davidian massacre and home of the Masonic Grand Lodge of Texas—was widespread.

THE GRAND LODGE OF TEXAS
ANCIENT FREE & ACCEPTED MASONS

Grand Lodge Memorial Temple

The Grand Lodge of Texas, Ancient Free and Accepted Masons, Waco, Texas

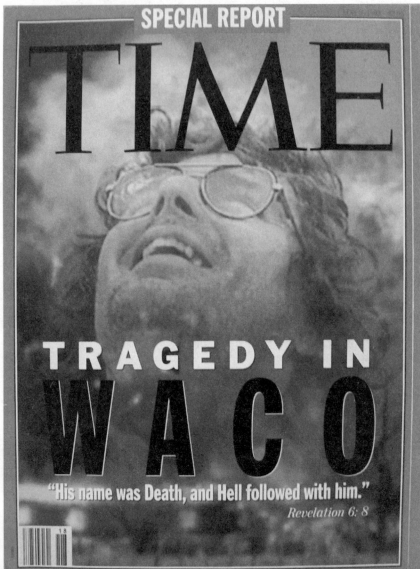

Authorities had few clues to work with; there was practically nothing left at the site of the explosion. Was it an industrial accident? An act of terrorism? We may never know.

After everything that had already happened that week, however, there was little doubt in Kent's mind: no matter what the official story turned out to be, whether investigators figured out what happened or it remained an unsolved mystery, this was no accidental commercial disaster. This was part of an ongoing false-flag terror operation rolling across the American countryside.

Listen All Y'all, It's a Sabotage...

"Sabotage," a 1994 song by the Beastie Boys, was in 2004 ranked by *Rolling Stone* magazine as one of their 500 Greatest Songs of All Time, and the music video is a parody of '70s crime dramas such as *Hawaii Five-O*, *The Streets of San Francisco*, *S.W.A.T.*, *Baretta* and *Starsky and Hutch*.

"Sabotage"

I can't stand it, I know you planned it
I'm gonna set it straight, this Watergate
I can't stand rocking when I'm in here
'Cause your crystal ball ain't so crystal clear ...

'Cause what you see you might not get
And we can bet, so don't you get souped yet
You're scheming on a thing that's a mirage
I'm trying to tell you now, it's sabotage

Why, our backs are now against the wall?
Listen all y'all, it's a sabotage
Listen all y'all, it's a sabotage
Listen all y'all, it's a sabotage
Listen all y'all, it's a sabotage

THIRD AND THREE

The staged terror attacks of 9/11 had been crammed into a single jam-packed day. This was different, although according to Kent's extensive research, not unprecedented. He was familiar with similar incidents uncovered by conspiracy researchers investigating the Unabomber case and others.

No, this was good old-fashioned industrial sabotage, and the third—in the span of just three days—in a string of false-flag terror attacks perpetrated against the unsuspecting public. Kent was willing to bet money on it, in no small part because he was well aware that in Masonry, and in the lore of the Egyptian jackal-god Anubis, a person who dies is said to have "gone west."

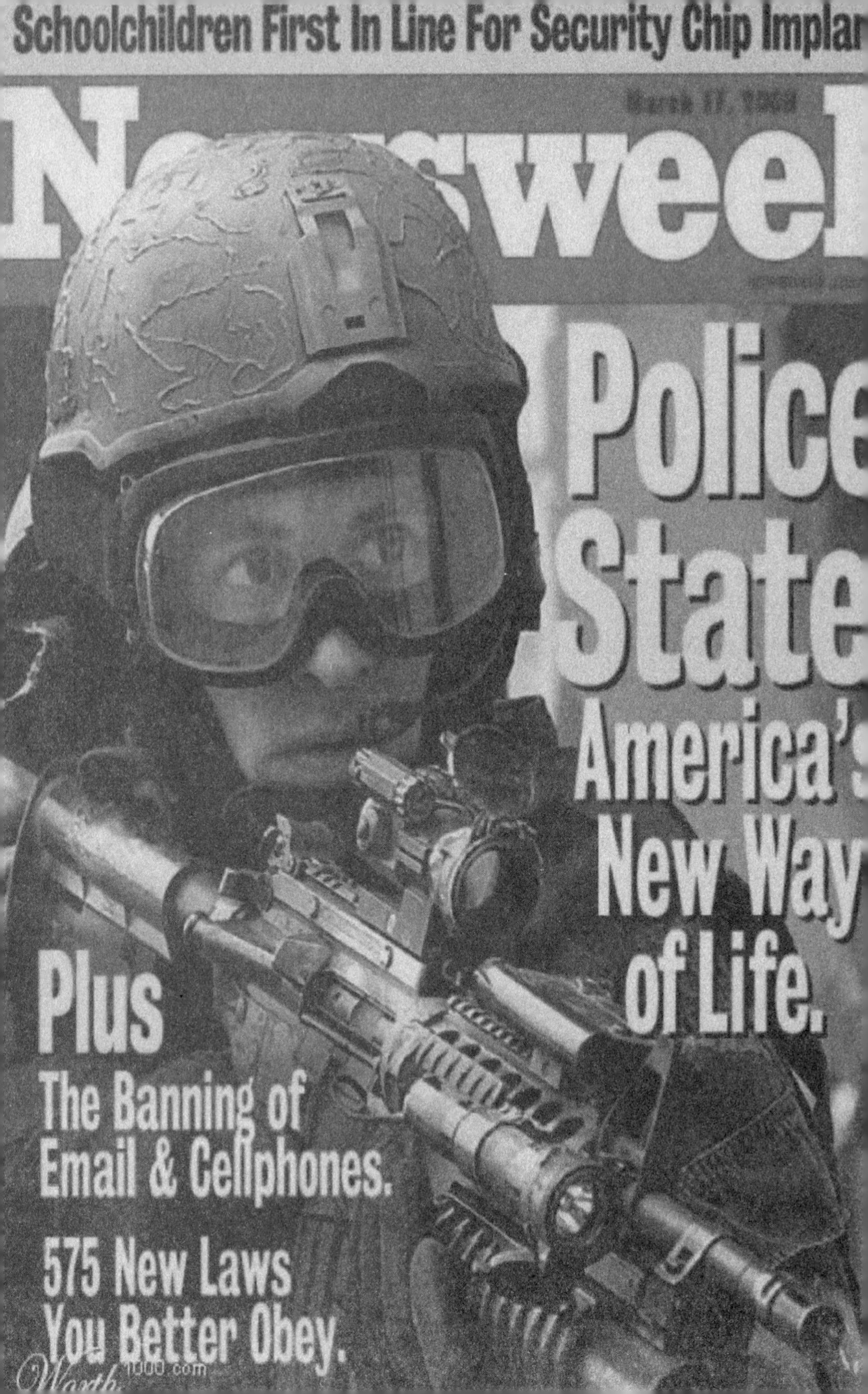

Schoolchildren First In Line For Security Chip Implant

Newsweek

March 17, 1969

Police State

America's New Way of Life.

Plus
The Banning of
Email & Cellphones.

575 New Laws
You Better Obey.

CHAPTER 8

ORWELL STRONG

… in some ways Julia was far more acute than Winston, and far less susceptible to Party propaganda. Once when he happened in some connexion to mention the war against Eurasia, she startled him by saying casually that in her opinion the war was not happening. The rocket bombs which fell daily on London were probably fired by the Government of Oceania itself, 'just to keep people frightened'. This was an idea that had literally never occurred to him. 1984, George Orwell

I n the wake of the Boston Bombings, the city was put on lockdown. An entire American metropolis was shut down, paralyzed, as the enormous extent of the domestic police state was on full display for the whole world to see. Officials would later reveal that at the time they feared a major sleeper cell had gone active. Whether true or not, Kent thought, somewhere George Orwell was smiling.

MORE THEATRICS

Thursday, April 18th, in Boston brought the obligatory visit from President Obama and the First Lady, with Michelle making a special visit to one particular Saudi national, a "person of interest" in the bombings, in the hospital (this after a reported unscheduled visit between the president and the Saudi ambassador).

On Friday, April 19th,* Dzhokhar Tsarnaev was killed, supposedly run over by his brother, Tamerlan, who was captured hours later hiding in a

---

* So, there it was, April 19th, a mere two days after the West, Texas conflagration, and wouldn't you know it, it's the anniversary of the Waco Tragedy and the Oklahoma City Bombing (April 20th is the anniversary of Columbine and Hitler's birthday, but let's not get too carried away).

boat behind a house on Franklin Street. Unfortunately for investigators, Tamerlan couldn't speak as he'd been shot in the throat, although some observers thought the injury looked more like a knife wound. In any case, he was lucky to be alive considering there were more holes in that boat than a block of Swiss cheese.

MORE HOLES

There were all sorts of holes in the official storyline, as well, in addition to conflicting accounts of almost every related event, which Kent knew was to be expected when the disinformation/misinformation component of a psychological warfare campaign kicks into high gear.

Intriguing side-stories and conspiracy theories, disinformation or otherwise, cropped up all over the place: some amateur researchers claimed to have dis-

Ride 'Em, Cowboy

Prominent Bush-era anti-war activist Carlos Arredondo (born Carlos Luis de Los Ángeles Arredondo Piedra), once an undocumented immigrant from Costa Rica, became a U.S. citizen with the help of U.S. Senator Edward Kennedy. In this now iconic photograph (above left), Arredondo, sporting a cowboy hat, assists in rushing a gravely injured Jeff Bauman toward a waiting ambulance.

Arredondo was present as a spectator, there to cheer on members of the National Guard and Samaritans, Inc., a suicide prevention group, who were running in honor of his two deceased sons.

His elder son, Alexander, a Marine, was killed in Operation Iraqi Freedom on Carlos' 44th birthday. Upon being informed of his son's death at his Hollywood, Florida home that same day, Arredondo became so distraught that he grabbed a hammer and began destroying a Marine Corp van. He then climbed inside the vehicle, doused the interior with gasoline, and at that point the propane torch he'd brought with him ignited; accidentally, claims Arredondo.

Before being pulled to safety by the Marines, Carlos received second- and third-degree burns to 26% of his body. Arredondo and his wife both spent time as psychiatric in-patients, and their youngest son committed suicide five years later. Carlos' story is featured in the documentary film, *The Prosecution of an American President.*

And you thought he was just some yahoo in a cowboy hat…

Actually, Kent reflected, he's a self-immolating, mentally imbalanced, former rodeo clown, former illegal-immigrant yahoo in a cowboy hat from Hollywood—who just so happened to get his citizenship with the assistance of JFK's brother, and who serendipitously found himself at the finish line of the Boston Marathon when the bombs went off, whereby he subsequently achieved international attention and quasi-celebrity status for assisting one of the worst-wounded victims of the bombings (although if you've watched any video of the aftermath of the bombings, his actions aren't all that heroic).

Now, things like this can certainly just happen, but this sounded to Kent like it might be one of those too-good-to-be-true scripted storylines that he so often found woven into the fabric of staged-terror incidents.

But, then again, Carlos might be exactly what he appeared to be: someone who was in the wrong place at the wrong time. Or, would that be the right place at the right time?

covered evidence of the use of green screens and fake blood at the bombings, along with fake wounds; others swore they'd identified various crisis actors who had appeared at other staged events; still others asserted that the brothers had an uncle with connections to the  CIA, and that Dzhokhar's wife was the granddaughter of a member of the infamous Skull and Bones secret society at Yale, which, of course, both Bush Sr. and Jr. belong to.

Kent had read that at least one Boston hospital had been evacuated on the day of the bombings, which could have been due to a real threat, or a convenient cover under which to remove crisis actors from the facility.

Who the hell knows, Kent thought, understanding that the only thing for certain was that nobody was ever going to figure it all out or be able to sort fact from fiction. These operators were too good for that; you might pick up clues here and there, but you'll never find hard evidence, unless they wanted you to for some reason. And, even if you did find something, you'd never get it on the evening news.

Were the Tsarnaev brothers set up? Did they believe that they were participating in a drill? Was Dzhokhar truly a radical Islamist, and, if so, was his radicalization facilitated in some way by parties within one of our national security or intelligence services, or individuals working for them? Did Tamerlan really run  over Dzhokhar during a battle with police?

Kent knew that there were a million questions that might never be fully answered, but he also knew not to get too caught up in the details—that is precisely what is supposed to happen, and is an intentional part of the overall strategy to prevent the truth from ever seeing the light of day.

In the midst of all the swirling media accounts, dead-end leads and rabbit holes, Kent couldn't help but recall the words of then-candidate Barack Obama: "We cannot continue to rely only on our military in order to achieve the national security objectives that we've set. We've got to have a civilian national security force that's just as powerful, just as strong, just as well-funded."

Yep, and this is exactly how you get it.

JACK NICHOLSON

ONE FLEW OVER THE CUCKOO'S NEST

IF HE'S CRAZY...
WHAT DOES THAT
MAKE YOU?

FANTASY FILMS PRESENTS

A MILOS FORMAN FILM JACK NICHOLSON IN "ONE FLEW OVER THE CUCKOO'S NEST"
STARRING LOUISE FLETCHER AND WILLIAM REDFIELD SCREENPLAY LAWRENCE HAUBEN AND BO GOLDMAN
BASED ON THE NOVEL BY KEN KESEY DIRECTOR OF PHOTOGRAPHY HANSKELL WEXLER MUSIC JACK NITZSCHE
PRODUCED BY SAUL ZAENTZ AND MICHAEL DOUGLAS DIRECTED BY MILOS FORMAN

R RESTRICTED

NOW AVAILABLE IN SIGNET PAPERBACK AND VIKING/COMPASS TRADE PAPERBACK

Chapter 9

"I don't even eat rice."

U pon being informed by authorities that he had been arrested for the production of ricin, and its subsequent use as a weapon through the U.S. Mail, Kevin Curtis reportedly exclaimed, "I don't even eat rice." Whether at that point or somewhere down the line investigators began to figure out they had the wrong man is unclear, but they soon realized that Curtis, as whacky as he is, was innocent.

They also soon found that Everett Dutschke, who Curtis had identified as someone who'd be interested in framing him, was guilty as hell, or at least it sure appeared that way. Dutschke, who made it a point of advertising his Mensa membership (and telling everyone who'd listen that Kevin Curtis, who also claimed to be a member of the high-IQ organization, was *not* in fact a member),

apparently thought it would be sufficient to mail a few letters containing ricin with KC's signature phrase, "I'm KC and I approved this message," and that'd be the end of it.

So sure of his scheme and his own brilliance was he, we're told by law enforcement and mainstream media sources, that he didn't even bother to get rid of a whole boatload of incriminating evidence at his former karate studio or residence, including receipts for castor beans (used to make ricin), a coffee grinder use to grind the beans into powder, rubber gloves, the printer used to print the letters, and a note saying that he was going to frame Kevin Curtis.

Okay, so the last item in that list isn't real, but it might as well have been, because it seems as though it never crossed Dutschke's mind that suspicion might at some point fall on him. Evidently, he was also completely oblivious to modern electronic surveillance tactics and capabilities, because after investigators swooped in and began searching his apartment, he got on a cell

There Ain't Gonna Be No Grease!

In his GQ article, "The Elvis Impersonator, the Karate Instructor, a Fridge Full of Severed Heads, and the Plot 2 Kill the President," Wells Tower recounts how ricin suspect Everett Dutschke's less-than-stellar musical pursuits, at least in once instance, oddly foreshadowed subsequent criminal behavior:

 Dutschke tried to make a name for himself with a blues act he called Dusty and the RoboDrum. The RoboDrum was unbeloved in the local music scene. "It was horrible. Every time he got up there the entire bar just flooded outside," says Brock Robbins, owner of the Boondocks Grill, whose open-mike night Dutschke used to frequent. "My open-mike night was his first act of terrorism. He killed it."

 The jacket of a demo CD characterizes the music of the Robo-Drum as "progressive guitar funktronica for smart people." This reviewer would characterize it as very ghastly. Still, the music of the RoboDrum is not without the power to haunt the listener. The song "2 Young" is the chilling lament of a man evidently in love with a girl below the age of consent. The song seems to presage a suite of disturbing events in the life of Everett Dutschke, events unrelated to ricin, events that the courts in Tupelo are still sorting out.

The grim particulars are these: In the fall of 2012, according to sworn testimony, school-age girls walking near Dutschke's home were occasionally dazzled by the green beam of a laser pointer. Glancing about for its source, the girls would spy Everett Dutschke standing in a window, nude. The neighbors recall it vividly. "You see there in the back of the place?" says Dennis Carlock, grandfather to one of the plaintiffs. He pointed down the block at Dutschke's home, an unprepossessing ranch with high grasses in the yard. "That's where he done all his exposure, through the window. When them window shades were up, you knew something was fixing to go on."

Asked about the exposure charge, Dutschke replies, "I would much rather you not even go there." But when pressed, he avers that if anyone had been victimized it was Dutschke himself, persecuted by neighbors peeping, unbidden, into his windows "for years."

The courts were not convinced by Dutschke's claims. In January 2013, he was sentenced to ninety days in jail for indecent exposure and ordered to pay a fine of $364. No sooner had he filed his appeal than he was picked up on graver charges of fondling minors. He had, at his dojo, the charges ran, improperly touched three girls under the age of 16. The police took him into custody in lieu of $1 million bond.

Might the child molestation charges have provided Dutschke with a motive for orchestrating and then purposely bungling his hugely incompetent ricin letter frame-up attempt?

Tracy Morgan on Saturday Night Live in "Scared Straight: Mac Attack," explaining to three male juvenile delinquents that if they persist in their criminal activity and end up in prison, their fellow inmates aren't going to do them the courtesy of using lubricant during sexual assaults – "There ain't gonna be no grease!"

[continued] ... for all Dutschke's local renown as a "genius," the ricin plot is not a masterwork of diabolical cunning. The ricin itself was so impotent that 80-year-old Sadie Holland huffed it with no ill effects. And there are probably junior high schoolers who would have covered their tracks more shrewdly than the ricin letters' sender did. So, one wonders: If Everett Dutschke loathed Kevin Curtis passionately enough to risk life imprisonment, can we really believe that he would have framed Curtis so bunglingly as to leave such a flagrant trail to his own front door? The perpetrator's plot was so maladroit, so easily unraveled, that it's hard not to wonder: If Dutschke did it, did he want to get caught?

So goes one local theory: Some speculate that, facing the possibility of forty-five years for child molestation in Mississippi's Parchman state farm, an especially unhappy home for pedophiles, Dutschke may have hit upon the ricin scheme as a route to a gentler bid in a federal pen.

... most everyone agrees that if Dutschke does any time, they will not be easy years. "I believe he's gonna go in a tight end and come out a wide receiver," mused Rep. Steve Holland, Dutschke's former political rival. "But that's pure conjecture. I couldn't say for sure."

This is certainly one possible explanation, but it could go deeper than this. Dutschke might not have been worried about his child molestation activities in the first place because he knew well in advance that he was going to the Federal penitentiary as part of another scheme. Or, maybe not.

In any case, There ain't gonna be no grease, Everett!

* * *

"When them window shades were up,
you knew something was fixing to go on."

phone and told his wife to start a fire so he could get rid of some papers, and later proceeded to his now-closed karate studio—which had been shuttered due to allegations against him of multiple counts of child molestation (see sidebar)—to bag up a bunch of items and toss them in a nearby dumpster, with FBI officials watching and listening the whole time.

Now, there's stupid, and then there's arrogant stupidity, and beyond that there's just plain dumb-ass. Where Dutschke falls in that spectrum was never entirely clear, but if Kent had learned one thing, it was never to take anyone or anything at face value—not alleged perpetrators, not investigators, victims, mommas, dogs, cats, nobody.

To be sure, not everything that happens is the result of a conspiracy, and not every criminal is other than what they seem. But not infrequently, there's a deeper aspect to the story that most people miss altogether.

THE PUPPETEERS' TOOLBOX

Those who are up on their Elvis lore will know that the King, a karate black belt, had his own personal nemesis, estranged-wife Priscilla's boyfriend, Mike Stone, karate instructor. During a 1973 concert, several men climbed on stage and Elvis fought them off alongside his bodyguards. He was sure they had been sent by Stone.

Fast forward to 2013 and in the middle of a week filled with acts of staged terrorism, a martial-artist Elvis impersonator is framed by an arch-rival karate instructor. Now there's one big damn coincidence, Kent thought. This was exactly the type of mocking dark humor Kent had found over and over again in his research, and discussed at some length in his book.

Staged terror scenarios often involve inside jokes, subtle and not-so-subtle references to prior staged events or other crimes, occult symbols and numbers, or all of the above. Yes, but *how* do they pull off these sorts of things, one might wonder. As Kent had discovered, the orchestrators of such acts are logistical wizards who spare no expense and expend untold resources to successfully execute their sophisticated, diabolical plans, and they are evil comic geniuses, as well.

As difficult as this was for Kent to accept, he knew it to be true: not only that, he found it was not just a recent phenomenon. There is a wealth of historical precedent of this nature. The *how* is hardly ever readily apparent, but suffice it to say that these operators have every tool under the sun in their toolbox, and they don't hesitate to use any of them.

From simple methods of suggestion and subtle manipulation to advanced behavioral modification protocols, from coercion to threats and acts of extreme violence, from brainwashing techniques to psychotropic drugs (and other pharmacological implements), they can get just about anybody to do anything, anytime, anywhere.

HIDDEN MEANING

Kent had resisted the urge to blog about the happenings in Tupelo, right under his nose, or to go snooping around trying to interview people. He'd drawn enough attention to himself already, he figured, no need to make things worse. He also knew that his understanding of the events would change over time, and sensed that something larger was going on—what it was, he wasn't quite sure yet.

The Elvis meme that'd been incorporated into the entire scheme was obvious, but he saw possibilities for additional memes, ones that'd be right in keeping with the whole JFK theme. Kent knew to look for clues and markers in a whole range of places: surnames, place names, street numbers and the like.

Certainly there are genuine coincidences and not every number is significant or used intentionally, and not every graphic icon is an occult symbol imbued with evil intent—in the overall scheme of things, this is rarely the case, in fact. But when numbers and symbols are employed purposefully, we'd be wise to recognize it and understand what they mean and why they're present.

Based on prior investigations and what had already happened in 2013, several things had caught Kent's attention about this particular episode. He wasn't entirely sure any of them meant anything, but, as he saw it, they were "imbued with possibilities."

MEMES-R-US

First, it wasn't uncommon in these situations to find a direct or oblique Nazi reference: "Dutschke" means "german." A bit of a stretch, admittedly, Kent thought, but there was also this fact: Lee Harvey Oswald was once famously arrested on Canal Street in New Orleans, and Dutschke lived on Canal Street in Tupelo. Coincidence? Again, maybe: there was no way to know for certain.

Even if these two items were pure coincidence and not intentionally incorporated, as might well be the case, the larger point is that these are exactly the types of signatures or markers the orchestrators of these staged events actually *do* integrate into the environment on a frequent basis.

There was one other aspect of the case that Kent was curious about, one that his intellect told him to let go but that his instincts wouldn't leave alone. He knew that it was probably not something done intentionally, but he couldn't resist the thought that perhaps it was an actual meme that had been ingeniously woven into the script for the event.

"I don't even eat rice," Curtis had told investigators, a line that made it into news stories, and some headlines even, across the country. With all of the other JFK connections trotted out thus far, Kent was curious: was this part of a rice meme, a means of referencing Kennedy's impromptu visit to the Rice Hotel in Houston on November 21st, 1963, the day before his assassination? Or, perhaps, his moonshot speech, at Rice University in 1962? Or both?

YOU WANT CREAM AND SUGAR WITH THAT?

In what might seem a slightly in-bred set of circumstances even for Mississippi, not only did Kevin Curtis' wife, Laura, work at his brother's insurance agency, Everett Dutschke was employed there, as well. After her divorce from Kevin, she admittedly contemplated having an affair with Dutschke. "I thought about it," she said. Why didn't she? "Because he's short," she explained. "He's short and hairy."

Laura Curtis also admitted that, "I forgot to tell the FBI even that [Dutschke] doesn't drink coffee, why would he have a coffee grinder? I just remember how I would ask him if he wanted a cup of coffee and he would go, 'That stuff's poison,' and he would always look funny when he said it."

"THIS PLACE IS CRAZY"

Writing in the *Los Angeles Times* on April 28th, 2013, in a piece entitled "With new arrest, ricin case takes a strange turn," reporter Matthew Teague shared the following:

> "Tupelo is a kaleidoscope," said sociologist Mark Franks, who grew up in nearby Booneville. There are true geniuses walking the streets of Tupelo, he said, and incredibly wealthy, generous people. But also, "every wall-eyed uncle and 'yard cousin' — just referencing the local pejorative — makes it into Tupelo, Miss. It creates a peculiar culture."

After providing that fairly accurate characterization, Teague later closes his piece with an exchange with Dutschke that echoed this sentiment:

> Hours before his arrest, Dutschke answered his door by opening it just enough to look out with one dark eye. He held a kitten, which also looked outside. "I'm sorry, I just...," he started. His voice was soft. "I can't talk. I'm so, so sorry."
>
> Could he say, at least, what started this mess?
>
> "Just look around you," he said. "This place is crazy."

Left: Dutschke and U.S. Congressman Roger Wicker. Right: Dutschke and former Chair of the Republican National Committee and Mississippi Governor Haley Barbour.

Dutschke and former U.S. Senator Trent Lott. Dutschke and former Arkansas Governor and Republican presidential candidate Mike Huckabee.

Dutschke and former President George W. Bush? (Kinda looks Photo-shopped.)

* * *

"… every wall-eyed uncle and 'yard cousin' … makes it into Tupelo, Miss. It creates a peculiar culture."

* * *

Yeah, Mac, I got a bunch of questions, too.

CHAPTER 10

CRIME SCENE REVISITED

April 25, 2013: Dallas, Texas

In the shadow of the main story of the day on Tuesday, April 16th—the ricin letter scare—this story was essentially lost, but it certainly grabbed Kent's attention: American Airlines had been completely shut down, with all flights cancelled, due to a "computer glitch."

Having covered the subject in his book, Kent was fully familiar with the role American Airlines' aircraft played in the attacks of 9/11—American Airlines Flights 11 and 77 had hit the North Tower and the Pentagon, respectively. But there was a good deal more to the story than these mere facts, as Kent had detailed in his book.

The orchestrators of the 9/11 attacks had chosen American Airlines, and the two involved flights with their specific numbers, for very definite

reasons, and Kent strongly suspected that the same was true in this instance. Involving American Airlines in another staged event, even if it was just through a form of industrial sabotage, was certainly a creative means through which to invoke the memory of the airline's role in 9/11, but there's this, as well: American Airlines' main hub is the Dallas-Fort Worth International Airport, and Dallas is, of course, the location of JFK's 1963 assassination.

GRAND OPENING

W as he getting carried away with the JFK associations, Kent wondered? He almost wished that this were the case, but he knew from experience that he was most likely onto something, and that his observations were probably valid.

His suspicions were substantially reinforced when, on April 25th, a mere ten days after the Boston Bombing, all five living U.S. Presidents gathered for the dedication of the George W. Bush Presidential Library ... in Dallas ... less than a mile from Dealey Plaza. Bingo.

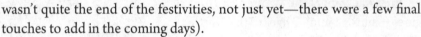

Years in planning and construction, and it just happens to open *now*? Come on.

Starting line: birthplace/Boston, John F. Kennedy Presidential Library. Finish line: deathplace/Dallas, George W. Bush Presidential Library (except that this wasn't quite the end of the festivities, not just yet—there were a few final touches to add in the coming days).

Too bad there were no fireworks to accompany the closing ceremony like there were in Boston...

Oh, but there were...

TRIUMPH!

T he early morning hours of April 25th, 2013, Mobile, Alabama: twin barge explosions (boy, they sure seem to come in twos, don't they?) rock the waterfront as huge fireballs erupt from two docked vessels. Coincidentally, or not, the Carnival cruise ship *Triumph* is moored nearby, undergoing repairs

following the "Cruise from Hell" earlier in the year.

Kent couldn't help but think that this was a purposeful echo of an event that had reportedly occurred during Kennedy's assassination ride in his motorcade: for four minutes, as the story goes, Police Band #1 was jammed, and immediately following the shooting, the Morse code for

"Victory" went out across all police radios. Channel #1 subsequently came back online and resumed regular transmissions. *Triumph!*

THE RISE OF THE…

As if that weren't enough fun with boats and their names, there was the name of the fireboat dispatched to help battle the blaze in Mobile: Phoenix. Kent had written an entire chapter on this potent symbol and its deep occult significance.

Hell, for all he knew, the names of the two boats were to be considered together as a single statement: the Triumph of the Phoenix (a well-known symbol of the Illuminati), but he wasn't so sure about that one, and anyway, each did a fine job by themselves.

WHY MOBILE?

Why Mobile, why not some place in Dallas, or closer to it? More JFK lore. Bringing in Alabama automatically evokes the memory of Kennedy-antagonist Governor George Wallace, about whom much need not be said, except that he took his oath of office standing on the exact spot where Jefferson Davis had been sworn in as president of the Confederate States of America, and that in his inaugural speech, Wallace delivered one of the most widely known lines of hate-speech in American history:

> In the name of the greatest people that have ever trod this earth, I draw
> the line in the dust and toss the gauntlet before the feet of tyranny, and
> I say segregation now, segregation tomorrow, segregation forever.

Kennedy was also an honorary University of Alabama letterman, but the more pertinent connection is this: just four months before Kennedy's assassination, Lee Harvey Oswald was invited by Spring Hill College[*] in Mobile to speak about his time living in Russia, and only hours after the assassination, FBI agents swarmed the campus.

As Kent was quickly learning, the year 2013 was going to be all JFK, all the time (well, not quite, but it sure seemed like it at the moment).

---

[*]   Also in 1963, on April 16th, Dr. Martin Luther King, Jr. wrote his famous "Letter from Birmingham Jail," in which he cited Spring Hill College for its leadership in the civil rights movement.

Chapter 11

Mr. Not-So-Funny Guy

April 27, 2013: Washington, D.C.

Twelve days after the Boston Bombings, on the twelfth of what Kent would come to refer to as "The Twelve Days of Terror" (and for all he knew, that's how those who planned the damn thing referred to it, as well) and …

The nation's political elite, Hollywood celebrities and top journalists are gathered for the annual White House Correspondent's Dinner in Washington, DC.

The featured comedian this evening is Conan O'Brien, which in itself is a bad joke because he's really never been all that funny. But, in reality, Conan himself is indeed the joke in the room that night: in this year, the 50th anniversary of the JFK assassination, *50-year-old* O'Brien is from Brookline, Massachusetts, Kennedy's birthplace.

Not only that, but he also serves on the board of, wait for it, the JFK Presidential Museum Foundation. *Badda bing.*

Another Marathon Explosion

All that was missing from the occasion, then, were the fireworks. But wait, what's this? An explosion and fire at the *Marathon (as in Boston Marathon, get it?)* Detroit Refinery only several hours before the Correspondent's Dinner? *Badda BOOM!*

Two days after the twin barge explosions in Mobile, and the very evening of the White House Correspondent's Dinner, it's more industrial-sabotage-for-kicks.

Why, you might ask yourself, the Detroit facility and not one of Marathon's other refineries? Perhaps because it is located approximately 20 miles from both the John F. Kennedy School and John F. Kennedy Park, and less than 10 miles from both the John F. Kennedy, Jr., Library and the Caroline Kennedy Library in Dearborn Heights.

As important to the event's orchestrators, however, who never tire of the radical Muslim theme, is that the refinery sits less than a mile from neighboring Dearborn, home of the Arab American National Museum, the American Moslem Society and the Islamic Center of America, the oldest Shia mosque in the United States and the largest mosque in North America. Dearborn, with its large Shia Arab population, is often referred to as "the heart of Shiism" in the U.S.A.

99 Problems

In April 2013, singer-rapper power couple Beyonce and Jay-Z celebrated their fifth wedding anniversary with a trip to Cuba.

The visit was highly criticized, and sparked speculation that the two may have violated a 51-year embargo making it illegal for U.S. citizens to travel to Cuba solely for tourism. Under current law, travel to the island nation is permitted only under license.

However, it was subsequently revealed that the couple had obtained official permission for their trip, leading some critics to believe that Obama had personally provided authorization for the visit.

The controversy prompted Jay-Z, among whose many hits is "99 Problems" ("I got 99 problems but a bitch ain't one"), to record a song entitled "Open Letter," slamming critics who suggested that the couple's clearance came from President Obama rather than the Treasury Department:

> Obama said, "chill you gon' get me impeached.
> You don't need this sh*t anyway.
> Chill with me on the beach."

The episode provided great fodder for Obama's script writers, and in his monologue at the White House Correspondent's Dinner the President referenced it, joking, "Some things are beyond my control. For example, this whole controversy about Jay-Z going to Cuba. It's unbelievable. I've got 99 problems and now Jay-Z's one."

Mr. and Mrs. Illuminati: "Do what thou will," indeed, my brother.

Hmm. April. Cuba. Kennedy. Ring a bell? (I'm not even gonna' touch the Amanda Berry-Castro brothers thing.)

THAT'S NOT FUNNY

Speaking of bad jokes, only four days before the White House Correspondents Dinner, on April 23rd, someone hacked the Associated Press's Twitter account and posted a fake report stating that there had been two explosions (again with the twin explosions) at the White House and that President Obama had been injured. The dramatic news produced a stock market flash crash, which, understandably, nobody on Wall Street found amusing.

(Left) The tweet. (Right) A graph showing the drop in the US markets after the fake tweet was released.

MEL GIBSON   JULIA ROBERTS

JERRY FLETCHER SEES CONSPIRACIES EVERYWHERE. ONE HAS TURNED OUT TO BE TRUE.
NOW HIS ENEMIES WANT HIM DEAD. AND SHE'S THE ONLY ONE HE CAN TRUST.

CONSPIRACY THEORY

A RICHARD DONNER FILM

WARNER BROS. PRESENTS

A SILVER PICTURES PRODUCTION IN ASSOCIATION WITH SHULER DONNER/DONNER PRODUCTIONS MEL GIBSON JULIA ROBERTS A RICHARD DONNER FILM "CONSPIRACY THEORY" PATRICK STEWART
MUSIC BY CARTER BURWELL CO-PRODUCERS DAN CRACCHIOLO J. MILLS GOODLOE RICK SOLOMON EDITED BY FRANK J. URIOSTE A.C.E. PRODUCTION DESIGNER PAUL SYLBERT DIRECTOR OF PHOTOGRAPHY JOHN SCHWARTZMAN A.S.C.
EXECUTIVE PRODUCER JIM VAN WYCK WRITTEN BY BRIAN HELGELAND PRODUCED BY JOEL SILVER AND RICHARD DONNER DIRECTED BY RICHARD DONNER

CHAPTER 12

IN THE CROSSHAIRS

During the latter part of the week of April 15, 2013, and the following week, the Twelve Days of Terror, Kent observed caravans of dark blue pickups and SUVs, many pulling matching enclosed trailers, passing by his office window as they travelled down Main Street. These were, he knew, unmarked FBI and Homeland Security vehicles transporting evidence-collection and hazmat teams.

In that same time-frame, Kent also noted unusual police activity around his building: a patrol car sitting in front of his office for two hours one day; another day, an officer walking down to the end of the hall where his office was located, looking around briefly, then leaving.

Great, they've put my ass on the Domestic Terrorism Watch List, he thought to himself. Actually, he already had other, very good reasons to believe that such was the case—but that's a story for another chapter. All he could do now was sit and watch, and wonder: did the subjects of his book have something special in store for him?

STAGED TERROR PLUS

To Kent, everything he'd seen in the past couple of weeks bore clear signs of being false-flag terror—without a doubt. Yet, his instincts told him that there was another still-undiscovered level to what he believed the perpetrators must view as one big game.

He recognized the classic hallmarks of a staged-terror operation, but he knew that these frequently had an occult or ritualistic aspect to them. Upon deeper analysis, these events often were incredibly sophisticated, multi-layered affairs, with the occult aspects increasing exponentially the logistical challenges involved.

DON'T FALL ASLEEP

A NIGHTMARE on
ELM STREET

R.I.P.
J.F.K.

MISS YOU
LANCE
CARAS

Dealey Plaza, a ritual killsite, getting set-up for the 50th anniversary of JFK's murder.

Could the "Twelve Days of Terror" also be a mass ritual? There were the multiple instances of false-flag operations, the JFK references, the inside jokes and that same unmistakable mockery—was there also an occult component?

If all of this somehow constituted a type of mass ritual, Kent didn't see it yet. He'd written briefly about certain ritualistic aspects of the JFK assassination in his book, but he realized that in order to understand what was going on now, he needed to gain additional insight into the events of November 22, 1963. He needed to return to the scene of the crime.

PART THREE

THE GOLDEN JUBILEE OF THE KILLING OF THE KING

SECRET SOCIETIES
and
Psychological Warfare

Michael A. Hoffman II

CHAPTER 13

HOFFMAN LENSES

Michael Hoffman is a former reporter for the New York bureau of the *Associated Press* and author of *Secret Societies and Psychological Warfare*, the first edition of which was published in 1989, long before September 11, 2001.

Kent referred to Hoffman in his book as "The Prophet of 9/11," but clarified what he meant by this, writing, "His work was prescient not in that it actually predicted 9/11, but in that it clearly defined the motives and *modus operandi* of those ultimately responsible for the terror attacks..." although, "much of *Secret Societies* reads as though it were written specifically about 9/11."

Kent quoted liberally from Hoffman's work, and this served as a guiding companion for the reader. *Secret Societies* helped Kent more clearly understand 9/11 as both psychological warfare and mass ritual, and contributed significantly to

his understanding of occult/Masonic practices and the subject of mass mind control.

A BLUNT INSTRUMENT

Now faced with the task of further analyzing the Kennedy assassination as a public ritual and as an act of "mind war," Kent turned once again to *Secret Societies* for guidance and illumination on the details of the assassination, those responsible for the killing, and the resulting deleterious effects on our country. Regarding the final point, Hoffman wrote:

> What ought to be unambiguous to any student of mass psychology is the almost immediate decline of the American people in the wake of this shocking, televised slaughter. There are many indicators of

71

this transformation. Within a year, Americans had largely switched from softer-toned, naturally-colored cotton clothing to garish-colored artificial polyesters. Popular music became louder, faster and more cacophonous. Drugs appeared for the first time outside the Bohemian subculture and ghettos, in the mainstream. Extremes of every kind came into fashion. Revolutions in cognition and behavior were on the horizon, from the Beatles to Charles Manson, from "Free Love" to LSD.

Hoffman is not implying that these were incidental effects of the assassination, however, but rather is pointing to an even more disturbing reality: JFK's brutal public killing was the blunt instrument of mass trauma delivered to the unsuspecting citizenry as part of a trauma-based mind-control operation of unthinkable proportions. His death was the psychic wound that opened up the mass mind for programming by the elites, and their coming assault on the collective psyche of the nation would be both multi-pronged and relentless.

Hoffman continued:

The killers were not caught, the Warren Commission was a white-
wash. There was a sense that the men
who ordered the assassination were
grinning somewhere over cocktails, and
out of this, a nearly-psychedelic wonder
seized the American population, an awe-
some shiver before the realization that
whoever could kill a president of the United States in broad daylight
and get away with it, could get away with anything.

Indeed, they could get away with anything, they did get away with it
and they're still getting away with it; "it" being not only the Kennedy assassination, but numerous incidents of a similar nature that followed and continue to this very day, including the killings of RFK, MLK, the Oklahoma
City Bombing, the Waco Massacre and 9/11, *et alia.*

In short, as you prepare to delve into the material that follows, if your
only question regarding the Kennedy assassination is whether or not there
was a second shooter involved, you'd better go take a couple of Xanax, because you're going to need them.

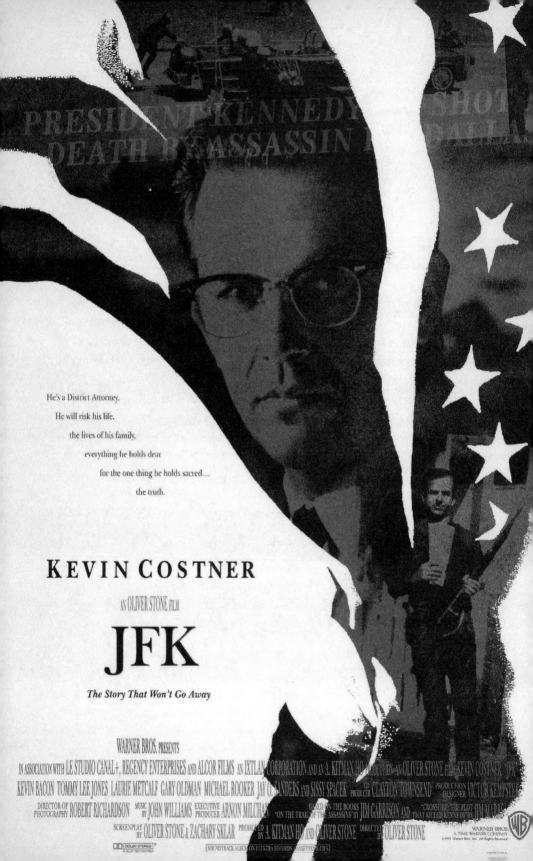

CHAPTER 14

FIDELITY. SECRECY. SILENCE.

November 22, 1963: Dealey Plaza, Dallas, Texas

The Presidential limousine rounds the corner onto Elm Street. Two shots ring out. No, three. No, four. A shot was fired from the Grassy Knoll. No, it wasn't. And on and on and on… What the hell did actually happen?

NO CLOSER

As the 50th anniversary of the JFK assassination approached, the pressing questions surrounding the murder of the President were apparently no closer to being answered than they were in 1963. Despite the passage of five decades, two Congressional investigations, untold millions of hours of research, the publishing of thousands of books and articles, the production of dozens of documentaries and the release of a major motion picture, in the year 2013 the mainstream media was still posing *exactly* the same questions half a century on: Did Lee Harvey Oswald act alone? Was there a conspiracy involved? Who killed JFK?

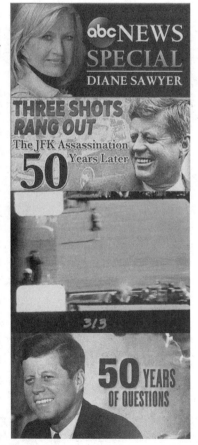

In an article published prior to the anniversary, author Vincent Bugliosi estimated that at least 42 different groups, 82 assassins and 214 individuals have been accused in various conspiracy theories concerning JFK's assassination—and this well may be an underestimation. The bottom line: the public still has no solid answers and, perhaps as a direct result, the horrid spectacle still captivates us as powerfully as ever.

How Big?

A massive amount of media coverage accompanied the year of the 50th anniversary of President Kennedy's assassination, and to the extent that the original event had lost any of its potential to mesmerize and enthrall the American public, the extensive programming served to reanimate the spell and re-open the psychic wound.

The question for Kent was not, Was there a conspiracy behind the assassination of JFK? Rather, Just how damn big was it? Years earlier he had moved well beyond asking whether Oswald was the only shooter, but had not done the research necessary to properly evaluate all the alternative theories. He *had* done enough superficial investigation to fully understand that he could spend the rest of his life reading JFK conspiracy books and still never arrive at the truth of what happened that day.

Kent knew from his research that Kennedy's killing had been more than just the most infamous assassination in modern history. There was clear evidence of occult ritual and psychological warfare that mirrored in multiple respects what he'd uncovered in analyzing 9/11.

Kent had written briefly about the ritual elements involved with the JFK assassination, drawing parallels between the occult components incorporated into both events:

> President Kennedy was shot on Elm Street, which forms one of the forks of the trident design of Dealey Plaza, site of the first Masonic Lodge in Dallas (the site also features an obelisk and a reflecting pool). The significance of the trident and the number 77 having already been discussed, one should not be terribly surprised to learn that, upon leaving Dealey Plaza, Elm Street runs directly under US Route 77 (John Hinkley bought the .22 caliber pistol he shot President Reagan with at Rocky's Pawn Shop on this same Elm Street, but that's another story). In some of the amateur footage and photographs taken on November 22, 1963, roads signs bearing the number 77 are clearly visible.

The obelisk at Dealey Plaza.

Kent also recognized clear evidence of the employment of psychological warfare tactics against the American public, first and foremost being a well-engineered campaign of misinformation and disinformation.

The trident design of Dealey Plaza. (Right) Road sign for U.S. Route 77. According to Aleister Crowley, 77 is "magical power in perfection"

Abundant Signs

As 11/22/13 approached and Kent's further research helped him better understand the complexity of the assassination, he accepted an invitation to appear on author Daniel Estulin's television program on the Spanish-language channel of the Russia Today network. Estulin is best known as author of *The True Story of the Bilderberg Group*, and Kent had previously appeared on his program to discuss his first book.

In his second appearance on the show, the topic was the occult symbolism in the JFK assassination and Kent shared information he was planning to incorporate into his next book.

Estulin's questions to Kent during the program included this one: "Dealey Plaza was the former site of a Masonic Lodge of the Scottish Rite. Did it represent anything else?" Kent answered,

It was also an outdoor temple: built in the shape of a trident, with an obelisk representing the phallus of Osiris. The sectioned obelisk has 14 levels, clearly representing the 14 pieces into which Osiris was cut. There is a flame atop the obelisk, representing illumination, the Light-Bearer, Lucifer himself. There are also two reflecting pools, symbols of Isis and the moon, which reflects the light of the Sun.

In fact, Dealey Plaza was not only the site of the first Masonic Lodge in Dallas, but is also named in honor of a 33rd degree Freemason, George Dealey, a Dallas businessman and the long-time publisher of the *Dallas Morning News*, whom the *New York Times* called "the dean of American publishers." (Dealey was also a Knight Templar, Shriner and member of the Red Cross of Constantine.)

Dealey Plaza: a site of historical significance to Freemasons, named for a prominent Freemason, constructed on a trident design, incorporating multiple symbols of significance within Freemasonry (obelisk, reflecting pool, torch of illumination, numerous Blazing Stars). It is indeed an outdoor temple, and as such a fitting location in which to conduct a ritual assassination.

And it was not merely an assassination, but a uniquely Masonic assassination. James Shelby Downard, who along with *Secret Societies* author Michael Hoffman decades ago penned a seminal work deciphering many of the ritual aspects of the Kennedy assassination in an essay entitled, "King Kill 33," wrote:

> Masonry does not believe in murdering a man in just any old way and in the JFK assassination it went to incredible lengths and took great risks in order to make this heinous act of theirs correspond to the ancient fertility oblation of the Killing of the King.

So, Dealey Plaza is an outdoor Masonic temple in which a Masonic ritual sacrificial ceremony was conducted on November 22, 1963: a conclusion with which Michael Hoffman would concur, writing in his own book that the assassination is "a masonic riddle several magnitudes above the pedestrian, CIA-Mafia-Anti-Castro-pro-Castro-KGB-Texas right wing, etc. political 'solutions' pushed by the various books and movies which

The obelisk is at the site of Dallas' first Masonic Lodge.

sometimes only serve to confuse and demoralize us all the more."

THE TEMPLE OF DOOM

The initiatory ceremony for the Third Degree of Freemasonry involves a dramatic re-enactment of the killing of Hiram Abiff, who they claim to be the chief architect of King Solomon's temple (this is not Biblically accurate) and who is a messianic figure within Freemasonry derived from the Egyptian Osiris myth.

President Kennedy was killed at precisely 12:30 p.m., as can be clearly seen on the clock on the Hertz Rent-a-Car sign atop the Texas School Book Depository. That's one, two, three as in "one, two, three, shoot!" Or, as in one, two, three degrees, the Third Degree of Freemasonry, Master Mason. (Don't forget the Triple Underpass or the Trinity River.)

During his television interview, Estulin asked Kent, "Was anything symbolized by the manner in which Kennedy was killed?" Kent replied:

Kennedy's killing was intended to mirror that of Freemasonry's Hiram Abiff, whose blood was shed within Solomon's Temple—it was a Masonic re-enactment of the murder of Hiram Abiff. The three unworthy craftsmen, or ruffians—Jubela, Jubelo, and Jubelum—each struck Hiram a blow. The first was to the throat, the second to the breast and the third to his forehead—almost precisely the three locations where Kennedy was struck.

79

This interpretation of the event is strongly reinforced by the presence of three unnamed 'hoboes' at Dealey Plaza on November 22, 1963, who were paraded by police through the plaza immediately following Kennedy's assassination.

The three hoboes (pictured below) were never officially identified, and an enormous amount of speculation has taken place regarding their true identities (see photo caption).

(Left) Dealey Plaza, November 22, 1963: The three "unworthy craftsmen" of Masonic lore are marched through the plaza. Some researchers claim that the first hobo is a top French assassin. The middle hobo is purported to be hit-man Charles Harrelson, father of actor Woody Harrelson, who died while serving a life sentence for the murder of a federal judge. The rear hobo is said to be E. Howard Hunt of Watergate fame. (Right) It is perhaps worth noting that filmmaker Oliver Stone directed both JFK and Natural Born Killers, in which the younger Harrelson starred.

While it is difficult to make a definitive identification of any of the three individuals based on the photographic evidence alone, there are additional facts to consider, including the following:

Among those who believe that Charles Harrelson was one of the three hoboes is author-researcher Michael Hoffman, who wrote of the photograph above:

> [It] is a ritual accompaniment of the Black mass that was the ceremonial immolation of a king, the unmistakable calling card of masonic murder, the appearance of ... the three 'unworthy craftsmen' of Temple burlesque, "that will not be blamed for nothing."

Hoffman met with Woody Harrelson (who once told the press, "My father was a CIA agent") at a San Francisco café in an attempt to gain access to the elder Harrelson, imprisoned for the murder of Judge John Wood. When Hoffman asked Harrelson point blank if his father killed Kennedy, the actor began to weep, and subsequently refused to facilitate Hoffman's request to visit his incarcerated father.

Given the family heritage, one might find it more than a little fitting that Woody reprised his role as Haymitch Abernathy in the sequel to The Hunger Games, entitled Catching Fire, which was released on the precise date of the 50th anniversary of the JFK assassination, November 22, 2013.

THE ULTIMATE WHO-DONE-IT?

Even if the elder Harrelson was in Dealey Plaza on November 22, 1963, he may have been a prop versus an actual shooter—as could well be the case with the other two hoboes. As James Shelby Downard noted, the symbolism of the three unworthy craftsmen "is at once a telling psychological blow against the victim and his comrades, a sign of frustrated inquiry—the supposedly senseless nature of any quest into the authentic nature of the murderers—and a mirror or doppelganger of the three assassins who execute the actual murder."

The trio photographed being marched through Dealey Plaza may have been purely symbolic figures representing three real shooters, for, as Downard notes, "It is a prime tenet of Masonry that its assassins come in threes." (One, two, three.)

If this sounds a bit odd and you find yourself asking, *Why would they go to all that effort?*, get over it, because it's only the tip of the iceberg. In fact, the orchestrators of the murder coordinated a veritable assassins' convention in Dallas on 11/22/63, with so many potential suspects/shooters it makes the mind reel. The place was crawling with intelligence operatives, as well, far beyond the number that would be associated with the advance teams that accompany a Presidential visit.

As Kris Millegan, publisher of TrineDay books, noted in an article about the 50th anniversary of the event:

One of the most effective tactics employed by the conspirators was to "muddy the waters" by bringing in as many "suspicious" individuals as possible into the assassination arena, even having different reasons for each person's presence — if there were a covert reason for being in Dallas on November 22, 1963, all the better. Scores of people were engaged in varied peripheral plots and sub-plots, many of which were related tangentially or not at all to the actual assassination. As a result, the pertinent facts drowned in a contrived whirlpool of suspicious, but not necessarily related, activity.

The result was a fog-of-war effect, a key strategy of the overall psychological warfare campaign, designed—quite successfully—to prevent anyone trying to navigate the maze from ever getting close to figuring out what actually happened or who was ultimately responsible.

This was combined, of course, with the fact that there were nearly a dozen very powerful interests with a possible motive for killing Kennedy, including the Central Intelligence Agency—about which JFK was reported as saying, "I want to splinter the CIA into a thousand pieces and scatter it to the winds"—and the military-industrial complex, major players in which were highly displeased with Kennedy's actions in Cuba and concerned about his approach to dealing with the Soviet Union, in general, and his potential stand-down of American forces in southeast Asia, in particular.

Others considered as potential suspects/conspirators include the Chicago Mafia and Vice-President Lyndon B. Johnson.

(Left) You'll get yours, pretty boy. (Right) President and First Lady Johnson on Air Force One with Jacqueline Kennedy and long-time crony Texas Congressman Albert Thomas immediately following the swearing-in ceremony, during which Johnson took the oath of office with his hand not on a Bible, but rather on a small Roman Missal, or Book of Mass. When asked about the wink, the White House photographer who took this photo, Cecil Stoughton, commented that it could have been "innocent, or sinister, and I have leaned to the latter." Johnson's own behavior aboard Air Force One that day was similarly inappropriate, with General Godfrey McHugh, the officer in command of the aircraft, complaining that the new President's behavior had been "obscene."

Roses Are Red...

"**T**hree times that day in Texas we were greeted with bouquets of the yellow roses of Texas. Only in Dallas they gave me red roses. I remember thinking: How funny—red roses for me," recalled Jacqueline Kennedy as she reflected on the events of November 22, 1963.

It's too bad she didn't pick up on the whole blood-red thing, and that she was apparently unaware of the flower's symbolic significance within Freemasonry and various other secret societies, wherein it primarily represents, among other things, both silence and secrecy.

The rose as a symbol of secrecy has ancient origins. In Roman legend, Cupid is said to have given Harpocrates, the god of silence, a rose as a token of gratitude for not revealing the indiscretions of Cupid's amorous mother, Venus (variously, Cupid gives Harpocrates the rose as a bribe).

Especially among Freemasons, the rose is a symbol of silence, which the candidate has promised to faithfully observe. As one Masonic author explains, "The three Rosettes [an imitation of a rose by means of ribbon or other material] on a Master Mason's Apron indicate that every Master Mason has thrice been obliged to Fidelity, to Secrecy, and to Silence: Fidelity to the Craft,

The Scottish Rite's 18th degree is "The Knight of the Rose Croix."

Secrecy as regards our sacred Secrets, and Silence as to the proceedings of the Lodge, which should never be disclosed to the profane."

The phrase "*sub rosa*" is Latin for "under the rose," and originated from the age-old practice of suspending a rose, chosen for its ancient association with confidentiality, from the ceiling of a council chamber to admonish all present to secrecy.

Sub rosa has come to denote that which is carried out in secret, and, in more modern times, the term has become a byword for covert operations, typically referring to those carried out by security services, such as the CIA.

The Egyptian goddess Isis had a deep connection to the symbolism of the rose, and roses were used extensively in the temples, rites and festivals dedicated to her.

"How funny—red roses for me."

A CRAFTY AFFAIR

Regardless of who was or wasn't involved in the conspiracy or related distractions, the reality is that great efforts were made to conform the manner, location and timing of Kennedy's assassination to Masonic convention.

It is also important to note that the seven-member Warren Commission—named for its chairman, Supreme Court Chief Justice Earl Warren, a 33rd degree Freemason and Grand Master of California from 1935-1936—whose official conclusion pinned all the blame for the assassination on lone gunman Lee Harvey Oswald, included at least two other high-level Freemasons, one being future U.S. President Gerald R. Ford. Also on the commission was former CIA director Allen Dulles, who, incidentally, JFK forced to resign following the Bay of Pigs fiasco. (J. Edgar Hoover, FBI director at the time, was a Thirty-Third Degree Inspector General Honorary in the Southern Scottish Rite Jurisdiction.)

Freemasons Earl Warren and Gerald Ford, who found out what it was like to be the target of a Presidential assassination attempt on two separate occasions, in the first instance thanks to Charles Manson Family cult member Lynette "Squeaky" Fromme. J. Edagr Hoover had a Masonic altar next door to his office.

There's a real surprise: an investigation led by Masons into a Masonic crime lays full blame on the scapegoat (a favorite Masonic ploy), Lee Harvey "I'm just a patsy" Oswald, who was himself, while under heavy police protection, almost immediately silenced following the assassination by a local mafia-connected night club owner.

So there's the main suspect, walking around the police station telling everybody he's a patsy, after which he takes a slug in the guts in the first-ever live televised murder from a thug named Jack Ruby, which just so happens to be a jeweler's term for a fake gemstone. The message? *Everything's* fake (except the killing—and some conspiracy theorists will even argue that point).

A COLLECTIVE TRAUMA

Whether Kennedy's assassination was a reenactment of the murder of Hiram Abiff alone, or was also intended to double as a twisted Killing-of-the-King fertility ritual designed to invoke the favor of the dark gods (or some such shit), Kent recognized the pattern from his deep research into the events of September 11, 2001: a staged act of terror that doubles as occult ritual accompanied by aggressive psychological warfare tactics targeting the American public.

When Kent first began digging more deeply into the JFK assassination, he naïvely assumed that because the event occurred half a century earlier, it would necessarily be less sophisticated—it was an assumption he soon found to be dead wrong.

Although the act of terror in this instance didn't fit the accepted post-9/11 mold of airplanes slamming into buildings and similar such acts, the public murder of the King of Camelot had been a psychologically traumatizing event collectively suffered by the entire nation.

John F. Kennedy was the first telegenic President, handsome and infallibly charming, whose very essence was transmitted directly into our living rooms through the flicker of that now-universal magic box. We felt that we knew him personally; he was part of our family.

On Monday, September 2, 1963, only a couple of months before his death, Kennedy appeared in a pre-recorded interview with Walter Cronkite, leading off the very first 30-minute evening news broadcast. He was there, among us, so personable and hopeful, and then he was cruelly and violently snatched away. Our technologically-induced sense  of familiarity with him, combined with the brutal manner in which he was ripped from us, triggered an immediate and lasting mass trauma, which was exacerbated by the ensuing confusion.

Michael Hoffman, writing in *Secret Societies*, observed, "...all this combined to leave the American people in the psychic condition of a rape victim; like a masonic initiate stripped of his clothes, lying in a coffin, terrorized by intimations of death and ready to be re-made in the image and likeness of his overseers."

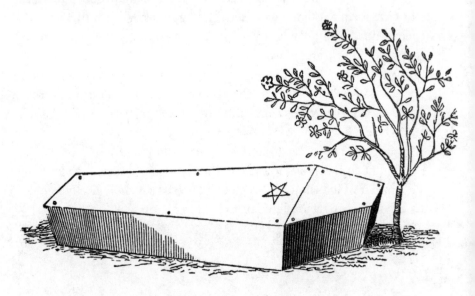

In an article in Hoffman's newsletter entitled, "King-Kill/33 Fifty Years Later: Symbolism, Psychological Warfare and Revelations in the John F. Kennedy Assassination Conspiracy," he further noted:

> The killing of President Kennedy was hugely demoralizing to the American people. Despite his many transgressions and foibles, he was a standard-bearer for a future vision of peace, prosperity, and health. He was endeavoring to return America to the dimensions of a Jeffersonian Republic rather than a National Security State fueled by a cryptocracy reaping enormous material prizes from perpetual wars and empire.

Ultimately, President Kennedy symbolized hope, and they allowed us to gain an intimate familiarity with its standard-bearer, bringing him into our living rooms on a frequent basis, and then blew his brains out right in front of us in a massive trauma-based mind-control operation, robbing us of our innocence and subsequently replacing hope with sex, drugs and rock'n'roll.

As James Shelby Downard noted, Kennedy's assassination involved far more than the killing of a sitting American President:

> ... the ultimate purpose of that assassination was not political or economic but sorcerous: for the control of the dreaming mind and the marshalling of its forces is the omnipotent force in this entire scenario of lies, cruelty and degradation.
>
> Something died in the American people on November 22, 1963— call it idealism, innocence or the quest for moral excellence. It is the transformation of human beings which is the authentic reason and motive for the Kennedy murder and until so-called conspiracy theorists can accept this very real element they will be reduced to so many eccentrics amusing a tiny remnant of dilettantes and hobbyists.

Certainly not to be counted among "so many eccentrics," Hoffman adds further weight to Downard's assessment, observing that in the assassination "we observe an elaborate ceremonial work of enchantment, replete with the theatrical elements of staging, choreography, iconography, *dramatis personae* and cryptic language freighted with arcana ..." cautioning us that "the plot of this bardic psychodrama has more influence over us than we may imagine ... it is an initiator and signifier of a process of human devolution whereby the earth is prepared for Elizabethan Dr. John Dee's prophecy of the coming Reign of Dead Matter and the subjugation of humanity."

Dr. John Dee was a mathematician, astronomer, astrologer, occultist and adviser to Queen Elizabeth I, devoting much of his life to the study of alchemy, astrology, divination and Hermetic philosophy.

THE SUBJUGATION OF HUMANITY

French intelligence officer Herve Lemarr once wrote that, "President Kennedy's assassination was the work of magicians. It was a stage trick, complete with accessories and false mirrors, and when the curtain fell the actors, and even the scenery, disappeared. But the magicians were not illusionists but professionals, artists in their way."

As Michael Hoffman warned, the ultimate aim of these demented artists is "the subjugation of humanity," and Kent now better understood why so much effort had gone into marking the 50th anniversary of the event, "the Golden Jubilee of the Killing of the King."

The JFK assassination was indeed a mass ritual, and the commemoration of that day encompassed not only the act itself but all that had by design been accomplished in its wake. Upon its foundations had been constructed the framework to conquer not only the most powerful nation in world history, but all of mankind.

Yet, even with this newfound comprehension, Kent was still to discover the full extent of the dark machinations at work on November 22, 1963...

FUNHOUSE U.S.A.

Commenting in *Secret Societies and Psychological Warfare* on the after-effects of the Kennedy assassination, Michael Hoffman wrote:

> A hidden government behind the visible government of these United States became painfully obvious in a kind of subliminal way and lent an undercurrent of the hallucinogenic to our reality. ...There was a transfer of power in the collective group mind of the American masses: from the public power of the elected front-man Chief Executive, to an unelected invisible college capable of terminating him with impunity. ...Now the American people were forced to con-

front a scary alternative reality, the reality of a shadow government, over which they had neither control or knowledge.

Hoffman expanded on this point, noting that this "scary alternative reality" was reinforced through the popular culture:

> Avant-garde advertising, music, politics and news would hereafter depict (especially in the electronic media)—sometimes fleetingly, sometimes openly—a "shadow side" of reality, an underground amoral "funhouse" current associated with extreme sex, extreme violence and extreme speed.
>
> The static images of the suit-and-tie talking heads of establishment religion, government, politics and business were subtly shown to be subordinate to the Shadow State, which the American people were gradually getting a bigger glimpse of out of the corner of their collective eye. The interesting function of this phenomenon is that it simultaneously produces both terror and adulation and undercuts any offensive against it among its percipients, which does not possess the same jump-cut speed and funhouse ambiance.

The overall impact, according to Hoffman, is that "there is a sense of existing in a palace of marvels manipulated by beautiful but Satanic princes possessed of so much knowledge, power and experience as to be vastly superior to the rest of humanity. They have been everywhere. They have done everything."

A1071

Every Book Complete

ALDOUS HUXLEY

35¢

Brave New World

The mighty novel
of a soulless,
streamlined Eden—
and two who
escape it

A BANTAM GIANT

CHAPTER 15

QUITE A DAY

The Kennedy assassination indeed ushered in a Brave New World, which, as everyone knows, is the title of Aldous Huxley's best-known novel in which he presents a dystopian vision of techno-logical tyranny where the human spirit is crushed less by brute force than by endless pleasure and distraction.

"Most men and women will grow up to love their servitude and will never dream of revolution," reads *Brave New World*, elsewhere adding, "A really efficient totalitarian state would be one in which the all-powerful executive of political bosses and their army of managers control a population of slaves who do not have to be coerced, because they love their servitude."

Speaking in 1962, a year before Kennedy's death, Huxley observed:

> Today we are faced, I think, with the approach of what may be called
> the ultimate revolution, the final revolution, where man can act di-
> rectly on the mind-body of his fellows. ...
>
> If you are going to control any population for any length of time,
> you must have some measure of consent—it's exceedingly difficult

to see how pure terrorism can function indefinitely. It can function for a fairly long time, but I think sooner or later you have to bring in an element of persuasion, an element of getting people to consent to what is happening to them.

It seems to me that the nature of the ultimate revolution with which we are now faced is precisely this: That we are in process of developing a whole series of techniques which will enable the controlling oligarchy, who have always existed and presumably will always exist, to get people to love their servitude.

This is, it seems to me, the ultimate in malevolent revolutions ... there seems to be a general movement in the direction of this kind of ultimate revolution, a method of control by which a people can be made to enjoy a state of affairs by which any decent standard they ought not to enjoy.

Huxley spoke presciently of precisely the type of world that the mass trauma of the Kennedy assassination helped birth, which Kent found more than a little interesting given that Aldous Huxley also died on November 22, 1963.

Seemingly profound coincidences do of course occur on a routine basis, as Kent well knew, but a simultaneous death that packs this level of symbolic value and is practically a statement-of-purpose for a ritual public murder, now that's a different story altogether, and, one would think, a statistical improbability of gigantic proportions.

In 1953, Huxley, well known for his use of psychedelic drugs, experimented with mescaline, the active ingredient in peyote, which was widely used for ritual purposes among American Indians. Huxley later wrote a famous essay describing his experience entitled, "The Doors of Perception," from which the rock group 'The Doors' took its name. Some researchers claim that Huxley was actually introduced to peyote over two decades earlier by English occultist Aleister Crowley in October 1930 when the two dined in Berlin.

NUMBER TWO

Kent would also discover that, further compounding the incredulity of these already suspicious circumstances, was *yet another* death of extreme symbolic value on that very same day, that of author C.S. Lewis—then and still, as the *New York Times* phrased it, "the most famous Christian apologist in the modern English-speaking world."

"They died in their homes," the *Times* article began, "not from an assassin's bullet, and in their 60s, not in their prime."

When C. S. Lewis collapsed in his Oxford bedroom, the presidential motorcade was leaving Love Field. When Aldous Huxley requested a final shot of LSD, a TV set in the next room had just blared the news that the president had been shot. And then the coincidence of two of modernity's keenest critics dying on the same November day was lost in a storm of headlines and public grief.

Huxley and Lewis did not share a worldview … but they shared a critique of contemporary civilization, and offered a similar warning about where its logic might end up taking us.

Lewis laid out his ominous vision of the future in *That Hideous Strength*, which George Orwell reviewed for the *Manchester Evening News* two years before writing *Nineteen Eighty-Four*. "Plenty of people in our age do entertain the monstrous dreams of power that Mr. Lewis attributes to his characters," wrote Orwell, "and we are within sight of the time when such dreams will be realizable." Orwell's review was written shortly after the bombings of Hiroshima and Nagasaki and makes reference to both.

Brave New Insanity

Two world-renowned literary visionaries with similar cautionary tales of the techno-fascist, hyper-stimulating world into which man was about to enter, both of whom died on the same day as The King of Camelot, whose very death would help usher in this new reality.

Kent suspected that this was perhaps an as-yet-unrecognized aspect of the 11/22 Mega-Ritual, dripping with that familiar sadistic Hellfire-Club black humor. True, both Huxley and Lewis were both in ill health (Huxley on death's door), but hastening the death of the dying to coincide with a particular date would still be murder and would still count for symbolic-ritual purposes, although it is admittedly not nearly as impressive as blowing somebody's brains out in broad daylight while they're in their prime.

While Kent was fully aware that there has never been any indication of foul play in Huxley's or Lewis's deaths, he was also aware that there has never been any reason to suspect wrongdoing. And although he knew how easy it would be to conceal evidence of a crime under such circumstances, it also occurred to him that if the

> ### Getting Randy
>
>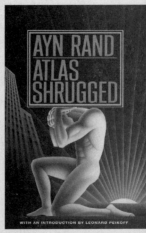
>
> Speaking of dystopian novels, *Atlas Shrugged* is a 1957 work by Ayn Rand, her fourth and last novel, and her longest. Rand considered the book to be her magnum opus in fiction, and in it explored an imaginary post-econom-ic-collapse United States which was increasingly socialist and where society's wealthiest refuse to pay skyrocketing taxes and reject restrictive new regulations, eventually disappearing altogether, resulting in the shutdown of the country's vital industries. The libertarian hero of the novel is John Galt, who seizes the airwaves and reveals himself to the nation on … November 22.

orchestrators of Kennedy's murder had not subtly engineered the simultaneous passing of these two cultural icons, then perhaps the dark forces whom they serve *did*.

This was no chance occurrence, no mere coincidence: it was synchronicity, real or manufactured.

It was either ritual murder or Satanic synchronicity—or both.

Lewis' death not only invoked *That Hideous Strength*, but marked the commencement of an all-out cultural and institutional assault on Christianity. Likewise, Huxley's death added the exclamation point after the powerful statement made by the simultaneous demise of Kennedy and Lewis—this is a Brave New World!

* * *

"God isn't compatible with machinery and scientific medicine and universal happiness. You must make your choice. Our civilization has chosen machinery and medicine and happiness."

–Aldous Huxley

HAPPY BIRTHDAY, EDWARD!

The nephew of Sigmund Freud, Edward Louis Bernays, "the father of public relations," combined research on crowd psychology with the psychoanalytical concepts of his uncle to, among other noteworthy accomplishments, help convince the public that bacon and eggs was the true all-American breakfast.

Bernays was also a pioneer in the related field of propaganda, and according to his 1965 autobiography, was highly dismayed to learn directly from a reputable source—a foreign correspondent for Hearst newspapers with first-hand knowledge of the matter—that Nazi Reich Minister of Propaganda Paul Joseph Goebbels was using his book *Crystallizing Public Opinion* "as a basis for his destructive campaign against the Jews of Germany" (Goebbels had personally shown the correspondent his propaganda library).

In Bernays' appropriately titled seminal work *Propaganda* (1928), he argues that the manipulation of public opinion was necessary to the proper functioning of democracy:

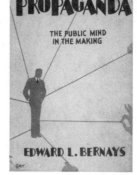

> The conscious and intelligent manipulation of the organized habits and opinions of the masses is an important element in democratic society. Those who manipulate this unseen mechanism of society constitute an invisible government, which is the true ruling power of our country. ...We are governed, our minds are molded, our tastes formed, our ideas suggested, largely by men we have never heard of. This is a logical result of the way in which our democratic society is organized. Vast numbers of human beings must cooperate in this manner if they are to live together as a smoothly functioning society. ...In almost every act of our daily lives, whether in the sphere of politics or business,

in our social conduct or our ethical thinking, we are dominated by the relatively small number of persons...who understand the mental processes and social patterns of the masses. It is they who pull the wires which control the public mind.

While Goebbels wasn't big on democracy, one might imagine that he would have given the general idea expressed above a big thumbs-up, as would many elitists and authoritarians. In fact, in a review of a biography on Bernays, the authors state, "It is impossible to fundamentally grasp the social, political, economic and cultural developments of the past 100 years without some understanding of Bernays."

Edward Bernays: the Father of Public Relations, the Father of Propaganda, on whose shoulders would stand the likes of Joseph Goebbels and on whose labors the framework for modern psychological warfare would be constructed.

Indeed, the JFK assassination and its aftermath was nothing if not a psychological warfare campaign that itself incorporated powerful propaganda (repeat after me: lone gunman, lone gunman, lone gunman). The scientific, psychological manipulation of the masses—precisely what the killing of JFK was designed to accomplish, at least in part.

So just exactly how perfectly appropriate is it that the simultaneous demise of John F. Kennedy, C.S. Lewis and Aldous Huxley—three enormously popular international public figures whose departures from this life were all cruelly synchronized to suit the dark purposes of the Cryptocracy (and/or their masters)—took place on the birthday of Edward Louis Bernays, who entered into this world on November 22, 1891.

Yet another completely overlooked aspect of the Brave New World Mega-Ritual, brought to you by our good friends in the New World Order.*

---

* The New World Order? That's yet-to-come, isn't it—under construction, awaiting full implementation—touted by Bush Sr. and many others before and since as a future development? Friends, you're living in it, and have been since November 22, 1963.

CHAPTER 16

THE ULTIMATE THREESOME

C.S. Lewis, Aldous Huxley and John F. Kennedy: three synchronized deaths (ritual murders all?) of global political/cultural icons, each carrying its own powerful symbolic significance. As Kent further contemplated everything he'd uncovered, he had an intuition that there was perhaps even deeper symbolism involved.

OUR GRAND MASTER

In the ritual ceremony for the Third Degree, it is explained that the symbolic structure of Masonry is supported by three pillars: wisdom, strength and beauty. Each pillar is represented by one of three Biblical characters: the pillar of wisdom by Solomon; the pillar of strength by Hiram, King of Tyre; and, the pillar of beauty by Hiram Abiff, the widow's son.

These three figures form a counterfeit trinity, a Masonic Trinity, in which Solomon also represents the Holy Ghost; Hiram, King of Tyre, the Father; and, Hiram Abiff, the Christ. (Both Christ and Abiff were killed, buried and resurrected.)

During the Freemasonic ritual of the Legend of the Third Degree, the candidate portrays Hiram Abiff and at the conclusion of this ritual, the Worshipful Master, portraying King Solomon, says:

Then, finally my brethren, let us imitate our Grand Master, Hiram Abiff, in his virtuous conduct, his unfeigned piety to God, and his inflexible fidelity to his trust; that, like him, we may welcome the grim tyrant, Death, and receive him as a kind messenger sent by our Supreme Grand Master, to translate us from this imperfect to that all-perfect, glorious, and celestial Lodge above, where the Supreme Architect of the Universe presides.

BRAVE NEW TRINITY

As Kent observed, "Dealey Plaza is less than 3,000 feet from the Trinity River." He'd also noted that, "Trinity Church (on Trinity Place) in downtown Manhattan is less than 1,000 feet from where the Twin Towers stood," and that "the third person of the Hindu 'Great Trinity' is Shiva the destroyer, whose symbol, like Satan, is the trident"—which, of course, is the symbol upon which Dealey Plaza's layout was based. (Freemasonry mixes and matches a broad range of religious precepts and symbols, including Egyptian, Hindu, Christian and others.)

Had the Brave New World Mega-Ritual also been a Masonic Trinity Mega-Ritual, with C.S. Lewis representing Solomon, wisdom and the Holy Ghost; Aldous Huxley representing Hiram, King of Tyre, strength and the Father; and, John F. Kennedy representing Hiram Abiff, beauty and the Christ?

That JFK was a handsome stand-in for Hiram Abiff was already clear, and Kent felt that the notion of symbolically blowing Christ's brains out would have had tremendous appeal to Kennedy's killers.

Christian icon C.S. Lewis as the Holy Ghost also seemed like a darn good fit in Kent's opinion, and symbolically ridding the universe of the Christians' spirit-in-the-sky likewise would have been deliciously attractive to the mega-ritual's fiendish organizers.

But Aldous Huxley as the Father? Why the hell not, Kent thought. From the perspective of the murderous occultists who may well have planned the entire spectacle, if the Israelites could fabricate Yahweh out of whole cloth, what in the world would it matter who they had playing him? Then again, on the other hand, having a psychedelic drug enthusiast portraying God the Father was just too  good for words. (You gotta' admit, the often-quite-bizarre behavior of the God of the Old Testament could lead one to believe that he was on drugs … or insane … or both. And, yes, I know what a demiurge is.)

CRAFTINESS APPLAUDED

The beatified (woops, wrong religion) Clive Staples Lewis as the Spirit in the Sky, Aldous L.S.D. Huxley as the cantankerous Yahweh (there was no equivalent for the letter "j" in the Hebrew alphabet so there was no Jehovah, okay?) and Playboy President John Fitzgerald Kennedy as the Messiah … Kent simply couldn't help but think that this was very much an intentional aspect of what he suspected had been a Lewis-Huxley-Kennedy triple murder/mass ritual.

And it would seem that he may be correct in his assessment, at least if Michael Hoffman is a reliable guide. Hoffman included a quote from Stephen Knight's *Jack the Ripper: The Final Solution* in his book, which implicates Freemasonry and British Royalty at its highest level in the gruesome murders and their cover-up (remember this point for future reference). This particular quote also aptly provides the rationale behind the entire horrifying, half-century-old episode we've been exhuming:

> … Freemasons applaud violence, terror and crime providing it is carried out in a crafty manner … humor is all-important and the most appalling crimes may be committed under its cloak.

Well that just about explains everything, doesn't it?

NARRATED BY TOM HANKS

KILLING
LINCOLN

BASED ON THE NEW YORK TIMES BESTSELLER

NATIONAL
GEOGRAPHIC
CHANNEL

SUNDAY FEBRUARY 17 8P

CHAPTER 17

A NATIONAL KNIGHTMARE

President Abraham Lincoln admired John Wilkes Booth, a prominent actor whom Lincoln had watched perform in a number of plays at Ford's Theatre. Following one particularly impressive performance, the President sent a note backstage inviting Booth to the White House, an invitation that, not surprisingly, the Confederate sympathizer declined. Booth reportedly didn't provide a specific reason, and later commented, "I would rather have the applause of a Negro to that of the president!"

Two days after Lee's army surrendered to Grant, on April 11, 1865—and three days before the assassination—Booth attended a speech at the White House in which Lincoln endorsed enfranchising former slaves. This apparently sent Booth over the edge, as his response to the speech would indicate:

> That means nigger citizenship. Now, by God, I'll put him through. That is the last speech he will ever give.

Also three days before his assassination, Lincoln discussed with Ward Hill Lamon, his friend and biographer, an ominous dream:

> About 10 days ago, I retired very late. I had been up waiting for important dispatches from the front. I could not have been long in bed when I fell into a slumber, for I was weary. I soon began to dream. There seemed to be a death-like stillness about me. Then I heard subdued sobs, as if a number of people were weeping. I thought I left my bed and wandered downstairs. There the silence was broken by the same pitiful sobbing, but the mourners were invisible. I went from room to room; no living person was in sight, but the same mournful sounds of distress met me as I passed along. I saw light in

all the rooms; every object was familiar to me; but where were all the people who were grieving as if their hearts would break? I was puzzled and alarmed. What could be the meaning of all this? Determined to find the cause of a state of things so mysterious and so shocking, I kept on until I arrived at the East Room, which I entered. There I met with a sickening surprise. Before me was a catafalque, on which rested a corpse wrapped in funeral vestments. Around it were stationed soldiers who were acting as guards; and there was a throng of people, gazing mournfully upon the corpse, whose face was covered, others weeping pitifully. 'Who is dead in the White House?' I demanded of one of the soldiers, 'The President,' was his answer; 'he was killed by an assassin.' Then came a loud burst of grief from the crowd, which woke me from my dream. I slept no more that night; and although it was only a dream, I have been strangely annoyed by it ever since.

The day of Lincoln's assassination, the President, who had for months looked pale and haggard, was uncharacteristically upbeat, with his new Secretary of the Treasury, Hugh McCullough, later commenting, "I never saw Mr. Lincoln so cheerful and happy."

That same fateful day, Lincoln told his bodyguard, William H. Crook, that for three straight nights he'd had dreams of being assassinated. As Lincoln left for Ford's Theatre that evening, he said to his bodyguard, who had advised him against going, not the usual "Good night, Crook," but, rather, "Goodbye, Crook."

UNDER THE DARK OF KNIGHT

Following Lincoln's assassination, a number of conspiracy theories emerged claiming the involvement of a range of powerful interests, including the Freemasons and the Rothschilds, and the supposed motives—related to everything from the Civil War to monetary policy—were as varied as the alleged conspirators, much as with the JFK assassination.

At the time, there were certainly indications and allegations of Masonic involvement in Lincoln's assassination and in what many believed to be a major cover-up that followed the killing, and it is unquestionable that high-level Freemasons were swirling all about, just as with JFK.

Kent didn't research the Lincoln assassination extensively, but he saw quite a few parallels between Lincoln's and Kennedy's killings, and not the usual well-worn list of Lincoln-Kennedy associations that has circulated for years, most of which are overblown or nonexistent in any case (Lincoln had a secretary named Kennedy and Kennedy had a secretary named Lincoln, blah blah blah).

One of the most compelling aspects of the entire incident from Kent's perspective was this: John Wilkes Booth was a known member of the Knights of the Golden Circle (KGC), a pro-slavery secret society with some fairly grandiose strategic and political objectives that included annexing large portions of Mexico and South America.

Although KGC was founded by one George W. L. Bickley on July 4th, 1854, evidence exists to indicate that the true organizing force behind the group was Albert Pike, who, as Kent noted,

…was a prominent Freemason and author of *Morals and Dogma of the Ancient and Accepted Scottish Rite of Freemasonry*. Pike was elected Sovereign Grand Commander of the Scottish Rite's Southern Jurisdiction in 1859, a position he held for the remainder of his life.

Some researchers assert that Booth was also a 33rd degree Freemason, and although Kent was unable to independently verify this claim, the photograph at left probably tells us all we need to know.

Booth was then very possibly a KGC assassin, and also, either directly or by association, a Masonic

assassin and part of a much larger conspiracy. (He was most certainly a step or two up the conspiratorial ladder from Lee Oswald.)

Booth reportedly did not die in a tobacco barn in 1865, but was spirited away by his brother Knights to Texas, and was later killed by fellow KGC member Jesse James in Oklahoma for repeatedly failing to honor his oath never to discuss his membership in the KGC

(Left) Jesse James. (Right) Nathan Bedford "Wizard of the Saddle" Forrest, Grand Wizard of the Ku Klux Klan, was, like John Wilkes Booth and Jesse James, a member of the Knights of the Golden Circle. (How in the hell did they keep order at their meetings?)

and never to speak of his role in the assassination of President Lincoln.

Booth's body was laid out in a local mortuary and its owner charged curiosity-seekers 10 cents a peek, with some intrepid gawkers stealing collar buttons and removing locks of hair as souvenirs (one even tried to sever an ear with his pocket knife). Booth's mummified corpse was later rented out to carnivals and traveled for years as part of a circus sideshow, in one instance emerging unscathed from a train wreck that killed eight passengers. As if that weren't indignity enough, Booth's mummy was even kidnapped and held for ransom.

The Knights of the Golden Circle—cross us and we'll send Jesse James to kill your ass and parade your corpse around the country as a freak-show attraction.

If anybody should have known better, it was John Wilkes Booth.

NOT-SO-GOOD FRIDAY

In considering the suspicious circumstances surrounding Lincoln's death, it did not escape Kent's attention that Lincoln's assassination had occurred on Good Friday—which of course was not so good for Jesus Christ, as it marks the day upon which the Savior was systematically tortured and crucified—a fact that most observers have chalked up to pure coincidence but which struck Kent as smacking of the same black humor and sacrilege that was smeared all over the Kennedy assassination.

A slain president, Freemasons, a murdered scapegoat, wicked humor ... sound familiar?

Some Sirius Sh*t

If the Lincoln assassination could be considered as a precursor of the ritual murder of John F. Kennedy, then the potentially coordinated killings of C.S. Lewis and Aldous Huxley might find precedent in the deaths of John Adams and Thomas Jefferson, the second and third presidents of the United States, who both died on July 4th, 1826, the 50th anniversary (that'd be the Golden Jubilee) of the signing of the Declaration of Independence, which Adams assisted Jefferson in drafting, and of which both were of course among the 56 signers (others included John Hancock and Benjamin Franklin, both Masons ... a minimum of nine signers were Freemasons).

From Here to Hell

The Secrecy Oath for the Knights of the Golden Circle:

Whoever dares our cause reveal,
Shall test the sword of Knightly steel,
And when the torture proves too dull,
We'll scrape the brains from out his skull,
And place a lamp within the shell,
To light his soul from here to hell.

As Kent covered at some length, the Dog Star, Sirius, is of utmost significance in Freemasonic belief (as well as in numerous other occult organizations), and

> In the modern era, the date on which Sirius conjuncts with the Sun, which esoterically is considered the embrace of our physical and spiritual Suns, is ... July 4th.

It is also worth noting that our fifth President, James Monroe, likewise died on July 4, 1831, the 55th anniversary of the signing of the Declaration of Independence. (That's a lot of fives. By the way, the Washington Monument is 555 feet tall, a fact mentioned four times in Dan Brown's *The Lost Symbol*.) And remember, the Knights of the Golden Circle was also formed on July 4th.

Now that's some Sirius shit.

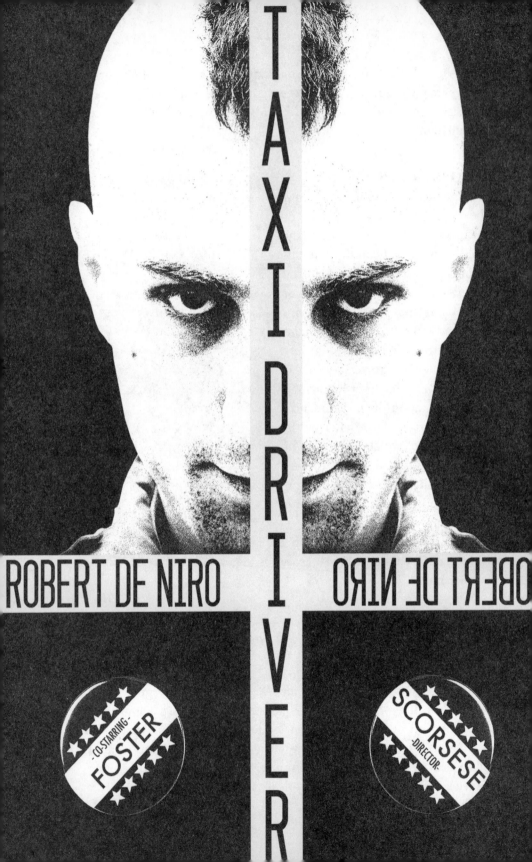

CHAPTER 18

BUSH-WHACKED

"Somewhere in Texas," is how President George Bush, Sr., responded when asked his whereabouts on the day of the Kennedy assassination. There is, however, documentary evidence that places him in Dallas on November 22, 1963, and further proves that he was affiliated with the CIA at that time, despite his claims that he was not associated with the agency until President Gerald Ford appointed him director in 1976.

An advertisement published in the *Dallas Morning News* on November 20, 1963, stated that George Bush, president of the Zapata Off-Shore Company, would be speaking the following evening at 6:30 p.m.—the night before the assassination—at the Sheraton-Dallas Hotel.

Additionally, a memo from an FBI Special Agent to the FBI's Houston bureau, dated the day of the assassination, reads:

> At 1:45 p.m. Mr. GEORGE H. W. BUSH, President of the Zapata Off-Shore Drilling Company, Houston, Texas, residence 5525 Briar, Houston, telephonically furnished this following information to writer by a long distance telephone call from Tyler, Texas.

Tyler is a small town about 100 miles east of Dallas, and one might suspect that this could have been an attempt by the future President to establish an alibi, since the phone call could have in fact originated from anywhere. In the last paragraph of the memo, the agent confirmed that Bush was going to be at the Sheraton-Dallas Hotel on the day of the assassination, returning to his residence in Houston the next day.

Yet, contrary to what the newspaper ad stated, Bush indicated that his visit to Dallas on November 22nd would begin many hours after the shooting, rather than the night before. It is also worth noting that the tip Bush gave the FBI regarding the assassination concerned a seemingly harmless man who lived with his mother, and after a cursory investigation, turned out to be totally useless.

Also of interest is an FBI memo written by J. Edgar Hoover himself on November 29, 1963, referencing "Mr. George Bush of the Central Intelligence Agency" as having provided background information contained in a report sent by the FBI office in Miami to the Department of State on November 23rd, 1963, one day after the assassination.

Spokespersons for the former president have asserted that this was a reference to a "George William Bush," who was a CIA employee in 1963. However, this George Bush, who was apparently a lower-level researcher at the agency, submitted a signed statement in a legal action before the U.S. District Court for the District of Columbia stating that he carefully

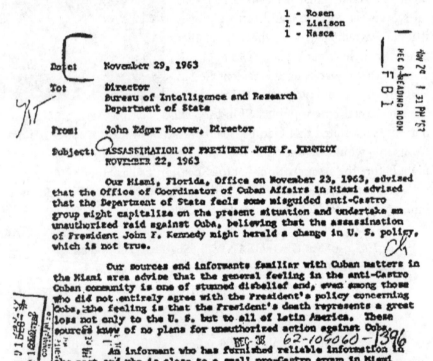

reviewed the memo and that he did not recognize its contents and was thus not the source of the information—a statement he repeated to other investigators.

SELF-INCRIMINATION

In *9/11 as Mass Ritual*, Kent had made a number of unflattering remarks concerning the Bushes, including Bush Sr., at one point even intimating, at least partially in jest, that the former president is perhaps Lucifer incarnate.

As a high-level intelligence operative and former director of the CIA, it is unsurprising that we find Bush Sr.'s fingerprints (at least partial fingerprints) on a range of suspicion-arousing incidents in recent American history, including the Bay of Pigs Invasion. Bush's involvement in the conspiracy to assassinate JFK has of course never been definitively proved; then again, what in the entire episode has?

The former president was not only in Dallas the day of the assassination, but lied to the FBI about when he was going to be in town. Bush's own untruthful and evasive statements about his involvement with the CIA and regarding his whereabouts on the day of JFK's killing ("Somewhere in Texas," my ass) provide perhaps the most incriminating evidence that he played some role in the incident.

As it turns out, however, the murder of John F. Kennedy was not the only Presidential assassination plot that George H.W. Bush would be implicated in.

* * *

"George Bush is a satanic, sadistic, brutal monster. Compared to George Bush, Adolf Hitler was a true gentleman."

-- Michael Boren Williams, former Campaign Manager for Senator Gary Hart and Bush murder attempt victim

BLOODY ELM

A postcard postmarked 1911 depicting "Elm Street looking East, Dallas, Texas." Referred to as "Bloody Elm" by the locals long before Kennedy took his fateful ride down its path, the road had obtained its moniker as a result of

the many gun fights, stabbings and other acts of violence that occurred along it during the days of the Wild West.

As Kent noted in his book, "John Hinckley bought the .22 caliber pistol he shot President Reagan with at Rocky's Pawn Shop on this same Elm Street…"

If you weren't already aware of that fact, you might be a bit incredulous that, of all the places in the United States to obtain a gun, Hinckley bought his on Bloody Elm. On the other hand, you might be thinking that Reagan's would-be assassin could have made his purchase here precisely because of its connection with the JFK assassination. Either way, that's just the beginning of the peculiarities surrounding this incident, which might lead one to believe that there was some deeper-level programming going on.

The attempt on Reagan's life came almost twenty years after the JFK assassination and over ten years after RFK's assassination, and in both cases there was speculation that the alleged assassins were in fact mind-controlled patsies.

Some researchers theorized that Oswald may have been programmed during his time in Russia, but, if he were in fact subjected to some sort of psychological manipulation, it could just as easily have occurred in the United States—particularly given that the CIA was involved in the assassination—or anywhere, for that matter.

Sirhan Sirhan had contact with a whole slew of interesting characters connected to government mind-control programs and occult organizations leading up to his rendezvous with RFK in the kitchen of the Ambassador Hotel in Los Angeles on June 5th, 1968, and his attorneys have argued in court in recent years that he was indeed subjected to various forms of pharmo/hypno psychological coercion.

UNHEALTHY OBSESSION

John Hinckley obviously had some serious mental issues to contend with, and it has been theorized that he was also a programmed assassin, or "Manchurian candidate," which Kent found to be a compelling hypothesis given that Hinckley was obsessed with Martin Scorsese's 1976 *Taxi Driver*, the plot of which was strikingly similar to real-world events involving Hinckley.

Jodie Foster in Taxi Driver. *(Maybe we should cut Hinckley a little slack…)*

Although the media tended to focus on Hinckley's intense obsession with actress Jodie Foster, who played a child prostitute in *Taxi Driver*, the entire movie captivated him to an unhealthy degree. Hinkley watched the movie at least fifteen times, read and re-read the book it was based on, and even purchased the film's soundtrack, listening to it for hours on end.

In the movie Robert De Niro plays Travis Bickle, a socially-isolated cab driver who plots to assassinate a presidential candidate and whose character was based partly on the diaries of Arthur Bremer, the would-be assassin of George Wallace.

Bickle becomes infatuated with a woman who works in the candidate's office, and after unsuccessfully attempting to win her affections, decides that assassinating her boss would be the best way to obtain her admiration, but he is ultimately impotent in that effort, as well.

No, we're talking about you.

THE BICKLE FINGER OF FATE

At his trial, one of Hinckley's defense experts stated that Hinckley's own social isolation had led him to subconsciously adopt the identity of Travis Bickle and model certain aspects of his behavior and actions on the him. Hinkley began to wear army-fatigue jackets and boots, developed

(Left) That would have saved everybody a lot of trouble. (Center) Hope that's not loaded. (Right) Hinckley's Röhm RG-14 revolver, on display at the Ronald Reagan Presidential Library.

a fascination with guns, adopted Bickle's preference for peach brandy and began keeping a diary.

More disturbingly, Hinckley adopted Bickle's strategy for gaining the attention and affections of his own unrequited love interest, Jodie Foster.

When Foster began attending classes at Yale University, home of the Skull and Bones secret society (of which George W. Bush, George H.W. Bush, Prescott Bush and a whole gaggle of Bush relations have been members), Hinckley moved to New Haven, Connecticut, and enrolled in a writing course. He slipped poems and messages under Foster's door and phoned her repeatedly.

Failing to elicit any meaningful response, Hinckley began considering more drastic measures to attract her attention, such as hijacking an airliner or committing suicide in front of her, the latter of which he quickly realized would be self-defeating. He eventually settled on presidential assassination

Like Mark David Chapman, John Lennon's killer, John Hinckley owned a copy of J.D. Salinger's Catcher in the Rye, *although unlike Chapman, Hinckley did not have his copy on his person at the time of the shooting. It would also be reasonable to assume that Hinckley would have purchased one or more copies of the March 1982 issue of* High Society *magazine, which featured a young Jodie Foster in the buff, had he not been in prison for shooting President Reagan in March of the previous year. (Shortly before shooting Lennon, Chapman met with, and offered a gift of live bullets to, experimental filmmaker Kenneth Anger.)*

as the most efficacious means to win her heart, believing that as an historical figure he would become her equal and thus worthy of her attention.

Hinckley began trailing President Jimmy Carter around the country, but was arrested in Nashville, Tennessee on a firearms charge and had to abandon his quest, at least for the moment.

He returned home penniless and underwent treatment for depression, but his mental health failed to improve. He subsequently started researching President Kennedy's assassination and came to view Lee Harvey Oswald as his role model.

WORLD'S CREEPIEST LOVE LETTER

The day of the assassination attempt, Hinckley wrote the following letter to Foster:

Hinckley posing in front of Ford's Theatre.

3/30/81
12:45 P.M.

Dear Jodie,

There is a definite possibility that I will be killed in my attempt to get Reagan. It is for this very reason that I am writing you this letter now.

As you well know by now I love you very much. Over the past seven months I've left you dozens of poems, letters and love messages in the faint hope that you could develop an interest in me. Although we talked on the phone a couple of times I never had the nerve to simply approach you and introduce myself. Besides my shyness, I honestly did not wish to bother you with my constant presence. I know the many messages left at your door and in your mailbox were a nuisance, but I felt that it was the most painless way for me to express my love for you.

I feel very good about the fact that you at least know my name and know how I feel about you. And by hanging around your dormitory, I've come to realize that I'm the topic of more than a little conversation, however full of ridicule it may be. At least you know that I'll always love you.

Jodie, I would abandon this idea of getting Reagan in a second if I could only win your heart and live out the rest of my life with you, whether it be in total obscurity or whatever.

I will admit to you that the reason I'm going ahead with this attempt now is because I just cannot wait any longer to impress you. I've got to do something now to make you understand, in no uncertain terms, that I am doing all of this for your sake! By sacrificing my freedom and possibly my life, I hope to change your mind about me. This letter is being written only an hour before I leave for the Hilton Hotel. Jodie, I'm asking you to please look into your heart and at least give me the chance, with this historical deed, to gain your respect and love.

I love you forever,
John Hinckley

Less than two hours later, one of the bullets from Hinckley's gun would miss President Reagan's heart by less than an inch.

DELAYED AMBITIONS

Did Hinckley's frustrated obsession with Foster in fact drive him to extreme action à la Travis Bickle, or might it be the case that he was programmed to kill Reagan using *Taxi Driver* as a psychological imprinting tool, in much the same manner that other films, such as *Alice in Wonderland* and *The Wizard of Oz*, have been, and still are, utilized in trauma-based mind-control programming—a fact Kent covered briefly in *9/11 as Mass Ritual*. (Hmmm, maybe this explains why Charles Manson believed that the Beatles' *White Album* contained messages specifically for him.)

A plot involving the assassination of a candidate for President of the United States by an unwitting victim of mind control—no, wait, that's *The Manchurian Candidate*, not *Taxi Driver*, and in any case that's the subject of a later chapter.

But before we leave Mr. Hinckley, we should consider two interesting facts related to the attempt on Reagan's life, which concern his Vice President, George H. W. Bush.

First, Hinckley's father, a fellow Texas oilman, had been a major financial supporter of George H. W. Bush in the 1980 presidential primary campaign and strove mightily to secure him the Republican nomination.

The Bushes and the Hinckleys were frequent dinner companions, but beyond their social connections, neither Bush nor Hinckley ,Sr., wanted Reagan in the White House due to his opposition to tax breaks for the oil industry.

Although Bush Sr. failed to get the top slot on the ticket, he and his backers got the next best thing: a job a heartbeat away from the presidency.

Fast-forward a couple of months after Reagan's inauguration, and if not for the single inch by which John Hinckley's bullet missed the president's ticker, Bush would have become Commander-in-Chief in 1981.

Following the assassination attempt, the Bush family crime syndicate reportedly put on a full-court press to prevent the Hinckley-Bush connection from becoming public knowledge, with some investigators listing this as one of the most-spiked stories of the twentieth century.

GETTIN' HINKEY WITH THE HINCKLEYS

The second point of interest regarding V.P. Bush and the Hinckley family is this: as an almost-bewildered John Chancellor reported on NBC Nightly News the evening of the assassination attempt, in a "bizarre coincidence," Bush's son, Neil, and another of Hinckley Sr.'s boys, Scott, had been forced to cancel dinner plans for the very next evening following the news of that day's shooting.

Neil, who worked for Amoco Oil, had met Scott approximately three weeks after the U.S. Department of Energy (DOE) had begun a routine audit of the Hinckley oil company, Vanderbilt Energy Corporation. On the morning of John Hinckley's attempt to assassinate Reagan, three representatives from DOE reportedly informed Scott, Vanderbilt's vice president of operations, that auditors had uncovered evidence of pricing violations on crude oil sold by the company over a three-year period, and that the federal government was considering a two-million-dollar penalty.

Scott requested additional time to explain the overcharges, with the meeting ending only a little more than an hour before his brother, John, put a bullet in President Reagan.

SURE YOU WOULD

Now, ask yourself, if you were Bush Sr., former director of the CIA, and had been beat out of the top job in the United States government by a two-bit Hollywood B-actor who was threatening to cut in on the profits of your oil enterprise, would you not at least consider winding up—through whatever means necessary, and you know the whole playbook—some convenient, unwitting hapless individual and turning them loose on the one man standing between you and the highest seat in the land? I mean, come on, especially if you'd personally seen it done, or even helped get it done, once before?

LIFE

Amid controversy over the Warren Report
Governor Connally examines for LIFE
the Kennedy assassination film
frame by frame

DID OSWALD ACT ALONE?

A MATTER
OF
REASONABLE DOUBT

FRAME 230

From the film:
A key moment in the controversy

NOVEMBER 25 · 1966 · 5C

CHAPTER 19

DID YOU SEE *THAT*?!

T he Zapruder film is without question the most-analyzed 26 seconds of film footage in history. In more recent years, high-resolution scans have been made of the individual frames, allowing the film to be scrutinized in greater detail than ever before.

The first frame in the Zapruder film in which Kennedy's limousine is visible.

For decades, researchers by the dozen, by the hundred—including those with varying degrees of professional qualification all the way down to those with absolutely none whatsoever—have claimed discovery of one anomaly after another, each one in their respective esteemed opinions proving without any question whatsoever that the film was tampered with.

Kent made a conscious decision early on in his research not to get sucked into the dark obsessive underworld of Zapruderism, with its numerous competing denominations, each it seems with its own hard-core evangelist(s) and devoted congregation, most of whom are all too willing to go to war with each other over the slightest variance from their own established orthodoxy.

Abraham Zapruder and his Bell & Howell Zoomatic movie camera, in the collection of the US National Archives.

TOO TECHNICAL

K ent would be the first to acknowledge that there do seem to be indications that the film has been manipulated, but amateur film analysis has the same potential to yield undesirable, counter-productive results as amateur cosmetic surgery.

If one does not possess detailed knowledge of the specific model of camera being used, including the variability of its frame rate, as well as the exact type of film being used, you're going to see a lot of things that you can't explain or that seem suspicious to you, but that doesn't mean these anomalies don't have perfectly legitimate technical explanations.

Kent discovered, much to his displeasure, that there are at least as many theories concerning the manipulation of the Zapruder film as there are about the JFK assassination in general. He studied some of them, but quite frankly didn't have the technical expertise, or patience, to be able to make an informed assessment, much less to perform any type of useful comparison between the oft-conflicting theories.

A SECOND VERSION

A select group of researchers claim to have seen a second Zapruder film: ostensibly an original, unedited version. The one we're all familiar with was supposedly intercepted in Chicago on its way to Time-Life, which had purchased it, and spent the weekend in Washington, DC, being doctored by professional film technicians under the guidance of CIA agents.

In this version, so state those who claim to have viewed one of several supposed extant copies, the president's limousine comes to a full stop as it turns the corner onto Elm Street, almost hitting the curb. At that moment, Kennedy is struck twice in the head, and then the driver accelerates rapidly and quickly exits Dealey Plaza.

Certainly possible, Kent thought, but then who got their brains liquefied in what would then be the fake Zapruder film? A Kennedy look-alike? How could they have staged two separate shootings in Dallas? Or was it Hollywood magic? Was the entire Elm Street episode recreated on a production set hidden away somewhere?

In light of the possibility of the existence of an unaltered original in which Kennedy is shot in the turn, Kent did find it interesting that the actual sequence of the presidential limo turning onto Elm is missing from the Zapruder film. One frame the car's not even visible, the next, *presto!*, it's halfway down Elm Street (that's a tad of an exaggeration). Not knowing the characteristics of Zapruder's camera, however, and not caring enough to investigate the matter further, Kent decided, "to hell with that."

120

Yellow Streak

One theory that made a good deal of sense to Kent was that the film had been doctored to hide visual evidence of a blow-out in the right

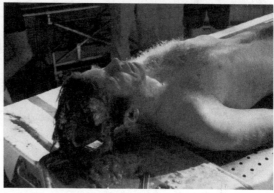

rear of Kennedy's skull, which numerous members of the medical staff at Parkland Memorial Hospital in Dallas reported witnessing (and which is pictured in the photograph at right). Such a wound would contradict the official single-shooter-from-the-rear theory, so it would need to be masked out of the film—which some researchers claim was done, and done sloppily, particularly by today's standards.

A handful of investigators have done excellent work and performed valuable technical analysis on the film itself, using what it shows to draw conclusions about what did and did not occur that day, not that Kent necessarily understood all of it, or claimed to.

He was more interested in some of the more obvious indications of treachery—such as the two short sections of yellow striping on the curb opposite Zapruder's position on the Grassy Knoll, placed approximately forty feet apart and clearly visible in the film. These two stripes are positioned precisely where the limousine was located when the kill-shot was made.

Kent noticed the stripes while reviewing digitized scans of the individual frames of the film, but others have noted them as well.

A Unique Anomoly

In viewing the frames individually, however, Kent did come across something that no one else seems to have discovered, and for good reason. It would take a very visually-oriented person, with a somewhat debased mentality, to make a find like this one, and once Kent was convinced of what he'd found, he wasn't entirely sure he wanted credit for the discovery.

A Rendevous with Death

During the 1960 presidential campaign, John F. Kennedy read Mary Renault's novel *The King Must Die*, in which several of the ancient societies involved in the plot practice the sacrifice of kings. The modern mythology that grew up around Kennedy after his death portrayed him as the "King of Camelot," an almost divine figure who, it has become clear, was sacrificed in an updated version of the "killing of the king."

Not surprisingly, Kennedy sometimes speculated that he would die at the hands of an assassin, perhaps intuiting that his own death was somehow inevitable. "Thank God nobody wanted to kill me today," he once told a friend on a return flight to Washington, DC.

One of Kennedy's favorite poems, which he often asked Jackie to recite, was by Alan Seeger—"I Have a Rendezvous with Death." And, indeed, he did.

I Have a Rendezvous with Death

I have a rendezvous with Death
At some disputed barricade,
When Spring comes back with rustling shade
And apple-blossoms fill the air—
I have a rendezvous with Death
When Spring brings back blue days and fair.

It may be he shall take my hand
And lead me into his dark land
And close my eyes and quench my breath—
It may be I shall pass him still.
I have a rendezvous with Death
On some scarred slope of battered hill,
When Spring comes round again this year
And the first meadow-flowers appear.

God knows 'twere better to be deep
Pillowed in silk and scented down,
Where love throbs out in blissful sleep,
Pulse nigh to pulse, and breath to breath,
Where hushed awakenings are dear...
But I've a rendezvous with Death
At midnight in some flaming town,
When Spring trips north again this year,
And I to my pledged word am true,
I shall not fail that rendezvous.

As he studied the frames, Kent paid particular attention to imagery in the sprocket area, which generally contains distorted impressions of the environs, either objects just outside the frame area, or from the frame above or below, or some combination thereof. It can be difficult to tell what you're looking at in some instances, but generally one can make some logical sense out of what they're seeing. Now, hold that thought.

As Kent looked closely at frame 350, or not-so-closely, rather, because it's damn obvious, he could see that a film technician had, in fact–– no question about it––colored the pavement around Secret Service agent Clint Hill's knee *grass green*, either accidentally, or, for whatever reason (and Kent had an idea why), on purpose. It wasn't a tiny dot of green, either, and the alteration also gave Hill's knee the appearance of being an odd, bulging protuberance in the vicinity of his loins.

As Kent pondered over this seemingly obvious error, which may or may not have also constituted a dirty joke, he referenced the sprocket area to the left for additional clues. Most of the film there was missing. It had apparently been cut out, with the excision having begun in the previous frame.

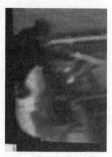

When he first looked at the small image that was visible at the lower left, he could make no sense of it whatsoever. He looked at the frame before, 349, and the frame after, 351. The image, or one very similar to it, was repeated at the top left in the sprocket area of frame 351. But neither of these practically-identical images bore any resemblance to anything in the frames before or after, or in the sprocket areas of those frames. Kent looked at frames further backward and further forward. No clues.

Kent scanned the sprocket areas of all 486 frames. There was nothing remotely resembling those two anomalous images. They were unique in the entire film.

By now, Kent was already completely convinced that the film had been doctored, at least to some extent. Frame 350 constituted the most glaring evidence of photographic manipulation, and there, in the sprocket area—the only thing in the sprocket area of this specific frame, in fact—was this anomalous image.

Damn peculiar, Kent muttered to himself. It was evident that the film technician(s) who had colored the pavement green, and perhaps given Clint Hill a boner, had spliced this image into the sprocket areas of frames 350 and 351. But why, and what was it?

Kent took the image and enlarged it in image-editing software. He zoomed in; he zoomed out.

Could it be? he thought. Surely not.

WELL, I'LL BE DAMNED

Those of us old enough to remember when films in movie theatres were shown from reels have all heard the stories of the boys in the projector room splicing in a single frame from a porn flick into a kiddie movie. The entire family is sitting there watching *Mary Poppins* and all of a sudden, Did you see that?

What Kent suspected he'd discovered is along those lines, although at first it's fairly difficult to grasp what you're looking at. But if you figure it out, you'll wish you hadn't.

PART FOUR

"Twelve Days" As Mass Ritual

CHAPTER 20

BENDING REALITY

The JFK assassination was so much more sophisticated than Kent had imagined before he began digging into it. He now better understood what was accomplished that day, and how foundational the event had been for everything that followed over the next 50 years.

Kent could see numerous common elements of JFK and 9/11, and between both of these and Twelve Days. His instincts told him that this was also a mass ritual. In his book, he'd written about 9/11 as a combined act of false-flag terrorism, psychological warfare and mass ritual.

He knew that Twelve Days was not a ritual in exactly the same way as 9/11 or the JFK assassination had been: it was also a commemoration, a grand celebration of the JFK assassination and everything that's been built on top of it since.

Kent had identified the false-flag and psychological warfare components of Twelve Days, but there were also readily identifiable occult ritual elements purposefully incorporated into the structure of the events, and he knew they were there for a purpose. What he didn't know was how they all fit together or how they functioned for ritual purposes. But he was determined to find out.

According to Julius Caesar in his Commentarii de Bello Gallico (*Commentary on the Gallic War*)*, the ancient Druids used the wicker man in ritual sacrifice.*

IT'S ON, BABY

Kent knew immediately that the game was afoot when he heard that one of the three recipients of the ricin letters was U.S. Senator Roger Wicker, whose district headquarters and main office is in Tupelo, where Wicker also resides.

Kent had been keenly aware of the Controllers' penchant for the word "wicker" well before this incident, and thus recognized its intentional use instantly. In his interview with Daniel Estulin on Russia Today dealing with the 50th anniversary of the Kennedy assassination, Estulin had asked about the ricin letters, and in his reply, Kent discussed the meaning of the word, saying:

> The word "wicker," according to Michael Hoffman, author of *Secret Societies and Psychological Warfare,* is a favorite meme of the cryptocracy. The wicker man was a construction used in human sacrifice, and is also the title of a 1973 British horror film starring Christopher Lee that has become a cult classic.

"The fiery Wicker Man," writes Hoffman, "the ancient symbol of human sacrifice and ritual murder, was resurrected into the Group-Mind consciousness during the 1970s. In 1977, the Son of Sam ritual murderers signed themselves 'Wicked King Wicker' in a well-publicized manifesto."

> Readers of the *New York Daily News* learned to associate "The Wicked King Wicker" with murder and terror. At the thought of King Wicker, millions felt fear. This fear was imprinted on their minds. This is the same control process hundreds of peasants were put through a thousand years ago while standing in front of a giant wicker effigy, inside of which was caged a doomed human sacrifice destined for burning.

"The alchemical processing of humans," Hoffman continues, "is performed with the props of time and space: what happens ritually in a series of significant places can 'bend' reality. That's what 'wicker' means in its most subterranean signification. Wicca (witchcraft) is just a description of the end-result of the function of bending reality."

"How is reality bent?" asks Hoffman. "By the placing of ritual props in ceremonial places. These places exist both in the mind and in physical space."

Reiterating elsewhere in his book, Hoffman states, "The word wicker has many denotations and connotations, one of which is 'to bend,' as in the 'bending' of reality. It is also connected to witchcraft through its derivative, *wicca*."

Swedish actress Britt Ekland, one of the stars of The Wicker Man, as Willow, does her famous "naked dance," which is well worth watching if you haven't seen it.

Wicker is derived from the medieval Scandinavian word *vika* ... Wicker is a symbol of ritual murder in northern Europe where sacrifices of humans were made in huge wicker effigies. The Son of Sam cult called its killers, "King Wicker" and the horror movie *The Wicker Man* helped to re-seed the legend in the modern mind.

Any questions about the real reason that Roger Wicker—one of a hundred U.S. Senators (not to mention hundreds of Representatives)—was singled out of the entire Congress as the recipient of one of three ricin letters?

* * *

Wick (Old Teutonic). 1. To bend.
Wick (Old English). 1. wicca, wizard (of which the feminine is wicce, witch).

--The Oxford English Dictionary

JUSTIFIED SUSPICIONS

Kent had actually thought about pro-actively employing the wicker meme himself when doing publicity for *The Most Dangerous Book in the World*, and considered using the Senator's name in his bio as having been instrumental in establishing the Mississippi Hills National Heritage Area. Kent had decided against this, however, out of respect for the Senator and out of concern that it might  somehow antagonize Wicker and have a negative impact on the project.

The fact that the wicker meme had been employed in conjunction with the ricin attacks didn't automatically make it a ritual, of course, but Kent strongly suspected that there was a deeper level of the game that he just hadn't uncovered yet. And, as usual, his suspicions were correct.

CHAPTER 21

THREE KINGS

Kent intuited that there was a major ritual aspect he was missing, one that would add a new level of dark meaning to the entire affair.

He was aware from his work how so much of the 9/11 Mass Ritual centered upon Sirius—the Dog Star, the Blazing Star of the Freemasons, the Silver Star of Aleister Crowley, the abode of Lucifer—and thought this might be a good place to start.

As just one example, on September 11, 2001, a bomb-sniffing police dog that just happened to be named Sirius had been the only such animal killed

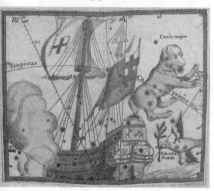

in the line of duty that day, and much attention was subsequently focused on commemorating the animal's demise. However, the whole affair was in fact but one creative, grotesquely humorous means through which the planners of the attacks integrated Sirius into the broader ritual. In fact, the date of September 11th itself is closely tied to Sirius, as Kent explained thoroughly in his book. Knowing how central Sirius is to the elite, in this instance he pondered, *Where's Sirius?*

Were the dates involved with Twelve Days tied to the star somehow? No, as Kent knew, July 4th, August 5th, the Dog Days of summer, September 11th, and New Year's Eve are, but nothing in April of which he was aware.

His mind came back to wicker ... Wicked King Wicker ... Elvis, the King of Rock'n'Roll ... both from Tupelo. Two kings—but what the heck did that mean? Then he remembered—this was all about JFK, the Golden Jubilee of the Killing of the King.

JFK, the King of Camelot; Roger "Wicked King" Wicker; Elvis, the King of Rock'n'Roll.

THE BITCH IS BACK

The Three Kings are the three main stars in Orion's Belt, called *Drie Konings* by Afrikaans speakers in South Africa and *les Trois Rois* in Daudet's 1866 *Lettres De Mon Moulin*. The ancient Germans called them the "Three Reapers," and the pre-Christian Maya referred to the belt as the "Three-in-Line," while after the Spaniards arrived they referred to the stars as *Tres Reyes* ("Three Kings").

Orion was associated by the ancient Egyptians with Osiris, the sun-god of rebirth and the afterlife, and the three pyramids of Giza are an exact representation of the three stars of Orion's belt (*mondo* As above, so below).

So, there we have it: the entire Twelve Days of Terror episode was not just a commemoration of the slaughter of the King of Camelot, it was a mass ritual invoking Osiris. Damn ingenious.

End of story? Not quite.

Actually, the Three Kings in Orion's belt point to a specific star in the heavens, one closely associated with Isis, wife of Osiris.

The name of this star? You guessed it—Sirius.

Hmmm, three kings following a "star of wonder" that will "guide us to thy perfect light," kind of like how the three stars of Orion's belt point to and follow Sirius, the brightest star in the sky, which immediately precedes the rising sun at dawn, ie., the daily birth of the sun—as opposed to the *annual* birth, widely observed as Christmas, which occurs three days after the Winter Solstice as the sun resumes its upward trajectory in the heavens after having been at its lowest point in the sky for three days

... Jesus rising after three days ... ring a bell? (In case you're wondering, it's called "astronomical allegory." Google that or "astrotheology.")

Star of Wonder

"We Three Kings," also known as "We Three Kings of Orient Are" and "The Quest of the Magi," is a Christmas carol written by the Reverend John Henry Hopkins, Jr., in 1857 and remains one of the most popular Christmas carols.

We Three Kings

We three kings of Orient are;
Bearing gifts we traverse afar,
Field and fountain, moor and mountain,
Following yonder star.

Refrain: O, star of wonder, star of night,
Star with royal beauty bright,
Westward leading, still proceeding,
Guide us to thy perfect light.

Born a King on Bethlehem's plain
Gold I bring to crown Him again,
King forever, ceasing never,
Over us all to reign.

Frankincense to offer have I;
Incense owns a Deity nigh;
Prayer and praising, voices raising,
Worshipping God on high.

Myrrh is mine, its bitter perfume
Breathes a life of gathering gloom;
Sorrowing, sighing, bleeding, dying,
Sealed in the stone cold tomb.

Glorious now behold Him arise;
King and God and sacrifice;
Alleluia, Alleluia,
Sounds through the earth and skies.

LET'S GET THE PARTY STARTED

Twelve Days followed a sophisticated script that ingeniously combined false-flag terrorism, psychological warfare and mass ritual. The script incorporated human sacrifice and industrial sabotage in new and innovative ways, and had been a grand commemoration of the Golden Jubilee of the Killing of the King.

However, Kent had noted what by all appearances were staged events earlier in the year, pre-Twelve Days. As he began to grasp the scope of Twelve Days, a thought occurred to him—was this it, or was there something more? Could the events earlier in 2013 somehow be related? What if Twelve Days had been the Main Show, with various sideshows leading up to and perhaps following it?

The Controllers are perpetually staging one event or another to keep the public in a constant state of fear and confusion, so Kent hadn't thought that the staged events he'd noted earlier in the year were necessarily connected in any form to the Golden Jubilee. But given the massive scale of Twelve Days of Terror, and the obvious importance placed on the Killing of the King, maybe the script for the Golden Jubilee had started earlier. What if, Kent wondered, the script covered the entire anniversary year? And with that question, he was about to discover when the party really started.

FUNNY GUY

A lot has been said and written about the "predictive programming" that preceded 9/11, particularly that which appeared in television and film. So the theory goes, intentional clues incorporated by those with advance knowledge of the attacks appeared in everything from episodes of *The X-Files* and *The Simpsons* to *The Matrix*.

Kent wrote briefly about the topic in his first book, but didn't discuss many specific examples, primarily because so much had already been said about it, some rather convincing, some not so much.

"Turban Cowboy" was an episode of *The Family Guy*, which aired on March 17, 2013, four weeks prior to the Boston Bombings. In the show, lead character Peter plows through a whole group of runners competing in the Boston Marathon, leaving a trail of carnage in the street.

Later in this same episode, Peter attempts to make two calls to his new Muslim friend with a cell phone given to him by this individual, who turns out to be a terrorist, and in both instances an explosion is heard in the background.

After the Boston Bombings, Fox promptly removed the episode from its website and *Hulu.com*. A YouTube video subsequently circulated showing the scenes from the marathon edited together with the explosion sequence to dramatic effect, which *Family Guy* creator Seth MacFarlane denounced as "abhorrent," and YouTube soon thereafter removed the clip.

That's all very interesting, and damn unlikely to be a coincidence, Kent thought, but then there's this little tidbit, as well: funny guy Mac-Farlane was supposed to be on American Airlines Flight 11, which struck the North Tower of the World Trade Center on September 11, 2001. Mac-Farlane claimed that he missed the flight due to a hangover and to his travel agent giving him an incorrect departure time.

"It was a very close call for me," MacFarlane explained, adding, "Alcohol is our friend. I think that's the moral of that story." (No, Seth, the moral of the story is that celebrities who may have willingly participated in mass rituals and the creation of predictive programming for those rituals shouldn't feign righteous indignation so zealously when someone highlights what they've done—it comes across as just a tad hypocritical.)

So, the creator of the *Family Guy*, an episode of which depicts a massacre at the Boston Marathon barely a month in advance of the real thing, was one of the handful of celebrities who miraculously escaped death on 9/11 …

PART FIVE

PRE-TWELVE DAYS

BRADLEY COOPER   SIENNA MILLER

A CLINT EASTWOOD FILM

AMERICAN SNIPER

THE MOST LETHAL SNIPER IN U.S. HISTORY

WARNER BROS. PICTURES PRESENTS
IN ASSOCIATION WITH VILLAGE ROADSHOW PICTURES A MAD CHANCE PRODUCTION A 22ND & INDIANA PRODUCTION A MAL PASO PRODUCTION
BRADLEY COOPER "AMERICAN SNIPER" SIENNA MILLER COSTUME DESIGNER DEBORAH HOPPER MUSIC SUPERVISOR MICHAEL OWENS
EDITED BY JOEL COX A.C.E. GARY D. ROACH A.C.E. PRODUCTION DESIGNER JAMES J. MURAKAMI CHARISSE CARDENAS DIRECTOR OF PHOTOGRAPHY TOM STERN A.F.C. A.S.C.
EXECUTIVE PRODUCERS TIM MOORE JASON HALL SHEROUM KIM AND BRUCE BERMAN BASED ON THE BOOK BY CHRIS KYLE WITH SCOTT MCEWEN
SCREENPLAY BY JASON HALL PRODUCED BY ROBERT LORENZ P.G.A. ANDREW LAZAR P.G.A. BRADLEY COOPER PETER MORGAN
DIRECTED BY CLINT EASTWOOD   DECEMBER

CHAPTER 22

AN ODE TO OSWALD

February 2, 2013: Glen Rose, Texas

The U.S. military's all-time top sniper and author of *American Sniper: The Autobiography of the Most Lethal Sniper in U.S. Military History*, Chris Kyle, and companion Chad Littlefield have taken 25-year-old fellow veteran and PTSD-sufferer Eddie Ray Routh, a former Marine, to the Rough Creek Ranch-Lodge-Resort shooting range on County Road 2013, not far from the small town of Glen Rose, Texas. At some point during the outing, Routh shoots Kyle and Littlefield, killing both, and then steals Kyle's pickup.

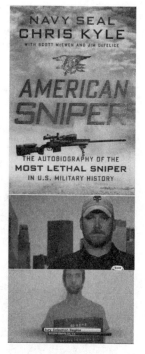

A memorial service was held for Kyle at Cowboys Stadium in Arlington, Texas, and he was buried in Texas State Cemetery in Austin after a 200-mile long funeral procession that began in Midlothian. Hundreds of local and out-of-state residents lined the route to view the procession, which traveled down U.S. Route 77—which also passes directly beside Dealey Plaza—and passed through Waco, the home (as previously mentioned) of the Masonic Grand Lodge of Texas and site of the Branch Davidian massacre.

A CAREFULLY-CRAFTED APPROACH

Kyle was the founder of Craft International, a private security contractor, and, interestingly, only three months after Kyle's death, personnel wearing Craft insignia were observed at the site of the Boston Bombings, ostensibly as part of the security detail.

Their role that day has been questioned, and they have been suggested as the potential perpetrators of an "inside job." Could Kyle have been eliminated for objecting to such a plan, Kent wondered?

The Craft International logo. Their slogan: "Despite what your momma told you.... Violence does solve problems."

Craft International wearing skull patches in Boston, a dead sniper, a jumbo-sized 50 and a whopping Blazing Star. Symbols don't kill people, people with symbols kill people.

Body Bag

During an interview in January 2012 following the release of his book, *American Sniper*, Kyle revealed the identity of an individual he had chosen not to name in the book, a man who Kyle claimed to have punched in a bar in Coronado, California in 2006. The bar, McP's, was popular with Navy SEAL personnel, and Kyle was attending a wake for a Navy SEAL and Medal of Honor recipient who had been killed in Iraq.

Kyle claimed the individual was "bad-mouthing the war, bad-mouthing (former President) Bush, bad-mouthing America" and that, when he asked him to tone it down because the families of military personnel were present, the person stated that the SEAL's "deserved to lose a few guys"—at which point Kyle punched him in the face.

The individual in question had himself been a member of the UDT/SEAL community, and was allegedly none other than former pro-wrestler, actor and Minnesota Governor Jesse "The Body" Ventura, host of the popular television series *Conspiracy Theory*.

Ventura took strong offense at the allegation that he'd made such comments regarding fellow soldiers, denying not only that he'd ever said those words, and that Kyle had ever punched him, but also that he'd ever met Kyle or even heard of him.

Ventura filed a defamation lawsuit against Kyle, which he continued following Kyle's death by adding his estate to the lawsuit. Although he was criticized for involving Kyle's widow in the suit, Ventura won and a jury awarded him $1.8 million.

Ventura's supporters claimed that the episode was part of a larger plot to discredit him. If true, Kent ventured, then perhaps Ventura's book, *They Killed Our President: 63 Reasons to Believe There Was a Conspiracy to Assassinate JFK*, was one of the primary reasons he was targeted.

GETTIN' CRAFTY

It is worth noting that Freemasonry is often referred to as "the Craft," and it is also worth noting that in 2013, the 50th anniversary of the JFK assassination—ostensibly perpetrated by lone sniper and former Marine Lee Harvey Oswald—Chris Kyle, another of America's most well-known snipers, is gunned down by a former Marine at a shooting range located on

County Road 2013, just months before Craft personnel are involved in an unknown capacity at the Boston Bombings.

* * *

"Despite what your momma told you...
Violence does solve problems."

DAILY●NEWS

NEW YORK'S HOMETOWN NEWSPAPER

LIGHTS OUT

SUPER BOWL XLVII

- **Ravens stop Niners**
- **The Dome goes dark**
- **Beyoncé is electric!**

Beyoncé wows crowd at the Super Bowl — a performance more powerful than the Superdome lights — as Ravens hold off 49ers, 34-31.

SEE FULL COVERAGE - PAGES 4-5 & SPORTS

CHAPTER 23

ODE TO OSWALD
(BOOTYLICIOUS MIX)

February 3, 2013: New Orleans, Louisiana

Despite admitting to lip-synching "The Star-Spangled Banner" at President Obama's second inauguration the month before, Beyoncé, along with a reunion of *Destiny's Child*, delivered a bootylicious halftime show at Super Bowl 47 in New Orleans, only minutes after which, with 13:22 remaining in the third quarter, the lights went out in exactly half of the Mercedes-Benz Superdome.

Hooked on You

(Left) The 26 members of the Sandy Hook Elementary School Choir sing for the crowd at Super Bowl 47. (Right) Later that year at the 2013 Boston Massacre, a special marker was placed at mile 26 in honor of the 26 people allegedly killed in Sandy Hook. (Wow, a unicorn and a rooster, symbol of Osiris.)

Earlier in the evening, Super Bowl spectators had been treated to a pre-game performance by the Sandy Hook Elementary School Choir, which was composed of 26 unnamed students to represent the 26 persons killed in the shooting the previous December.

Some keen observers commented on the startling resemblance of a number of the children in the choir to those who had reportedly been killed at Sandy Hook. Were these brothers and sisters of the alleged victims?

Another, less palatable possibility which would explain the likenesses had occurred to Kent and other researchers: the Sandy Hook shooting could have involved a drill held several years earlier (during which images and footage were captured for later use), and the children on the field at the Super Bowl were actually some of the very same children that the public was told were killed in December of 2012.

(If you don't know who this is or why it's very odd that he's grinning like a ninny in this photograph, Google "Robbie Parker" and "press conference.")

As 71,000 people sat in the semi-darkened stadium for over 30 minutes, it crossed more than one person's mind, including Kent's as he sat watching the game in his living room, that this location had been the scene of tremendous suffering in the aftermath of Hurricane Katrina. Was something far worse about to happen to this crowd?

The game eventually resumed and continued without further incident, but Kent and others noted the time of the blackout and the fact that it contained Skull & Bones' numerical signature, 322—which, coincidently, had put in an appearance in the football stadium-bombing scene in *The Dark Knight Rises*.

Others noted that the massive Mercedes-Benz logo emblazoned on the ceiling of the Super Dome, and on full display during the blackout, bears an uncanny resemblance to the inverted, broken Cross of Nero.

Few, however, made the connection between the half-dark stadium and the half-moon in the sky above that night, or realized that they were witnessing a lunar ritual unfolding before their eyes in the Crescent City.

The most relevant point of all, however, went completely unnoted: New Orleans was a center of activity for multiple individuals connected with the JFK assassination. The take-home: In 2013, the 50th anniversary of the JFK assassination, Chris "America's Sniper" Kyle is killed on County Road 2013 *the day before* the Super Bowl, which was played in New Orleans, the birthplace and old stomping grounds of Lee Harvey Oswald. Get it? Got it? Good.

Disney
OZ
THE GREAT AND POWERFUL
DISNEY PRESENTS A ROTH FILMS PRODUCTION IN ASSOCIATION WITH CURTIS-DONEN PRODUCTIONS JAMES FRANCO "OZ THE GREAT AND POWERFUL"
MILA KUNIS RACHEL WEISZ MICHELLE WILLIAMS ZACH BRAFF BILL COBBS JOEY KING TONY COX VISUAL EFFECTS AND ANIMATION BY SONY IMAGEWORKS INC.
SCOTT STOKDYK MUSIC BY DANNY ELFMAN COSTUME DESIGNERS GARY JONES MICHAEL KUTSCHE FILM EDITOR BOB MURAWSKI, A.C.E.
PRODUCTION DESIGNER ROBERT STROMBERG DIRECTOR OF PHOTOGRAPHY PETER DEMING, ASC EXECUTIVE PRODUCERS GRANT CURTIS PALAK PATEL PHILIP STEUER JOSH DONEN
PRODUCED BY JOE ROTH BASED ON THE WORKS OF L. FRANK BAUM SCREENPLAY BY MITCHELL KAPNER AND DAVID LINDSAY-ABAIRE DIRECTED BY SAM RAIMI
DISNEY.COM/THEWIZARD
IN CINEMAS SOON
IN DISNEY DIGITAL 3D, realD 3D AND IMAX 3D

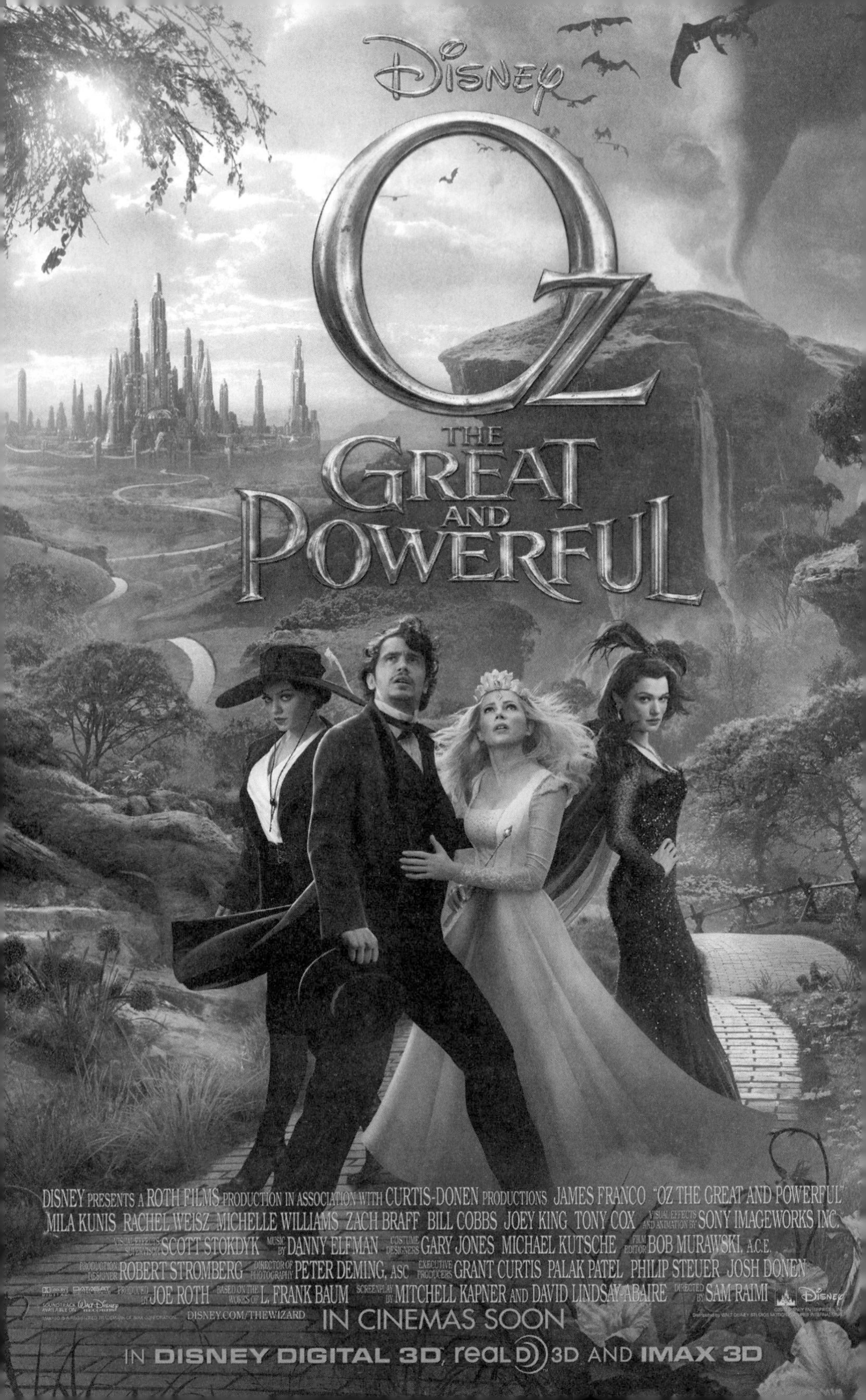

CHAPTER 24

CRAP SHOOT

February 14, 2012: Pretoria, South Africa

Eleven short days after the Big Game, in the early morning hours of Valentine's Day, Olympic athlete Oscar "Oz" Pistorius—sometimes callously referred to as "the fastest man on no legs"—shoots girlfriend Reeva Steencamp to death through the bathroom door in his home. (Steencamp, by the way, was a German occupational name for a stone-cutter ... as in "mason.")

"How funny—red roses for me."

Pistorius would later claim that he believed that she was an intruder and, fearing for his own life and that of his beloved girlfriend, fired multiple rounds in self-defense at this supposed interloper who, in Oscar's tenuous scenario, had broken into the home only to shut themselves up in the shitter.

One supposes that it would have been a little too obvious had he shot her through the heart with a bow and arrow. Reeva Steencamp, meet Sharon Tate. (You'll get that one later.)

The Nike Corporation of course immediately discontinued its latest advertising campaign featuring Pistorius, the text of which read, "I am the bullet in the chamber," followed by, "Just do it." ("Do What Thou Wilt" = "Just Do It"?)

Oz Squared

Later this very same Day of Love, half a world away, Disney's *Oz the Great and Powerful* had its world premiere at the El Capitan Theatre in Hollywood, which is owned by Disney as part of the El Capitan Entertainment Complex, fittingly housed in the former Hollywood Masonic Hall.

Actor James Franco, who played the Wizard, arrived at the premiere that evening in a hot air balloon and, fortunately for him, life failed to imitate art when the balloon did *not* come crashing to earth as happens in the movie.

Not so fortunate, however, were the 19 victims of the deadliest ballooning tragedy in history, who, just twelve days later on February 26, died tragically as their sight-seeing balloon went up in flames and then promptly dropped like a rock out of the sky over Luxor, Egypt, city of Amun Ra, King of the Gods.

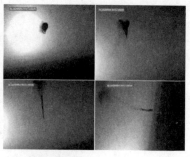

THE GOLDEN JUBILEE BIRTHDAY BOY

Kent had written about the significance of, and relationships between, Oz (no, not the wizard—it's a little complicated), the goat-headed deity Baphomet and the number 77. He also wrote about the *Wizard of Oz* and its well-document use as a tool in MK-Ultra mind-control. He was further well aware of the Cryptocracy's pattern of foreshadowing real-world events in books and film, and understood why they would integrate Oz so prominently into the Golden Jubilee celebration.

Kent also felt that it was no coincidence that James Franco had expressed an interest in playing the role of Pistorius in an upcoming biopic, or that Oscar Pistorius' birthday is … November 22.

Oz Pistorius, the Golden Jubilee Birthday Boy,* who sacrificed, whether knowingly or not, his gorgeous girlfriend on Valentine's Day, thereby achieving his 15 minutes in the occult spotlight.

---

* In his book, Kent wrote about former U.S. Solicitor General Ted Olsen, whose celebrity wife, Barbara, had supposedly been among those killed when American Airlines Flight 77 hit the Pentagon, and whose birthday was … September 11—the 9/11 Birthday Boy.

GIANT CONSOLIDATION

AND

RINGLING BROS

BARNUM & BAILEY

WORLD'S BIGGEST MENAGERIE

CHAPTER 25

MEGA DRIVE-BY

April 9th, 2013: Tupelo, Mississippi

Exactly one week before the ricin letters incident hit international headlines, an unprecedented incident took place in the normally sleepy little northeast Mississippi community of Tupelo.

The Ringling Brothers Circus was in town, and in the early morning hours of April 9th, an unknown assailant shot Carol the circus elephant. Fortunately, the injury was non-fatal but the perpetrator was never apprehended.

Kent had written about the connection between Sarasota, Florida, where President George W. Bush was on the morning of Sept. 11, 2001, and the Ringling Brothers Circus, and beyond that he knew that the Cryptocracy loves incorporating circus/clown elements into their staged events even more than the wicker meme.

In his interview with Daniel Estulin, Kent elaborated:

> The Ringling Brothers and Barnum & Bailey's circus was in Tupelo at that time, and someone shot Carol the circus elephant. If you've read my first book, 9/11 *as Mass Ritual*, you'll remember that Ringling also had a connection to September 11, 2001. The Ringling Brothers clown college is located beside Venice Municipal Airport in Florida, which has been a CIA base of operations for decades and where alleged 9/11 ringleader and mastermind Mohamed Atta sup-

posedly received part of his flight training. CIA recruits were often sent to the clown college to learn sleight of hand.

MAKING THE CONNECTION

The week of the shooting, Kent hadn't given the matter much thought, but in the weeks that followed the Boston Bombings, the incident kept coming to mind. *Who the hell shoots an elephant?*

Sure, Tupelo and the surrounding area has its fair share of rednecks, gangbangers and jackasses sorry enough to shoot an elephant, but the fact is that it hadn't happened before in Tupelo or anywhere else that Kent knew of.

Ricin, wicker, Elvis; Tupelo, Boston; Carol the circus elephant—what was the connection? Surely there had to be one. Timing and location are paramount in ritual: an elephant was shot in Tupelo *the week before* the Boston Bombings and the ricin incident *in Tupelo.*

Again, Kent recalled the familiar intentional interplay between fantasy and reality, between book and film and real-world events. He could recall many such instances in which a book or movie foreshadowed with uncanny accuracy the tragic events that would follow.

The Boston Bombings were false-flag terror attacks resulting in the shutdown of an entire major American city. Was this not George Orwell's *1984* brought to life? In the past decades, this question has been raised so frequently in so many circumstances that it has become a cliché, but that doesn't mean it wasn't true in this particular situation. Kent recalled seeing a police photograph of Lee Harvey Oswald's copy of *1984*, and his instincts told him that there was an Orwell reference in the midst of all this––and then it hit him.

George Orwell had once written an essay first published in the literary magazine *New Writing* in the autumn of 1936 and broadcast by the BBC Home Service on October 12, 1948. The essay describes the experience of the English narrator, possibly based on Orwell's own experiences, called upon to deal with a large aggressive animal while working as a police officer in Burma. The name of the essay? "Shooting an Elephant."

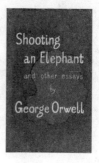

GEORGE ORWELL

> 1984 <

ROMAN

BÜRGERS TASCHENBÜCHER

CHAPTER 26

THE WORST THING IN
THE WORLD

Tuesday, April 16, 2013: San Jose, California

In the wee hours of the morning the day after the Boston Bombings, unidentified gunmen—in what military experts would later describe as a professional black-ops job—cut the fiber optic cable leading to the PG&E Metcalf Transmission Substation, thus defeating its security systems, and proceeded in the next 20 minutes to an hour to knock out 17 giant transformers that funnel power to Silicon Valley.

The special operators who pulled off this attack did so with surgical precision: they knew exactly where to shoot the transformers so that the cooling oil would leak out, thus causing them to overheat and shut down. One former PG&E vice-president of transmission put it bluntly: "This wasn't an incident where Billy-Bob and Joe decided, after a few brewskis, to come in and shoot up a substation."

SYSTEM FAILURE

Although for a variety of reasons this sniper attack didn't make major headlines until well into 2014, this act of industrial sabotage had been part of the Twelve Days of Terror.* However, unlike the Lights Out Super Bowl XLVII, in this incident, due to the power grid's redundancy and emergency backup systems, no one actually lost power.

Had this actually been an unprecedented *failed attempt* on the part of the Twelve Days planners? Through sheer bad luck (on their part) and/or

---

* A second potentially related incident that was under-reported at the time occurred a few days later on April 21st, 2013, when a security guard at TVA Watts Bar Nuclear Plant in Spring City, Tennessee was involved in a 2 a.m. shootout with an intruder. A TVA spokesperson reported that the subject had traveled to the plant by boat and walked onto the property. When the officer questioned the suspect, the perpetrator fired multiple shots at the guard, who returned fire and called for backup. The suspect then fled in his boat.

lack of planning, had they been robbed of the horrifying impact that a successful attack on the heart of the American technology sector would have yielded? Was this a Tribute to the Unabomer gone awry?

A WEAK LINK

Six days before he was elected in 1960, JFK gave a speech at the current site of the San Jose Public Library, less than ten miles from the location of the substation attack. The site was also less than ten miles from JFK University—not the main campus, though.

Yet, as almost anybody over 40 can tell you, Kennedy gave speeches all across the country, and there are so many buildings, institutions and roadways named for him that you could throw a dart at a U.S. map and just about be guaranteed to hit the location of one of his speeches or of

JFK drew a crowd of 20,000 that overflowed the San Jose Civic Auditorium parking lot.

something bearing his name. If the planners of this attack were looking to make a Kennedy Connection, they picked a fairly obscure one, to be sure.

Kent couldn't escape the thought that *these people do not make mistakes.* They do not leave things to chance; they do not fail. If they had truly wanted to disrupt the power to Silicon Valley, the lights would still be off. And the Kennedy link was weak, although not entirely negligible. There had to be something else in play here, something he had missed.

THE ONE-O-ONE

If not Kennedy, what then? Kent had written in-depth about the use of numbers and symbols in mass ritual, and began to scan the environs for clues. If not JFK, maybe Orwell? This had been, after all, almost certainly another in a series of highly-coordinated false-flag attacks during the Twelve Days in April.

Kent looked at a map of the San Jose area and the substation site: running beside it was US Route 101. 101, he thought, I know that number. And indeed he did, as do all readers of George Orwell's *1984*.

101

In the book, Room 101 is a torture chamber in the Ministry of Love, and due to the novel's popularity, the term "Room 101" has come to signify any place where unpleasant things are done. According to Anna Funder's book *Stasiland*, Erich Mielke, the last Minister of State Security (Stasi) of East Germany, had the floors of the Stasi headquarters renumbered so that his second floor office would be 101.

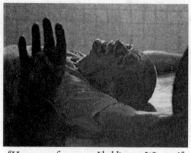

"How many fingers am I holding up, Winston?"

In *1984*, Inner Party member O'Brien says, "You asked me once, Winston, what was in Room 101. I told you that you knew already. Everyone knows. The thing that is in Room 101 is the worst thing in the world."

CHAPTER 27

WHAT'S NEXT?

merica's Sniper, gunned down the day before "Lights Out" Super Bowl XLVII in Lee Harvey Oswald's Crescent City; a sacrificial invocation of Oz on the Day of Love; Carol the circus elephant, shot in the hometown of the King of Rock'n'Roll and Wicked King Wicker; a sniper attack in Cali pointing to *1984*'s Room 101, "the worst thing in the world"... and all this was *pre*-Twelve Days.

More staged violence, more sabotage, more ritual invocation, more JFK, more Orwell...and the year wasn't even half over yet. "Good God," Kent muttered to himself. "What's next?"

Could it possibly get any worse? As Kent was about to learn, the unfortunate answer to that question was, *Hell yes.*

By now, it was abundantly clear that the script for the Golden Jubilee was an extravaganza of false-flag terrorism, psychological warfare, public ritual, human sacrifice, industrial and corporate sabotage and more. Yet, the point was not merely to commemorate/celebrate the 50th anniversary of the JFK assassination, or the literal realization of Orwell's worst nightmare.

No, the script for 2013 was something more—more than a tribute to Oz/Baphomet, or Sirius, or Amun Ra. It was a demonstration of Complete Mastery, the global elite's total mastery of our modern world and every aspect of it.

LETTIN' IT ALL HANG OUT

The months following the 12 days in April were to bring more of the same, as well as new material in the script for the remainder of 2013, which was equally (if not *more so*) creative and diabolical. There were more Satanic antics and crimes against humanity as the elite's shock troops galloped all over the planet, lettin' it all hang out.

One might observe that they absolutely outdid themselves, except *that's what they do*—they constantly innovate in a perpetual struggle to

159

perform more sophisticated in-plain-sight public rituals and morbidly humorous acts of terror, mocking us to our faces all the while.

Is this the *real* Hunger Games? No, this is worse. These games are not confined to an arena—your world is their arena. Everyone is a potential tribute, contestant, victim. The games are anywhere, anytime—everywhere, all the time. *May the odds be ever in your favor,* my ass.

(For those of you who may not be *Hunger Games* fans, this line is used throughout the trilogy to provide encouragement to the involuntary participants in the games).

Anywhere, anytime.
Everywhere, all the time.

Le génie du mal (installed 1848), or "The Genius of Evil," known informally as Lucifer or The Lucifer of Liège, was executed in white marble by Belgian artist Guillaume Geefs. (Art historians often refer to the figure as an *angedéchu*, a "fallen angel.")

CHAPTER 28

THE NEW GREAT AGE

The year 2013 was not simply the Golden Jubilee of the Killing of the King. As Kent explained, it was also the first year in the New Great Age—no, not the New Age, as in the Age of Aquarius, but the New *Great* Age, a new 26,000-year age, as marked by the cycle of procession.

Our masters, the global elite, are Luciferians. The much-anticipated One World Religion is here, and it is Luciferianism. We unknowingly worship at its altars, partake of its sacraments and participate in its sacrifices. This is the New Great Age of Lucifer, the Light Bearer, and we will all bathe in his glory, willingly or otherwise.

The Killing of the King marked the 50-year countdown to the Dawning of the New Great Age of Lucifer, and on that day John F. Kennedy, C.S. Lewis and Aldous Huxley were sacrificed for all they represented and to ensure the blessings of the Dark Powers as the great shift of the ages approached.

Have no doubt that the elite were successful in securing these blessings, for this game is far older and far darker than your worst imaginings.

Yet, should you doubt, you need do nothing more than look at the photo of Kennedy's Air Force One (below), aboard which he flew to Dallas, Texas on November 22, 1963, aboard which Vice President Lyndon B. Johnson was sworn in as the new president, and in which Kennedy's body and Johnson were subsequently flown back to Washington, DC.

President Kennedy's casket is offloaded at Andrews Air Force Base. Not wanting the casket to travel in the cargo hold, the crew made room for it in the passenger compartment by removing two rows of seats and a separating wall.

There, on the rear vertical tail fin you will see a number, the identification number for this aircraft, and it reads, simply, "26,000." *This little light of mine, I'm gonna let it shine…*

PART SIX

POST-TWELVE DAYS

CHAPTER 29

NOT EVEN HALFWAY

As Kent reflected on the true nature and import of the JFK assassination, and of the year 2013 itself, it again occurred to him: the year's not even half done yet. Pre-Twelve Days was bad, Twelve Days worse yet. What would Post-Twelve Days bring for the country (or the world, for that matter) and for him and his family?

His mother's apartment burned the day he signed the contract for his book, which was all about 9/11 as false flag, psych warfare and mass ritual. The book had been released on September 11, 2012, and barely six months later, the next major staged event unfolded in part on his doorstep.

While in DC, Kent had worked in the same office with the Project for a New American Century, co-founded by *Weekly Standard* editor William Kristol, which many viewed as a war-mongering neoconservative cabal situated at the beating heart of the 9/11 attacks. He'd subsequently written an alarming book that presented 9/11 in a startling new light, appearing to reveal information that the perpetrators of the attacks would not want exposed to the light of day.

IS IT OVER YET?

Now, at the end of April 2013, he sat looking out his office window contemplating everything that had just unfolded, staring at the parking lot where Carol the elephant had been shot, and watching dark blue pickups with utility trailers—unmarked FBI evidence-collection and HazMat units—speed by, going to and from ricin-laden crime scenes. There'd been unusual police activity directly outside his office and in his building, and he strongly suspected he was the focus of it.

The circus *had* come to town, and it wasn't the Ringling Brothers. Once again, it appeared that he had a front-row seat in the Main Tent; first in DC, now in Tupelo. *Were they through with Tupelo*, he wondered, and beyond that, *Were they through with him?*

167

CHAPTER 30

A CROWNING ACHIEVEMENT

May 10, 2013: New York City

Live on the *Today* show: Matt Lauer, several hundred feet in the air in Manhattan for the topping off of the One World Trade Center, with the final two sections of its communication tower about to be lifted into place. The date had supposedly been pushed forward several weeks to May 10 by some contractual dispute, but Kent knew why this specific date had been chosen for this particular act.

Kent had predicted in a lengthy piece on his blog that something significant would occur on May 10, an achievement in itself considering that the date is not one of traditional importance on the occult calendar and historically very little of ritual significance has taken place on this day.

Kent discovered in advance that there was a link between: a.) *The Dark Knight Rises* theatre shooting in Aurora, Colorado on May 20, 2012; b.) the Sandy Hook elementary school shooting on December 14, 2012; and c.) May 10, 2013—a link involving the crescent moon.

In his article, he had taken an educated guess, based on similar scenarios, as to what might happen on 5/10, but he'd known at the time he wrote it that he was probably wrong— and indeed he was wrong, although it was a worthwhile thought exercise nonetheless.

169

MEGA-SYMBOL

As Kent sat watching the spire being hoisted into place that morning, completing the full height of One World Trade at exactly 1776 feet tall, he understood full well the hidden meaning of the act: 1776, the year of the American Founding, true, but also, and of much greater importance to the global elite, the year of the founding of the Illuminati.

As he'd written in his book, the One World Trade building—with its massive upward-and-downward-pointing triangles—was an alchemical architectural statement, a massive concrete-and-steel representation of the penultimate occult/hermetic maxim, *As above, so below.*

And today, of all days, at the former site of the Twin Towers—on the date of the first annular "ring of fire" solar eclipse of 2013, as well as the third in a series of Friday crescent moons which connected prior ritual sacrifices in Aurora and Sandy Hook (all spaced exactly the same number of days apart),

The World's Tallest Minaret

With One World Trade's height of 1776 feet being achieved through the installation of its communication tower, it is interesting to note that the tower's design bears a striking resemblance to the minarets found in Islamic mosques

ONE WORLD TRADE CENTER   MUSLIM ISLAMIC MINARET

all over the world; and this, of course, is no coincidence.

In his book, Kent had written about the controversy surrounding the initial design of the Flight 93 memorial, which had been shaped like an Islamic crescent and named, adding insult to injury, "The Crescent of Embrace." (Some observers even claimed that the crescent had been oriented toward Mecca, as is common practice in Islamic architecture.)

Such a public uproar followed that the design was eventually changed, but the point had been made: those who had orchestrated the attacks on 9/11 were now rubbing our noses in the pile of crap they'd served us as the official story behind the attacks.

We'd been told that a bunch of Muslim terrorists with box-cutters had evaded the world's most powerful security and intelligence services over the course of years, had assumed control of multiple airliners and used them as weapons of mass destruction, which, we were informed by various figures in authority, nobody had ever thought

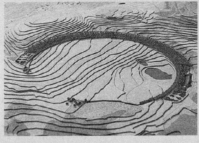

of, despite the fact that drills simulating this very thing had been conducted in the past and were in fact being conducted on the very day of September 11, 2001.

So, if you liked that, have some more: here's a memorial to your dead, designed in the shape of an Islamic crescent.

The communications tower on One World Trade is exactly the same thing: a slap in the face, bold mockery. On the very spot where thousands died on 9/11, our masters have erected what can accurately be referred to as the Tallest Minaret in the World. Take that, bitches.

constituting *a dual solar-lunar mass ritual*—the One World Trade Center was brought to its full symbolic height, a crowning achievement if ever there was one.

YES, ANNULAR

No, that's not a misspelling: an annular solar eclipse is one in which the moon doesn't entirely block the sun, creating a ring in the sky—a ring of fire, such as in the annular eclipse shown right.

Which, by the way, looks an awful lot like this ring of fire:

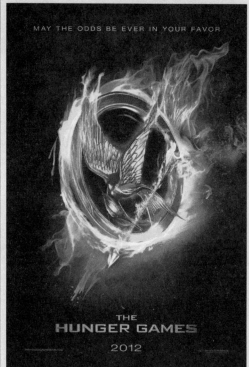

Or this one:

And is it just me, or does the bird in the above images—called a mockingjay in the The Hunger Games—remind anyone of anything?

Pictured above: the guest of honor at the 2012 XXX London Olympic Illuminati Extravaganza (otherwise referred to as the Closing Ceremony)

Yeah, that's what I thought, too. The only thing mocking about that bird is the way it's being used to mock all of us.

Take us out, Johnny…

I fell into a burning ring of fire
I went down, down, down and
the flames went higher
And it burns, burns, burns,
the ring of fire
The ring of fire

(With apologies, but I can't stop myself from sharing this, as well: "Ring of fire" is a colloquial term that refers to pain around the anus during and/or after defecation as a result of ingesting spicy foods. So, would that be anular pain?)

Magically, deliciously, the "ring of fire" eclipse on this day transpired, of all the places in the entire world, over Australia, the *Land of Oz* … a blessing from the dark gods.

TIMING IS EVERYTHING

Of more human origin that day was another orchestrated connection of import: the release of the latest screen version of F. Scott Fitzgerald's *The Great Gatsby*, a celebration, if you will, of the excesses of the super elite and the fine art of deception.

Interestingly, *Gatsby* had been scheduled for release on December 25, 2012, but the release date was pushed forward for reasons that weren't entirely clear to industry observers, but that were quite clear to Kent.

A ROYAL PAIN-IN-THE-ASS

It also struck Kent as quite fitting that a representative of the British Royal Crown, Prince Harry,* was in America on May 10, part of a weeklong trip. The site that the Prince visited on 5/10 also intrigued Kent.

Prince Harry stopped at Arlington National Cemetery that day, ostensibly to pay tribute to the fallen soldiers of

---

* In keeping with this being in part a lunar ritual, let us remember that Prince Harry is the son of Diana (who was herself sacrificed in an elaborate public ritual that was Great Britain's equivalent of the JFK assassination, but that's another story altogether)—that's Diana as in the crescent moon goddess Diana/Artemis.

THE EYES OF HORUS

In The Great Gatsby, the eyes of Doctor T. J. Eckleburg are a pair of fading, painted, bespectacled eyes on an advertisement for an optometrist's practice, plastered on an old billboard overlooking the Valley of Ashes: "… his eyes, dimmed a little by many paintless days, under sun and rain, brood on over the solemn dumping ground."

The eyes stare down on the main characters as they pass underneath on their way into New York City to carry on their illicit activities, with one character equating them to the eyes of God: "…God knows what you've been doing, everything you've been doing. You may fool me, but you can't fool God!," he says, to which his listener replies, "It's just a billboard."

The hollow eyes also suggest the emptiness of the American Dream—that it is a just a dream for the vast majority of Americans, represented by those toiling the blighted landscape below. And while they might also seem to symbolize the nation's loss of morality and the abandonment of values in an all-consuming pursuit of wealth, Fitzgerald implies throughout the novel that symbols only have meaning because characters instill them with it. Thus, the eyes come to stand for the essential meaninglessness of existence and the arbitrary manner with which common people invest objects with meaning … you know, the usual kind of nihilistic crap the global elite seem to thrive on.

Plus, the billboard also kind of reminds you of the Eyes of Horus.

Iraq and Afghanistan, the very wars initiated by 9/11 and the fall of the Twin Towers, which One World Trade replaced. Yet, as Kent was all too aware, Arlington is also the final resting place of JFK and site of the eternal flame dedicated to his memory; never mind that it's also the symbol of the Illuminati.

ALL IN THE FAMILY

Hecate is a Triple Moon Goddess, whose tripartite nature includes the Virgin/Maiden, the Mother and the Crone—the three stages of a woman's life—symbolized by the three lunar phases of the crescent new moon, the luminous full moon, and the waning moon.

The Greek goddess Artemis (whose Roman counterpart was Diana) is often viewed as the maiden aspect of Hecate, and her symbol is therefore the waxing crescent moon. Given the centrality of that symbol in this context, and knowing that Aurora is the mother of Lucifer, we should find it highly appropriate that Artemis is also known, wait for it, as the sister of Lucifer. This is just turning out to be one big family reunion, isn't it?

ARTEMIS   DIANA

Artemis: note the crescent moon in her hair.

But before we break up our little get-together, let's talk pets: Hecate is associated with Cerberus, the three-headed dog, and the Dog Star Sirius is also considered sacred to her. Guess which animal is among those traditionally associated with Artemis? The bat (and, no, I didn't make that up). Batgirl!

Postscript: The Programmers may have done the Batman-moon thing before: the second install-ment in The Dark Knight trilogy, starring Heath Ledger in a brilliant performance as The Joker, was released on July 18, 2008, a full moon. After filming had been completed, Ledger died tragically, under suspicious circumstances some have argued, of an apparent drug overdose on January 22, 2008 – a full moon – propelling interest in the upcoming film to even greater heights.

FIGHT THE DEAD.
FEAR THE LIVING.

THE
WALKING DEAD

RETURNS OCT 14
SUNDAYS 9/8C   aMC

CHAPTER 31

ZOMBIE APOCALYPSE

May 30, 2013: New Boston, Texas

As soon as Kent heard the words "New Boston" and "ricin," he knew the story that followed was 100% certain to be another installment in the 2013 Mega-Ritual.

April: Boston; May: New Boston. *Another* attempted ricin-letter frame-up, a slight variation on the theme established in Tupelo, wherein Everett Dutschke tried unsuccessfully to frame Kevin Curtis.

In New Boston, Shannon Richardson, a bit actress in the *Walking Dead* and *Vampire Diaries* TV series (and a good choice by casting directors judging from her police mug-shot), attempted to set up her husband Nathan in exactly the same manner as Dutschke had Curtis, mailing ricin-laced letters to President Obama and then-New York Mayor Michael "Give Me Your Guns" Bloomberg.

The letters, which were discovered before they reached their intended recipients, contained this message: "You will have to kill me and my family before you get my guns. The right to bear arms is my constitutional God-given right. What's in this letter is nothing compared to what I've got planned for you."

Could this have simply been a copycat crime? Sure it could. It worked so well for Dutschke that Shannon must have thought to herself, *I'll do exactly the same thing. And just like Dutschke, I'll leave evidence all over the place incriminating myself instead of the person I'm trying to frame.*

No, if you can't tell by now that this was part of the script, if you can't identify the telltale markers in the place name and other delicious details, just give up, there's no hope for you.

Exclusive

The whistleblower

I can't allow the US government to destroy privacy and basic liberties

theguardian

guardian.co.uk

- ● Edward Snowden, 29, emerges from hiding in Hong Kong
- ● IT contractor says his concerns were ignored and he had to go public

Glenn Greenwald Hong Kong
Julian Borger

The whistleblower behind the most significant US intelligence leak in modern times broke cover last night, saying he had decided to leave his position at a National Security Agency (NSA) contractor because he believed its unconstrained collection of electronic intelligence was destroying civil liberties and creating the conditions for tyranny.

Edward Snowden, a 29-year-old IT administrator for the defence contractor Booz Allen Hamilton, was speaking in Hong Kong after leaking a series of agency documents on the collection of telephone data on millions of Americans, the NSA's relationship with US internet providers and the Obama administration cyber-warfare policy.

"I can't allow the US government to destroy privacy, internet freedom and basic liberties," he said. "My sole motive is to inform the public as to that which is done in their name and that which is done against them."

Snowden said he felt compelled to speak out because in his job helping to run the NSA computer systems, he had witnessed a pattern of excessive and intrusive surveillance of Americans, and that his objections had been ignored by his superiors.

"When you're in positions of privileged access, like a systems administrator for these sort of intelligence community agencies, you're exposed to a lot more information on a broader scale than the average employee, and because of that you see things that may be disturbing but over the course of a normal person's career you'd only see one or two of these instances," Snowden said. "I, sitting at my desk, certainly had the authorities to wiretap anyone: you, your accountant, to a federal judge, even the president if I had a personal email."

He argued that NSA surveillance was not being effectively constrained by administration policy and would continue to grow as the technology improved. "And the months ahead, the years ahead, it's only going to get worse, until eventually there will be a time where policies will change - because the only thing that restricts the activities of the surveillance state are policy."

Snowden warned that if there was no greater awareness of what US intelligence was doing and not much greater oversight the "surveillance state" would outrun the ability of the American people to control it. "And there will be nothing the people can do at that point to oppose it. And it'll be turn-key tyranny," Snowden said.

He said he had given up a comfortable existence in Hawaii and now risked arrest and imprisonment. In a note accompanying the first set of documents he provided, he wrote: "I understand that I will be made to suffer for my actions."

But in an interview with the Guardian, Snowden declared: "I've no intention of hiding. I've done nothing wrong.

"The greatest fear that I have regarding the outcome of these disclosures for America is that nothing will change," he said. "People will see in the media a of these disclosures, they'll know th lengths the government is going to to gran themselves powers unilaterally, to create greater control over American society an global society, but they won't be willing t take the risks necessary to stand up an fight to change things, to force their repre sentatives to actually take a stand in thei interests," Snowden said.

He also sounded a warning to othe nations that the US intelligence establish ment does not view international treatie as being binding constraints on its opera tions. "Even our agreements with othe sovereign governments, we consider tha to be a stipulation of policy rather than stipulation of law," he said. "And becaus of that, a new leader will be elected, they'l flip the switch, say that because of the 'cri sis', because of the dangers we face in the world, you know, some new and unpre dicted threat, we need more authority, we need more power."

He defended his decision to go to Hon Kong to share his knowledge of NSA oper ations, pointing out that the enclave ha autonomies and freedom not shared b the rest of China. He insisted his inten tion was not to harm America's security and pointed out that he had access to a huge amount of information that coul have crippled US intelligence collection but had not given it away.

Snowden said that he had raised his concerns at work, but they had been shrugged off so he felt he had little choice but to go public.

2-5 »

9 770261 307712 24

MIF

MANCHESTER INTERNATIONAL FESTIVAL

4 – 21 July 2013

See page 3

CHAPTER 32

THE INTELLIGENCE
NON-APOCALYPSE

June 5th, 2013

The fifth of June, the day before the anniversary of the assassination of Robert F. Kennedy (see Chapter 46), the headline of the *Guardian* newspaper announces the leak of a whole slew of top-secret NSA documents by security contractor Edward Snowden.

Kent wasn't sure if this was coincidence or another carefully timed aspect of the 2013 Mega-Ritual, and he basically didn't care as he was beginning to suffer from Golden Jubilee burnout.

As it unfolded, the whole thing smelled a little funny to him, and he figured that, as usual, there was more to the incident than first met the eye. This was probably part of some super-sophisticated, three-dimensional, psychological warfare chess game being played by the Cryptocracy.

Snowden's leaks were portrayed as catastrophic for the American intelligence community and Department of Defense and, with multiple revelations angering friends and foes alike, were generally viewed as quite damaging to U.S. foreign policy.

OF COURSE BIG BROTHER IS WATCHING

Snowden's leaks were said to reveal sources and methods putting lives at risk all over the planet. We were told that our adversaries changed their methods of communication and other tactics as a result of the top-secret information being published.

Yet, independent of how true this may have been, the leaks also accomplished something else: they revealed to the general public, most of whom have their heads up their backsides or they would have known all

Snowden's girlfriend, Lindsay Mills. Whattaya' bet that the boys at the NSA kept an extra close eye on her?

this much earlier, that they were, and had been for some time, under comprehensive surveillance by their own government. Wow, there's a surprise.

In the name of securing our liberty, the NSA watches everything we say and do. (Did anybody actually read the Patriot Act?) But aren't there appropriate checks and balances in place? Yes, and there's a shadow government that does anything it damn well pleases, too, and it's not accountable to anyone.

The government listens to our phone calls and reads our email? Yes, and the sky is blue and bears shit in the woods. Snowden's revelations are yesterday's news. To Kent, this sounded a lot like Michael Hoffman's "Revelation of the Method," whereby our Controllers reveal what they're doing to us, and in many instances, how and why. Kent wrote about this subject in his book, drawing heavily from *Secret Societies and Psychological Warfare*.

THE EXORBITANT PRICE OF FREEDOM

Snowden's disclosures were likely not all that top secret, and the technologies and methods he revealed are probably at least ten years behind the cutting edge. Kent knew from his own research that much more exotic, sophisticated technologies had been under development for decades, and had been employed in the field for years in many instances.

He'd read about science-fiction-sounding stuff: satellite-based brainwave-interpretation mind-reading technologies, voice-to-skull microwave transmitters, and the like.

Which technologies actually existed and which were fiction didn't matter too much to him and he didn't spend a great deal of time trying to figure it out. What he suspected was that Snowden's leaks were less than the catastrophic revelations they were portrayed as.

Snowden put those who hadn't been paying attention (i.e. most everybody) on notice: *We see and hear everything you do. Freedom isn't free, and neither are you.*

The intended effect: a profound sense of violation, of uncertainty, of disillusionment, of fear. Precisely the frame of mind programmers want their victims in when they subject them to multi-spectrum brainwashing techniques.

PROJECT ECHELON

Kent had known through first-hand experience *pre-Snowden* that we're under constant surveillance. He'd proven it to himself through a hairbrained scheme which had in all likelihood gotten him placed on the Domestic Terrorism Watch List.

In his research, Kent had run across descriptions of Project Echelon, reportedly an NSA program of precisely the type Snowden had leaked about: an unconstitutional dragnet for all domestic emails and phone calls. Somewhat skeptical about it at the time in 2008, he knew how he could test for the existence of such a program, hopefully without getting himself thrown in prison.

In August of 2008, the first Presidential Debate between Barack Obama and John McCain was held in the Ford Center for the Performing Arts on the campus of the University of Mississippi in Oxford. Kent's brother was a staff photographer at Ole Miss, and he also knew the director of the Ford Center.

In the body of an email, Kent typed in hot-button keywords that would be certain to be flagged if it was run through any type of Echelon-style database program: Barack Obama, assassination, .50 caliber, red mercury, Ford Center, Oxford—and several others. He pulled up his brother's email address in the "To" box and clicked send.

"Echelon, my butt," he muttered, and didn't think much more about it—that is until several days later as he was walking to pick up his son at school.

179

An Unusual Sight

In tiny Blue Mountain, a rural northeast Mississippi town of 1,000, helicopters are a rare sight, and low-flying helicopters even rarer. As Kent walked down the old disintegrating sidewalk that afternoon, he heard the unmistakable sounds of a chopper in the distance, not paying much attention as it drew closer and closer. He finally stopped and turned. Was it a life-flight helicopter out of Memphis? He hadn't heard any sirens.

He looked back down the street he'd just walked up, and finally saw the chopper, less than a hundred feet off the ground, just over the tree tops, approaching him. At this point, he was still merely curious, wondering what the reason for this unusual sight was. Now that he thought about it, he couldn't recall witnessing anything like this in Blue Mountain before.

Flashback

Kent was standing near the three-way stop not far from the school grounds gazing upwards with his hand shielding his eyes from the intense sunlight.

He momentarily recalled the time as a small child living in Fort Worth, Texas that he'd successfully flagged down a police helicopter just to see if he could do it. Much to Kent's dismay, the concerned pilot had proceeded to circle his house at a very low altitude until a squad car arrived. Young Kent had been horrified by his unexpected success and cowered screaming on the porch while the incredibly loud noise flooded the neighborhood.

Back in the present, a slight wave of panic echoed from the past and then was gone, but the helicopter was not. It was now directly over the intersection, hovering. Kent was the only person on the sidewalk, and there were no cars on the road. Several things now stood out that he hadn't previously noticed: it was a black, unmarked helicopter, with no doors.

As the aircraft angled sideways to him, the pilot turned his head and looked down at him through his reflective aviator sunglasses and simply stared. He then rotated the chopper around facing the direction he'd flown in from, and proceeded slowly back down the street. *Shit, that was weird,* Kent thought as he turned back toward the school.

We Know Where You Live

It wasn't until later that evening that he remembered the email he'd sent to his brother and connected the dots: he was being sent a message, "We're watching you, and we know where you live and where your kids go to school."

And if Kent had harbored any doubts that the dots *were* connected, they would be erased altogether over the next nine months as the local police cruiser drove by his house multiple times a day, every day and every evening—something that hadn't happened before with *anywhere near* this regularity.

Although nothing much else came of the incident, Kent figured that his little experiment had gotten him put on the Domestic Terrorism Watch List. He'd proven the existence of Project Echelon, or whatever the hell its real name was, to his own satisfaction, and hadn't seen a need to seek any further confirmation.

In fact, he felt a little bit like the small kid who had flagged down the police chopper—they'd seen him, now what?

CHAPTER 33

HAPPY BIRTHDAY, MR. PRESIDENT

July 6, 2013: San Francisco, California and Lac-Mégantic, Quebec

As the Asiana Airlines Boeing 777 approached the San Francisco International Airport (SFO) that morning, both the weather and visibility were very good. There was only a light wind, no precipitation and no forecast or reports of wind shear.

At 11:21 a.m. PDT, the flight was cleared for a visual approach on runway 28L due to the instrument landing system's vertical guidance (glide slope) being out of service because of construction. At 11:27, when the plane was 1.5 miles out, a tower controller gave clearance to land.

Seven seconds from the runway, one of the pilots called for an increase in speed. Four seconds later, someone else in the cockpit called for a 'go around'—abort the landing—echoed by yet another crew-member 1.5 seconds later. Then…

The plane had come in too low and too slow. First the landing gear, then the tail of the giant airplane struck the sea wall. Both engines and the tail section separated from the aircraft, the vertical and horizontal stabilizers falling onto the runway. The remainder of the fuselage then pivoted on one of its wings and rotated counter-clockwise approximately 330 degrees as it slid across the tarmac, coming to rest 2,400 feet from the initial point of impact.

A minute or so later, a dark plume of smoke rose from the wreckage as the plane caught fire. Evacuation slides were deployed. Slides for the first and second doors on the right side inflated *inside* the aircraft, pinning some passengers and crew and blocking those exits until they were deflated.

VERY CONCERNED

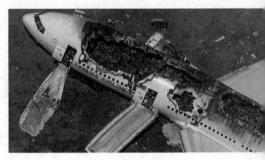

Of the 307 people aboard, two passengers died at the scene and a third in the hospital several days later; 181 were injured, 12 of them critically. Among the injured were three flight attendants who were ejected from the airplane while still strapped in their seats as the tail section broke off.

The two on-scene deceased were both 16-year-olds with Chinese passports. One allegedly died after being rescued from the plane alive, placed on the ground, inadvertently covered with fire-fighting foam and subsequently run over by an emergency vehicle.

It was only the second crash of a Boeing 777, the *first* resulting in fatalities, since the aircraft began operating commercially in 1995, and just the third fatal crash in Asiana Airlines' 25-year history.

Although the 45-year-old pilot, Captain Lee Kang Guk, had 9,793 hours of flying experience, only 43 of those were in a 777. Lee was in the process of receiving his initial operating experience (IOE) training and halfway through Asiana's IOE requirements. Lee *was* operating the controls that day under the supervision of 48-year-old Captain Lee Jung Min, who had over 3,200 hours of flying experience specifically in the 777 (over 12,300 total hours); however, this was his first flight as an instructor.

Although Captain Lee had previously landed at SFO in a Boeing 747 and other aircraft, when asked by investigators whether he'd been concerned about his ability to perform a visual approach without the runway's instrument landing aids, he said, "very concerned, yeah."

Lee conceded that he was also worried about his unfamiliarity with the 777's auto-flight system, and admitted that he had not studied it well enough and thus thought that the plane's auto-throttle was supposed to prevent the jet from flying below minimum speed as it approached the runway. "This pilot should never have taken off," remarked an attorney representing a group of passengers.

BLINDED BY THE LIGHT

Another Asiana pilot who had flown with Lee just two days before the accident told investigators that he wasn't sure if the trainee captain had been making normal progress and that he hadn't performed well on their trip together, describing Lee as "not well organized or prepared."

By all accounts, there were several rather unusual circumstances surrounding this flight, and then there's this little fact, which most people either discounted or assumed Lee made up to cover his ass: Lee insisted in interviews that, at 500 feet—35 seconds from impact—he had been blinded by a bright, piercing light from outside the aircraft.

NTSB investigators repeatedly questioned Lee about the light, but he was unable to pinpoint its origin or in precisely what manner it affected him. The NTSB referred to the effect of the bright light as "temporary" and reported that Lee did not believe that it had affected his ability to fly the aircraft. None of the other members of the flight crew made any reference to it either during interviews or in cockpit voice recordings.

RECIPE FOR CALAMITY

So, you take a pilot with 43 hours in the seat of a 777 and put him beside a *first-time* instructor, take away his vertical guidance system, shine a laser in his eyes right before landing, and BINGO, you've got yourself a major airline *catastrophe* (let alone the possibility that the airplane's controls might have also been manipulated remotely, as several white-hat hackers had demonstrated could be done earlier that year). And, just like when someone with a known mental illness is selected to be transformed into a programmed assassin and nobody suspects anything after the killing because the person had a history of being nuts, you've got the perfect cover story to keep anybody from looking any further.

All of this struck Kent as somewhat reminiscent of 9/11's American Airlines Flight 77 pilot Hani Hanjour, whose flight instructors stated couldn't fly a single-engine Cesna, but who, according to flight path recordings from the incident, performed fantastical aerobatic maneuvers in order to slam into the side of the Pentagon.

What had really gotten Kent's attention, however, was the flight number involved in this crash: Asiana Airlines Flight OZ214. *More Oz.*

First Oz Pistorius, then *Oz the Great and Powerful* followed by the film-foreshadowed Luxor hot-air balloon conflagration ... and now, Oz the Plane Crash, or Calamity, whichever you prefer, and the latter would be preferable, given the fact that the number 214, according to master occultist Aleister Crowley—who was featured prominently in both the 9/11

Mega-Ritual itself as well as Kent's book on the subject—connotes, as per Crowley's essay entitled *Gematria*, "*Calamity!*"

A specific flight number being chosen for its occult significance? As bizarre an idea as it may at first sound to the uninitiated, Kent knew full well that there was a powerful precedent for such, one he'd covered quite thoroughly in *9/11 as Mass Ritual*.

American Airlines Flights 11 and 77 and United Airlines Flights 93 and 175 had all been selected because of the potent occult meaning attached to these numbers, and in his book he'd gone into detail on each. Using numbers that were of particular importance to Crowley had also been a key feature of the ritual.

CITY OF SAINT FRANCIS

Speaking of significant numbers, it is noteworthy that the San Francisco International Airport sits on U.S. Route 101, less than 50 miles northwest of the PG&E electrical substation on Route 101 that was the target of a professional sniper attack on April 16th.

The airport itself is of course named for the City by the Bay, which sits some ten miles north. San Francisco is Spanish for Saint Francis, and city founders were intent upon honoring St. Francis of Assisi when they selected this name in 1776. However, the orchestrators of this staged event would be far more interested in evoking the memory of Sir Francis Dash-

wood, founder of one of the most notorious of the high-society gentleman's clubs, which would later come to be referred to, often in collective fashion, as "the Hellfire Club."

Sir Francis' club was never known by this name during its existence during the 1740s, 50s, and 60s, but rather went by several names, including the *Brotherhood of St. Francis of Wycombe* and *The Order of the Friars of St. Francis of Wycombe*, and later, after moving their meetings to Medmenham Abbey, the *Monks of Medmenham*.

The club motto was *Fais ce que tu voudras* ("Do what thou wilt"), a philosophy associated with 16th century Franciscan monk François Rabelais' fictional Abbey of Thélème, and later adopted by Aleister Crowley. The famous inscription was incorporated into a stained-glass window above the grand entrance of Medmenham Abbey, whose "monks" were satirically referred to as Franciscans and amused themselves with obscene parodies of Franciscan rites, and with orgies of debauchery and drunkenness.

Among the rumors circulated regarding the activities of these Hellfire clubs were: the practice of devil worship and other dark arts; the conducting of orgies, Black Masses and other mock religious ceremonies as well as pagan rites; and, partaking in meals featuring dishes with names like Holy Ghost Pie, Breast of Venus and Devil's Loin (while drinking Hell-fire Punch).

It was also reported that club members frequently attended such festivities dressed as characters from the Bible, and that female guests (ie. prostitutes) were dressed as nuns.

Founding Father Benjamin Franklin, to whom Kent is related through Franklin's older brother John, is known to have occasionally attended Sir Francis' club meetings in 1758 during his time in England. Franklin was a Freemason who rose to the rank of Grand Master of Pennsylvania in 1734.

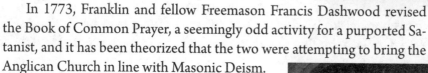

That same year, he edited and published the first Masonic book in the Americas, a reprint of James Anderson's *Constitutions of the Free-Masons*. During Franklin's stay in France, he served as Grand Master of the Lodge Les NeufSœurs from 1779 until 1781.

In 1773, Franklin and fellow Freemason Francis Dashwood revised the Book of Common Prayer, a seemingly odd activity for a purported Satanist, and it has been theorized that the two were attempting to bring the Anglican Church in line with Masonic Deism.

Whatever the case may be, it has also been theorized that Dashwood's Hellfire Club, as well as others, might have been Masonic Lodges in disguise, and not simply the Devil-worshipping bunch of hooligans many believed them to be. A more sophisticated interpretation of these clubs would take into account the rumors of sexual magic and kabbalistic teachings, as well as the recurring image of Harpocrates, god of silence.

HOME SWEET HOME

The City of St. Francis was thus the perfect location in which to establish the Church of Satan, founded by occultist, writer, actor, musician and ex-circus entertainer Anton Szandor LaVey on Walpurgisnacht: April 30, 1966. On this night, LaVey ritualistically shaved his head, presumably in the tradition of ancient executioners, declared the founding of the Church of Satan and proclaimed 1966 as "year one," Anno Satanas—the first year of the Age of Satan.

Underground experimental film maker, actor, controversial author and Crowley-enthusiast Kenneth Anger was a member of the church, which would subsequently give rise to the Temple of Set, led by U.S. intelligence asset and psychological warfare specialist Lt. Col. Michael Aquino.

San Francisco was also home to an outpost of the Process Church, an offshoot of the Church of Scientology, brainchild of the illustrious L. Ron Hubbard.

WHAT'S NOT TO LOVE?

During 1967's "Summer of Love," Charles Manson established himself as a hippie guru of sorts in San Francisco's Haight-Ashbury district. Prosecutor Vincent Bugliosi noted in his book *Helter Skelter* that Manson appeared to have borrowed philosophically from the Process Church, which is not in the least surprising given that the church was located two blocks down the same street where Manson lived.

The Church of Satan's home in San Francisco was the Black House and LaVey was the High Priest until his death in 1997. In 2001, a new high priest took over and the church's headquarters were moved to, where else, Hell's Kitchen* in Manhattan. The Church of Satan does not recognize any other

---

* Although several explanations exist as to how this area of the city received its name, an early use of the phrase appears in a comment made by another of Kent's famous relatives, Davy Crockett. According to the Irish Cultural Society of the Garden City Area, Crockett said the following in 1835 about another notorious Irish slum in Manhattan, Five Points: "In my part of the country, when you meet an Irishman, you find a first-rate gentleman; but these are worse than savages; they are too mean to swab hell's kitchen."

Franco's Anger: The Voyeur-King

James "Oz" Franco has taken on an interesting variety of film roles, including that of rapper-gangster "Alien" in the 2012 comedy *Spring Breakers*—but who could really blame him given the gaggle of hottie co-stars?

Franco is also always working on a wide range of personal projects, and in September 2012 his band, Daddy, released its first single, "Love in the Old Days." The music video Franco shot for the song depicts what he calls "The Marriage of Hell," which some might view as a full-on Satanic ritual.

The video features bizarre imagery and dizzying strobe-light effects, with scantily-clad and fully nude men and women wearing animal-head masks and carrying candles, circling a black-and-white checkerboard altar and gyrating on one another.

(Left) Anger. (Center and right) The soundtrack for Scorpio Rising, *a 1963 experimental short film by Anger, features Elvis Presley singing, "You're the Devil in Disguise."*

Franco cast film director and Crowley-disciple Kenneth Anger—who spent three months in Cefalu, Sicily in 1955 shooting a documentary about Crowley's frescoes in Thelema Abbey—as the priest overseeing the ceremony, and it was an opportunity for Franco to collaborate with one of his idols.

"Kenneth Anger has been an influence on me since I was first exposed to 'Kustom Kar Kommandoes' and 'Scorpio Rising', but especially 'Scorpio Rising,'" Franco explained. "When I went to NYU for film, I was always looking for ways to Anger up my films. My first one in particular, 'The Feast of Stephen' owes a lot to Anger, the way his camera transformed a gang of real 1960 bikers into homoerotic gods. In other films and projects I loved the way he took celebrity and the occult and fused them in [Sergei] Eisensteinian juxtapositions to achieve a greater, spiritual/aesthetic significance."

In Anger's 1954 38-minute short film, *Inauguration of the Pleasure Dome* (the phrase "pleasure dome" was taken from Samuel Taylor Coleridge's poem, *Kubla Khan*), the roles of The Scarlet Woman—also known as Babalon, the Great Mother or Mother of Abominations, a goddess in Aleister Crowley's mystical system of Thelema—and Kali are played by Marjorie Cameron, an actress, occultist and wife of rocket pioneer/occultist Jack Parsons.

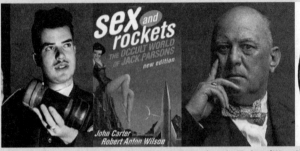

Crowley's friends, Jack Parsons and Gerald Brosseau Gardner, the "Father of Wicca," and director of the Museum of Magic and Witchcraft on the Isle of Man, was actively involved with OTO. Shortly before his death, Crowley elevated Gardner to the VII°. (Love that hair, Gerald.)

[continued] Parsons, a founding member of the Jet Propulsion Laboratory, was a devout follower of Aleister Crowley and head of the Agape Lodge, a branch of the Thelemite Ordo Templi Orientis (O.T.O.).

In 1946, Parsons engaged in a series of rituals with L. Ron Hubbard utilizing Enochian magic with the intention of attracting an "Elemental woman" to be his partner in a sex magick ritual, part of the "Babalon Working," a rite to invoke the incarnation of the Thelemite goddess onto Earth in human form.

Almost immediately after declaring that the first series of rituals had been successfully completed, Parsons met Cameron at his home, the Parsonage, and regarded her as the entity that he and Hubbard had summoned through the initial ritual.

Parsons and Cameron were instantly attracted to each other and spent the next two weeks in Parsons' bedroom, where Parson sought to continue the Babalon Working through the conception of a child by sex magick. Parsons came to regard Cameron as Babalon herself and the two were soon married. Two years after Parsons' premature death in 1952, Anger cast Cameron in the very same role in *Inauguration of the Pleasure Dome*.

Lucifer Rising, another short film by Kenneth Anger, was completed in 1972 but only widely distributed in 1980. Anger hired musician Bobby Beausoleil to compose the soundtrack, despite the fact that Beausoleil was in prison, having been convicted of killing Gary Hinman under orders from Charles Manson in 1970. Chris Jagger, brother of *Rolling Stones*' lead singer Mick Jagger, was originally slated for the role of Lucifer but had a falling out with Anger during filming.

"I could think of no one better to preside over the marriage of Hell than Anger," Franco concluded. "He is a force. A fusion of art, pop-culture, magik and sex. He is the voyeur-king."

(Left) The role of Egyptian god Osiris in Lucifer Rising was played by Donald Cammell, son of Charles Cammell, a friend and biographer of Aleister Crowley. (Right) Anton Lavey played "His Satanic Majesty" in Anger's 1969 Invocation of My Demon Brother.

Designed by La Boca, the Lucifer Jacket (left) pays homage to the original satin jacket featured in Lucifer Rising (center), and will only be produced as a very limited edition (less than 100). You can bet your ass that James Franco will be getting one of these, but if for whatever reason he misses out on the opportunity to purchase one, perhaps he can borrow Joaquin Phoenix's (right).

organizations as holding legitimate claim to Satanism and the practice thereof, although aspiring Satanists will be glad to learn that the church *does* recognize that one need not necessarily be a member of the church to be a Satanist.

So, from an occult perspective, there's lots to love about the City of Saint Francis and its sordid history, including the Zodiac Killer and the attempted assassination of President Gerald Ford, which took place in front of the St. Francis Hotel (not to mention that the city is the LGBT Capitol of the World). If you still have any questions as to why Flight OZ214 was brought down at the San Francisco International Airport, God help you.

UP IN FLAMES

Another interesting aspect of San Francisco's history with which many will be familiar is that the city was completely destroyed in 1906 by a major earthquake and the ensuing conflagration. The city flag, appropriately on several levels, features a phoenix.

Now, attempting to put ourselves into the same mindset as our adversaries, we might ask whether it might not have been more appropriate to crash Flight OZ214 into downtown San Francisco, setting it ablaze in a fitting act of conflagrational commemoration. Come on, though, crashing planes into buildings? Been there, done that.

Not that setting an entire town ablaze isn't an appealingly sinister idea in general, and a great way to evoke the memory of the burning of San Francisco—which is a particularly interesting thing to note at this juncture, given that this is precisely what the Cryptocracy did earlier that same day in the wee hours of July 6th, only hours before slamming Flight OZ214 into the tarmac.

Francis the First

Pope Benedict announced his historic resignation, the first in over 600 years, on February 11th, 2013, three days before Oz Pistorius' unfortunate Valentine's Day shooting of Reeva Steencamp and the Hollywood premiere of *Oz the Great and Powerful*. As it happened, April 11th was also the official release date of *Temper, Temper*, the latest CD by the band, Bullet for My Valentine.

Three days before his own resignation, Benedict accepted the resignation of Cardinal Keith O'Brien, the leader of the Roman Catholic Church in Scotland, amid allegations of sexual misconduct. This possibly ties into a then-recently completed private report prepared by three bishops for the Pope detailing the extent of sexual impropriety in the Catholic Church hierarchy, with the timing of its release leading some observers to wonder whether the information contained therein might have been a key factor in Benedict's decision to resign.

In any case, Benedict's successor, Argentinian Cardinal Jorge Mario Bergoglio, a former bouncer and janitor, also racked up a series of firsts: he is the first Pope to choose the name Francis, making this the first time since Pope Lando's 913-914 reign that a serving Pope holds a name not used by a predecessor. Francis is the first Jesuit Pope, the first Pope from the Americas, the first Pope from the Southern Hemisphere and the first non-European Pope since Pope Gregory III in 741.

A series of historic papal firsts, including an historic resignation and an historic name selection, all in the year of the Golden Jubilee of the Killing of the King. Kent couldn't help but wonder if there were more to the story than first met the eye. Pope Francis, Sir Francis Dashwood … nah, there couldn't be any connection he concluded after giving the matter more thought than warranted. Bergoglio's long-time fondness for Saint Francis of Assisi was well known.

But perhaps there was a broader point being made that Kent had missed altogether. Maybe the close interplay in time between the momentous occurrences within the papacy and the full deployment of the Oz meme within the popular culture were orchestrated by agencies human or otherwise to draw attention to conceptual parallels many would find uncomfortable.

The Emerald City, the Eternal City, what's the difference? The wizard, whose full name is Oscar Zoroaster Phadrig Isaac Norman Henkel Emmannuel ("god with us") Ambroise Diggs, rules over the imaginary Oz just as the Pope rules over—our occult masters would contend—a fairy-tale kingdom where a god-man walks on water, heals the sick and is resurrected from the dead. ("And the glow of an emerald circled his throne like a rainbow." Revelation 4:3)

From the perspective of the Controllers, is Oz not a metaphor for this world of illusion we occupy, a world they've created over centuries, a world in which roughly one-sixth of the population is under the sway of Roman Catholicism and an even greater number under Christianity in general—which is, at its core, an innovative derivation of the standard sun-god mythology of the ancient mystery religions? Is the Pope not the Wizard?

Maybe, maybe not, but just as Dorothy clicked the heels of her ruby slippers together to facilitate her departure from Oz, it was ceremoniously announced prior to Pope Benedict's historic resignation that he would cease wearing his trademark red loafers upon leaving the Vatican. *There's no place like home…there's no place like home…*

LE TRAIN D'ENFER

As Kent noted, geographic distance is no obstacle in occult ritual: these acts transcend space and time. The 9/11 Mega-Ritual unfolded at seemingly unconnected locations all over the countryside: Washington, DC; New York City; Shanksville, Pennsylvania; Sarasota, Florida; and, unbeknownst to many, Whitehorse, Yukon (Kent devoted an entire chapter to this episode). Yet, a cohesive ritual unity bound the acts committed at these various sites, connecting them through supernatural means in the astral realms (at least according to the beliefs of the perpetrators).

Given all of the above, Kent was not terribly surprised to read the news of the tragedy, nor to learn where the incident took place. In the early morning hours of July 6th, 2013, Canada's worst railroad disaster since 1884 struck the small town of Lac-Mégantic, Quebec (which, as the crow flies, is only ten miles or so from the U.S. border, but, hey, gotta give a little love to our northern neighbors, eh?).

HELL ON EARTH

At 1:14 a.m., an unmanned runaway Montreal, Maine & Atlantic Railway (MM&A) freight train consisting of five locomotives and 72 tank cars containing shale oil, travelling at an estimated speed of 101 kilometers per hour, derailed in the heart of downtown in this quiet little tourist village.

The tremendous momentum that the train had gathered barreling downhill hurled almost all of the black tankers off the tracks as the train hit the curve at high speed. The cars smashed into one another and stacked on top of each other, many rupturing and spilling their deadly cargo. Of the 70,000

193

barrels of Bakken sweet light crude oil, 50 thousand—2,500,000 gallons— poured into the middle of town.

A wave of petroleum three to four feet high was ignited as a series of massive explosions set off a ferocious fire. One survivor described it as a tsunami: "It was a wave of fire. It burned so hot there's no more asphalt on the street. There are only the foundations and nothing else."

Flaming oil poured into the sewer system and subsequently erupted from man-holes, drains and even chimneys. The white-hot inferno was so intense that it showed up clearly on NASA satellite imagery. Roughly 2,000 people, a third of the population, were ordered to evacuate their homes. The explosions and fire killed 47 and destroyed more than 30 buildings in the downtown area, including the public library.

HELL ON WHEELS

For many in this close-knit, French-speaking community, it became known as "le train d'enfer"—"the train from hell."

It had been left unattended overnight sitting on the main tracks roughly seven miles away in Nantes, Quebec. At around 11:00 p.m., the lone engineer had stopped the train, leaving a single diesel engine running to provide pressure to the air brake system. He reportedly applied a number of manual hand brakes on the locomotives and cars, although this has been disputed.

The engineer departed that night leaving one locomotive running to operate the air brakes, despite being fully aware that the engine was not functioning properly. The malfunction was not a minor one, either: the engine was spitting oil and emitting thick, black smoke, which the employee knew full well considering that he was, according to his taxi driver, covered in droplets of oil. Witnesses recalled having to slow down as they drove through the area because of the cloud of dark blue diesel exhaust hanging in the air, and they also reported seeing sparks flying out of the engine. (It would later be determined that this was due to a broken piston.)

Sometime after the engineer's departure, the Nantes Fire Department responded to a 911 call from a citizen who reported a fire on the first locomotive. Upon arriving, and following standard procedure, firefighters shut down the train's engine before attempting to fight the fire.

The fire department extinguished the flames and then notified MM&A's rail traffic controller, who had, in fairness to the engineer, been previously notified by him of the problem with the locomotive. The controller subsequently dispatched a track maintenance foreman to the scene who was reportedly unfamiliar with the operation of railway air brakes.

Case solved. Cause: incompetence. There's no conspiracy here, just another instance of human error causing catastrophe. And, indeed you could leave it at that, if you needed to for your own false sense of security. However, you could also see a set of circumstances so open to sabotage that it likely bored nearly to tears those who engineered this staged event.

But why is it necessarily sabotage? Why is this unfortunate incident necessarily related to the crash of OZ214? True, the Transportation Safety Board of Canada found that MM&A's operating plan was to leave the train parked on the main line, unattended, with an unlocked locomotive cab, alongside a highway where it was accessible to the general public. That doesn't prove anything.

Just because an entire town went up in flames in Quebec the same day that a plane crashed in San Francisco doesn't mean there's any connection. There's no proof that this was some sort of nefarious act designed to evoke the memory of the

> ## Whore of Babylon
>
>
>
> **B**orn Isabelle Fortier in Lac-Mégantic in March of 1973, the late Canadian novelist Nelly Arcan is arguably the small town's most famous former resident.
>
> Arcan's first novel, *Putain* (2001; *Whore* [2004]), was a critical success and literary sensation in France and Quebec, where Arcan would eventually become a literary star after the publishing of three additional novels. *Whore* was a finalist for both the Prix Médicis and the Prix Fémina, two of France's most prestigious literary awards.
>
> The book contains noted similarities between the main character, a prostitute named Cynthia, and Arcan's own experience as a professional escort sex worker. Writing in the *Globe and Mail* shortly after Arcan's death in 2009, author Linda Leith observed:
>
> > The literary world is hardly a stranger to feminine beauty, but the beauty we find among women writers tends to the intellectual, if not the ethereal, with distractions from the athletic, the angelic and the elfin. To find a figure comparable to Nelly Arcan, you have to imagine Marilyn Monroe as a writer—and no ordinary writer. Picture Marilyn Monroe at the age of 28 getting short-listed for the Booker Prize and the Dublin IMPAC prize for her first novel. And then writing a second novel that gets nominated for the Dublin IMPAC prize again. Marilyn Monroe crossed with Zadie Smith and—why not?—Colette.
>
> As they were deviously plotting the destruction of downtown Lac-Mégantic, perhaps somewhere in the recesses of their twisted minds the orchestrators of this tragedy took note that the town was the birthplace of Arcan, and envisioned her as embodying the spirit of the community and symbolizing the Whore of Babylon … "And the kings of the earth, who have committed fornication and lived deliciously with her, shall bewail her, and lament for her, when they shall see the smoke of her burning…" (Rev. 18:9) Or, maybe not, but this sure sounds like the kind of demented garbage they spend all their time coming up with.

burning of San Francisco or whatever. That's quite a stretch.

Connecting the Black Dots

Yeah, that's probably right, or at least Kent wished it were. Unfortunately, he suspected differently.

He was aware that this tragic incident marked a 50th anniversary connected to JFK, as set forth in the following article in the *Portland Press Herald*:

> WASHINGTON – The nation was on the brink of a crippling national strike by railroad workers in the summer of 1963 when Congress stepped in to settle a years-long battle over how many men it took to safely operate a train.
>
> The bill, signed by President John F. Kennedy in August 1963, set a historic precedent by forcing labor unions and railroad management into arbitration, a process that eventually allowed rail companies to trim their payrolls yet also protected the unionized workers who filled those jobs.
>
> Fifty years later, some of the same arguments over safety (and jobs) versus necessity (and money) still echo in Washington as the unions and railroads debate whether one person should be allowed to operate a train hauling hazardous materials.
>
> But the 2013 debate is taking place in the shadow cast by the 47 people killed by a Maine-bound train that barreled into Lac-Megantic, Quebec, derailed and exploded with tremendous fury.

Yet, although technically pertinent in context of the Golden Jubilee, he knew that this wasn't a prime factor in this act of railroad sabotage. And it was sabotage, as was the crash of OZ214, and the two acts *were* related.

How? July 6th is two days after July 4th, on which day Sirius conjuncts with our sun. Kent had written about the significance of this date in his book, about what it symbolizes to occultists and why this specific day was chosen for the founding of the United States.

But this really didn't have anything to do with the crash, either, Kent knew. The Cryptocracy is never late with their commemorations. No, these were no tardy Fourth of July fireworks, nor was July 6th some astrologically auspicious occasion, neither was this a ritual to honor some deity or another.

The attacks of 9/11 had been planned for that particular day due to its connections with Sirius, and, again, July 4th is a Sirius holiday. But July 6th?

On that day in 1885, WWII German Field Marshal Ernst Busch, recipient of the Knight's Cross of the Iron Cross with Oak Leaves, was born. And in 1944, the Hartford Circus Fire, one of the worst fire-related disasters in U.S. history, killed approximately 168 people and injured over 700 in Hartford, Connecticut. Nonetheless, Kent was certain that both of these historical events, although they generally fit the spirit of the occasion, were essentially irrelevant.

Flight OZ214 and the Train from Hell had been the main attractions in a good ole-fashioned birthday party, not for Ernst, but rather for a much more well-known Bush, George W., who was born July 6th of 1946.

WHAT A PARTY!

As Kent had detailed, W. presided over 9/11 from Paradise (Sarasota's nickname), conducting an in-plain-sight Black Mass under our very noses that morning. Kent had presented good evidence that George Junior not only had foreknowledge of, but direct involvement in, the events of and leading up to September 11, 2001.

Perhaps as a reward from George "Poppy" Bush, Sr., who himself has been implicated in the JFK assassination plot, the dedication of the GWB Presidential Library in Dallas on 4/25 had been a key component of the Twelve Days of Terror, and, now, a little over two months later, W. gets the Birthday Surprise of a lifetime.

As covered in *Mass Ritual*, 9/11 had also been a trib-ute to Aleister Crowley, and Kent knew from his research that the Cryptocracy had on prior occasions honored Crowley through various nefarious means on the dates of both his birth and death (speaking of the latter, the 7/6 Lac-Mégantic derailment wasn't the only suspicious one in 2013…more on that later).

Thus, the idea of throwing such a diabolical shindig as a birthday celebration was not a new one to Kent, and what an occasion it was: a train crash in Hell-on-Earth, Quebec, birthplace of the Whore of Babylon, followed by a plane crash in the City of Saint Francis of Wycombe, birthplace of the Church of Satan.

And there were other little meaningful details, too, like party favors scattered about, including this one: back up the tracks less than 80 miles from Lac-Mégan-tic on the same rail line is a little town called Magog, which, as it just so happens, was George Sr.'s nickname in the secret society Skull & Bones at Yale.

As delicious as that little tidbit was, though, the icing on the cake was yet to come.

WE TOO LOW

In its coverage of the Flight 214 crash, Bay Area television station KTVU decided to include the names of the flight crew, which, it was later claimed (and you will shortly see why if you're not familiar with this incident), they double-checked with the National Transportation Safety Board (NTSB) before airing.

In an incredible prank that cost three KTVU producers their jobs, the station broadcast the supposed names of the Asiana Airlines crew, only they weren't their real names, but rather-obvious, racially-offensive fakes: Captain Sum Ting Wong, Wi Tu Lo, Ho Lee Fuk and Bang Ding Ow.

As it happened, a representative at the NTSB *had* confirmed the names of the crew to the television station, but this representative turned out to be a summer intern who, according to an NTSB press release, "acted outside the scope of his authority when he erroneously confirmed the names of the flight crew on the aircraft." The release also stated that, "The NTSB does not release or confirm the names of crew members or people involved in transportation accidents to the media."

Ah, just like a locomotive left running on a downhill grade on the main line with its engine spitting oil and sparks, it's simple to understand how these things can happen so easily. Was this not just an incredibly funny racial joke at a local television station gone horribly awry? Gone global, more like it, as the story hit international media outlets like a runaway freight train (couldn't resist).

This wasn't some amateur prank gone viral, Kent chuckled. This was truly glorious, he reluctantly admitted to himself, one of the cryptocrazies' funniest gags ever. Easily enough accomplished as far as these sorts of things go, and put the icing on Georgie's birthday cake to boot. *Happy Birthday, Mr. President!*

CHAPTER 34

JFK, MOTHMAN AND MOUNT HOPE

July 15, 2013: The Summit Bechtel Family National Scout Reserve outside of Mount Hope, West Virginia

The 10-day 2013 National Boy Scout Jamboree was just kicking off, and Kent was paying close attention. Nevada gubernatorial candidate David Lory VanDer-Beek had several months prior posted an article on his website warning that, especially in light of the recent "obviously" government-staged false-flag attack in Boston, the Jamboree could well be the next target of such a state-sponsored attack.

After reading the article, Kent had done some investigating of his own, and uncovered some unnerving information. He had previously decided against blogging about the Boston Bombings, etc., but he now felt compelled to echo VanDerBeek's warning, and posted an entry on his book's blog page in hopes that, were the threat real, advance exposure of the plot might somehow thwart the attack. It wasn't the first time he'd gone public with such a warning, and he wasn't concerned what people thought about it, either.

2013 NATIONAL JAMBOREE SUMMIT BECHTEL RESERVE

The blog entry, entitled "JFK, Mothman and Mount Hope," was post-ed Friday, June 14, and read:

> When I first encountered this story, "National Scout Jamboree 2013 False Flag Insider Warning: Nevada Governor 2014 David Lory VanDerBeek," I wasn't particularly concerned. The author makes some fairly general observations, and at first I saw no reason why the 2013 Scout Jamboree would necessarily make any more compelling a target for a false-flag attack than any other major event. After an initial general inclination to ignore the matter, however, I decided to give it the smell test—and, boy, does it stink (well, it has all the ingredients for a good old rotter in any case).
>
> Without giving away the premise of my next book entirely, I can guarantee you that, just as Aleister Crowley was the guest-of-honor on 9/11, JFK was the focus of attention at the Boston Bombings. Being acutely aware of this, as I began to examine the circumstances surrounding the Scout Jamboree, intriguing possible JFK connec-tions began to materialize, but this was after I had identified certain other "run of the mill" markers, outlined below.
>
> **Checking Things Out**
> As discussed in the articles linked above, the Scout Jamboree will take place from July 15th through the 24th at the Summit Bechtel Family National Scout Reserve outside of Mount Hope, West Virginia. Now, the first thing to note is just how well the general framework here matches the familiar mold involving mockery and black humor that we've come to anticipate: "an attack on the Boy Scouts of America at Mount Hope." Check. Secondly, we should observe that hope is one of the three principle moral virtues of Masonic philosophy, the other two being faith and charity (Faith. Hope. Charity.) Check.
>
> Also worth mentioning is that while Bechtel co-owner Stephen D. Bechtel, Jr.—whose foundation donated $50 million to help pur-chase and develop the property that is now the National Scout Re-serve—is a member of the Eagle Scouts, his son, Riley, the current CEO of the Bechtel Corp., is reportedly a member of both the Tri-lateral Commission and Bohemian Grove. Check.
>
> **Another Ode to JFK?**
> Recalling U.S. Route 77's immediate proximity to Dealey Plaza (as well as the importance of the number 77 itself) … try to guess the number of the Interstate that passes less than five miles from Mount Hope, WV. That's right, Interstate 77. I-77 would be a bad omen under normal cir-cumstances, but combine it with the JFK-Golden Jubilee link and it spells double trouble.

That's just the start of the Kennedy connections, though: JFK was, of course, the first Boy Scout to become President, and he in fact delivered a presidential campaign speech in Mount Hope. Further, one of three major performances during the 2013 Scout Jamboree will take place on July 20, which, in addition to being the annual date of Satanic Revels and the one-year anniversary of the Aurora ("Mother of Lucifer") Dark Knight Rises theatre massa-

cre, is also, and perhaps most significantly, the 44th anniversary of the Apollo 11 moon landing, an event which came about as a result of Kennedy's vision and leadership.

And lest you think I'm blowing this out of proportion: 1.) the week of April 15th, the date of the Boston Bombing saga, was the anniversary of the Bay of Pigs invasion; and, 2.) in *Secret Societies and Psychological Warfare*, Michael Hoffman discusses the importance not only of "The Killing of the Divine King" but also of the "The Bringing of Prima Materia to Prima Terra" (ie., the moon landing) in Masonic philosophy. Check.

The F-Word

Unfortunately, we're not done here: Mount Hope is located in Fayette County, West Virginia, "Fayette" being one of the cryptocracy's favorite repetitively-employed memes/name games (such as, per Hoffman, "Wicker," as in "Wicked King Wicker" and "The Wicker Man" and Senator Roger Wicker, but that's covered further in the next book). Fortean philosopher William N. Grimstad, long-time associate of Michael Hoffman, was one of the first to write about "The Fayette Factor" in an article in a 1978 issue of *Fortean Times*.

What we're finding here is that familiar clustering of phonetic and memetic markers that are the hallmarks of our masters' occult tradecraft. Could all of this—Mount Hope, I-77, Fayette County, John F. "The Boy Scout President" Kennedy—be coincidence? Certainly, but, as we know all-too-well, these things could also be indicators of a sophisticated and sinister plot to do bodily and/or psychological harm to our fellow citizens.

The Mothman Prophecies, Continued?

Before we attempt to draw any firm conclusions, however, we should look deeper at the geographical area involved here, as we may gain additional insight from doing so.

Just over 100 miles northwest of Mount Hope is Point Pleasant, West Virginia, location of the bizarre events described in John A. Keel's book *The Mothman Prophecies*. However, the first sighting of the Mothman during that era was not in Point Pleasant, but in Clendenin, a little over half the distance, as the crow flies, from Mount Hope to Point Pleasant. To say that Mount Hope is in the heart of Mothman country would then be stretching things a bit, but it's certainly close enough to be worth considering in this situation.

We're well familiar with how fond the architects of reality are of re-visiting the sites of their past rituals and transgressions against human-ity (recall the Sarasota/Venice-9/11 link as but one example), and, as it turns out, it just may be that there was a good deal more going on in Point Pleasant than even most of those who are familiar with the book (or the movie of the same name) are aware—more than a giant flying red-eyed biped and strange phone calls.

The Mason County Black Op

The first thing I'd like to point out is that Point Pleasant is located in Mason County. The second fact I'd like to bring to your attention is that the wreckage analysis of the Silver Bridge showed that its collapse was due to a defect in a single link, eyebar 330. (Perhaps of increased inter-est in light of these facts are the statements of a witness who reported seeing two men climbing on the bridge the day before the tragedy.)

Investigative researcher/author Jim Keith was among the first to speculate that Point Pleasant was used as some type of "test tube," the setting for a black ops experiment, and to explore the CIA/Men-in-Black connection.

Writing in *Casebook on the Men in Black*, Keith states: "During the period of the Mothman encounters, black limousines prowled the Point Pleasant area, stopping at rural homes. Deeply tanned men pro-claimed themselves to be 'census-takers' and showed an inordinate in-terest in the children of the households." Keith continues: "People in the rural areas also reported seeing mysterious unmarked panel trucks which parked in remote locations for hours, and were rumored to be Air Force. Men in coveralls worked on telephone and powerlines.

"A thirtyish blond woman visited people in Ohio and West Virgin-ia, telling people she was John Keel's secretary, and filling out lengthy forms with information about health, income, family background, the types of cars the people owned, along with questions about UFO and Mothman sightings. Keel, naturally, did not have a secretary."

A JFK-Mothman Connection?

West Virginia native and investigator/author/filmmaker Andrew Col-vin ties together military intelligence and the nearby Defense Logistics

Agency as well as industrial concerns such as I.G. Farben, Union Carbide, General Motors and others—pointing to the possible use of a paranormal/UFO/MIB guise as a cover for post-war military-industrial projects.

In fact, some researchers assert that the architects who designed the WWII TNT Factory outside Point Pleasant also worked on both the Manhattan Project and the fabled Area 51.

Other researchers have even gone so far as to posit an actual JFK-Mothman link, asserting that certain suspected JFK-assassination-figures were active in Point Pleasant during the Mothman/Silver Bridge incident (claiming, for example, that David Ferrie was likely Mothman's "Frightwig" MIB, or that CIA pilot Fred Crisman was involved with both events), believing that the evidence points toward an international military intelligence-FBI-mobster-banker operation emanating partly out of Ohio and neighboring Toronto.

Jubilee at the Jamboree?

What does all this mean, though? It means that the general vicinity we're considering is the old stomping grounds of the folks that pulled off 9/11 and the Boston Bombings and dozens of other false-flag events/public rituals. It means that, in combination with all of the other evidence we've considered, we have, potentially, one more good reason to suspect that this particular locale would be laden with meaning and significance for the sadistic, occult-driven fruitcakes that make their livings pulling these sorts of things off in plain sight.

It means that the 50,000 plus Scouts and their families, which will temporarily balloon the population of Fayette County up to around 300,000 souls to over twice its normal size, could well be sitting ducks after all as they enjoy the festivities at the 2013 Scout Jamboree.

To put matters into even clearer perspective, we should note that these events have historically featured a heavy police and military presence, for both security and recruiting/indoctrination purposes, and this year will be no different. So, as I indicated at the outset, this event has all the ingredients necessary for a good-old-fashioned false-flag/public ritual/black op/psy-op.

IT NEVER ENDS

Fortunately, the Jamboree came and went, and there was no false-flag attack or incident of any kind. No Mothman sightings, no suspicious outbreaks of illness, zilch. But Kent didn't regret having sounded the alarm, given what he knew had gone on during the first part of the year and also knowing that the Cryptocracy wasn't finished yet.

Indeed, it had looked for all the world like the stage had been set for a mass casualty event: the geography was right, the place names were right, the occult markers were right. The only things missing were the lifeless bodies of dozens, or hundreds, or thousands of Boy Scouts and their families.

Just because there was no mass sacrifice doesn't mean it wasn't a ritual, , Kent thought. Perhaps it had been a mass ritual of the less lethal variety, with references to some obscure occult garbage he wasn't familiar with and thus didn't recognize, or perhaps it simply looked a whole lot like the ones he'd studied. Maybe it had been a part of the Golden Jubilee script, or, maybe not. In the final analysis, it probably didn't matter much anyway. As always, there would be more sacrificial killings, more staged terror and more ritual acts. It was only a matter of when and where.

POSTSCRIPT: BE PREPARED

For those who suspect that a shadow government-led war is in fact being waged against the Boy Scouts of America, it is telling that in 2014 former Secretary of Defense and former CIA director Robert Gates was appointed to lead BSA. During 2013, the organization faced increasing pressure over its stance on homosexuality, and, as it would happen, Gates led the Pentagon when it eliminated its long-standing Don't-Ask-Don't-Tell policy.

Interestingly enough, Gates' most-recent book, *Duty: Memoirs of a Secretary at War*, included several statements that his former boss, President Obama, was displeased with, and Gates spent the next six months appearing on TV news shows and at book signings wearing a neck brace after supposedly tripping down the stairs in his residence.

POSTSCRIPT TO THE POSTSCRIPT: SHOW'S OVER

Apparently Robert Gates got off easy. In June 2014, comedienne Joan Rivers finally cracked "a joke too far" about Obama being the first gay president and Michelle being a "tranny," and come September 4th, she's outta here. Show's over.

Ironically, Rivers made the fatal statement shortly after officiating at an impromptu gay wedding, but unfortunately that didn't buy her a "Get Out of Jail Free" card.

An unidentified reporter questioned Rivers about the ceremony, asking when the country would have its first gay president, to which she replied, "We already have it with Obama, so let's just calm down."

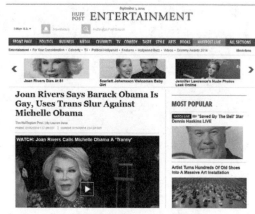

Unprompted, she then continued, "You know Michelle is a tranny." As the reporter attempted to clarify, she responded, "A transgender. We all know."

Yeah, well, anybody who's been paying any attention for the last six years has been told Obama's gay (or bi), and to suspect that Michelle may have two sets of equipment (or may have swapped one for the other), and that you don't connect the dots out loud, in public, not even jokingly.

Political correctness is one of the harshest, most *intoler-* ant political regimes ever devised by man/woman/he-she, and Rivers found out the hard way that some offenses may carry the death penalty.

Interestingly, Rivers reportedly went into cardiac arrest after her unnamed personal physician performed an unscheduled/"unauthorized" biopsy following the successful completion of an upper endoscopy by the staff of the clinic where the procedure was being performed.

Said physician also reportedly took a selfie with the unconscious Rivers before conducting the biopsy that killed her. Anyone want to take any bets as to whom he might've emailed the selfie; you know, as proof of a job completed?

PART SEVEN

INTERLUDE

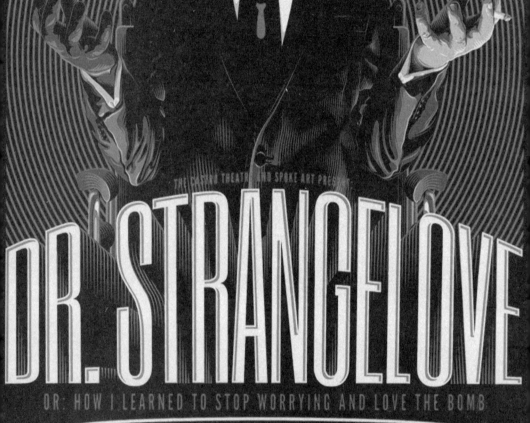

THE CASTRO THEATRE AND SPOKE ART PRES

DR. STRANGELOVE

OR: HOW I LEARNED TO STOP WORRYING AND LOVE THE BOMB

CASTRO THEATRE   429 CASTRO ST. SAN FRANCISCO, CA 94114   AUGUST 28TH 2013

CHAPTER 35

SOUTHERN-FRIED APOCALYPSE

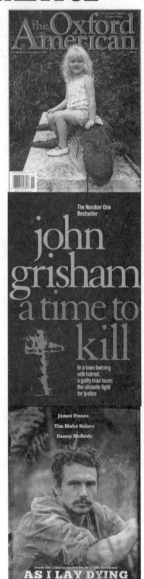

In the early 1990s, Kent attended the University of Mississippi in Oxford, affectionately referred to as "Ole Miss" by its fans, where he worked as graphic designer for *Living Blues* magazine, published by the Center for the Study of Southern Culture.

After college, Kent landed a job as art director for the *Oxford American* magazine, published at that time by best-selling author John Grisham; in Oxford, of course.

Oxford was the long-time home of Nobel-Laureate William Faulkner, and his former residence, Rowan Oak, has been fully restored and is owned and curated by the University of Mississippi.

Over the years, the town has acquired a reputation as a mecca for Southern literature, having served as home to a range of talented authors such as Larry Brown, Barry Hannah, Willie Morris and Pulitzer Prize-winning Donna Tartt.

Oxford's reputation as a hotspot for great Southern writing is bolstered by the presence of one of the finest independent bookstores in America, Square Books, located, as its name indicates, on the picturesque Oxford Square, directly across from the iconic Lafayette County Courthouse, which is referenced in several of Faulkner's works.

After achieving literary super-stardom, John Grisham continued his support of Square Books, whose owner had helped promote the then-struggling author's first book, *A Time to Kill*, which was eventually transformed into a box-office hit—one of many.

A new film adaptation of Faulkner's As I Lay Dying *was released in 2013, for which James Franco co-wrote the script; he also directed and starred in it.*

CONFRONTING RACISM

As one of the founders of the Mississippi Hills National Heritage Area, Kent was fully familiar with Oxford's rich heritage, literary and otherwise. He was also keenly aware of its dark side, of the community's unique place in the nation's tumultuous Civil Rights history.

On October 1, 1962, civil rights pioneer James Meredith, inspired by President Kennedy's inaugural address, became the first African-American to enroll at the University of Mississippi. A mob of white students and segregationists, many of whom had driven in from out of town and out of state, protested his enrollment by rioting on the Ole Miss campus over the next several days.

U.S. Attorney General Robert Kennedy called in 500 U.S. Marshals to take control of the situation, and the Marshals were supported by the 70th Army Engineer Combat Battalion from Fort Campbell, Kentucky. President Kennedy also ordered reinforcements from the U.S. Army's 2nd Infantry Division from Fort Benning, Georgia, under the command of Major General Charles Billingslea, and military police from the 503rd Military Police Battalion, as well as troops from the Mississippi National Guard, to Oxford.

Upon his arrival at the entrance of the university, the mob attacked the General's staff car and set it on fire. Trapped inside the burning vehicle, Billingslea and his officers managed to force open one of the doors and crawled 200 yards under gunfire to the Lyceum building, the first floor of which became filled with blood as the evening progressed. (Bullet holes from the riots are still visible on the building's exterior.)

Troops did not return fire during the incident. The General had established a strict protocol to prevent unnecessary loss of life: one code word was required for issuing ammunition to the platoons; another for distributing it to the squads, and a third for loading the bullets into rifles—none of which could take place without Billingslea's confirmation of the codes.

Although only two persons, a French journalist and another man, were killed in the violent clashes, one-third of the U.S. Marshals were injured, and 40 soldiers and National Guardsmen were also wounded.

I LOVE MISSISSIPPI

The Kennedys were opposed in their efforts to integrate the University by Governor Ross Barnett, the youngest of ten children of a Confederate veteran. A prominent member of the Dixiecrats, Southern Democrats who opposed integration, Barnett had arranged for the arrest of the Freedom Riders a year earlier in 1961.

The night before the Oxford riots, Barnett delivered his famous sixteen-word "I Love Mississippi" speech at an Ole Miss football game in Jackson. Over 40,000 fans, waving thousands of Confederate flags, cheered as a gigantic Rebel flag was unfurled on the field at halftime. As shouts of "We want Ross!" echoed through the stadium, the peoples' champion strode to the 50-yard line, grabbed the microphone and bellowed:

"I love Mississippi! I love her people! Our customs. I love and I respect our heritage."

Several years later in March of 1966, former U.S. Attorney General Robert Kennedy visited the University of Mississippi campus and spoke to a crowd of more than 6,000 students and faculty. Kennedy's talk addressed the topic of racial reconciliation, and afterwards he answered questions, including those concerning his involvement in the events surrounding the enrollment of James Meredith.

Kennedy, who had spoken with Barnett by telephone on numerous occasions during the crisis, recounted a plan the Governor had concocted in which the U.S. Marshals would aim their guns at him while Meredith enrolled so that the scene could be photographed. If that plan had been deemed infeasible, Kennedy continued to the great amusement of the audience, Barnett had proposed a second ruse whereby Meredith

213

would register in Jackson while he remained in Oxford, whereupon Barnett would feign surprise. At is turned out, both plans had actually been approved and only went unimplemented because of subsequent intervening events.

The day following RFK's address, Barnett vehemently denied his version of the events, saying, in part:

> It ill becomes a man who never tried a lawsuit in his life, but who occupied the high position of United States attorney general and who was responsible for using 30,000 troops and spent approximately six million dollars to put one unqualified student in Ole Miss to return to the scene of this crime and discuss any phase of this infamous affair.... I say to you that Bobby Kennedy is a very sick and dangerous American. We have lots of sick Americans in this country but most of them have a long beard. Bobby Kennedy is a hypocritical, left-wing beatnik without a beard who carelessly and recklessly distorts the facts.

(Left) O Brother's Gubernatorial candidate and head Klansman Homer Stokes: "Brothers! Oh, brothers! We have all gathered here, to preserve our hallowed culture and heritage—from the intrusion, inclusion and dilution of color, of creed and of our old-time religion! We aim to pull evil up by the root, before it chokes out the flower of our culture and heritage! And our women, let's not forget those ladies, y'all. Looking to us for protection—from darkies, from Jews, from papists, and from all those smart-ass folks say we come descended from monkeys!"" (Right) Stokes: "Is you is, or is you ain't, my constituency?"

WALKER, TEXAS RACIST

Ross Barnett wasn't the only, or even necessarily the most noteworthy, parody-inspiring racist villain opposing the integration of Ole Miss.

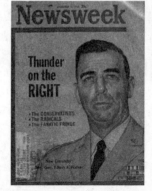

Major General Edwin Anderson "Ted" Walker was a U.S. Army officer who saw action in both World War II and the Korean War. Known for his ultra-conservative political views, he was criticized by President Dwight Eisenhower for using his official position to promote his personal ideology. Walker resigned in 1959, but Eisenhower refused to accept his resignation and gave him a new command instead.

In 1961, after being publicly admonished by President Kennedy for calling Eleanor Roosevelt and Harry Truman "pink" in print, and for violating the Hatch Act by attempting to influence the votes of troops under his command, Walker again resigned his commission; Kennedy accepted his resignation.

In early 1962, Walker ran against John Connally for governor of Texas and lost. Later that year, Walker was arrested for his involvement in the riots at the University of Mississippi.

RED SCARE, CONTINUED

Earlier in his military career, Walker had been made the commander of the Arkansas Military District in Little Rock. During his time at that post, although he dutifully carried out President Eisenhower's 1957 order to quell civil unrest during the desegregation of Central High School, he repeatedly protested the use of Federal troops to enforce racial integration.

Walker fed on a steady diet of anti-Communist literature and radio programming and, in 1959, met publisher Robert Welch, Jr., founder of the John Birch Society, who believed that Eisenhower himself was in fact a Communist, a claim Walker took seriously. Walker likewise believed the assertion of segregationist preacher Reverend Billy James Hargis that the Civil Rights movement was a Communist plot.

Walker subsequently teamed up with Hargis for "Operation Midnight Ride," giving political speeches all over the

---

Oxford Town

Bob Dylan's *Freewheelin'*, the second album by the legendary singer-songwriter, contained a song entitled "Oxford Town," about Meredith's enrollment at Ole Miss.

Oxford Town, Oxford Town
Ev'rybody's got their heads bowed down
The sun don't shine above the ground
Ain't a-goin' down to Oxford Town

He went down to Oxford Town
Guns and clubs followed him down
All because his face was brown
Better get away from Oxford Town

Oxford Town around the bend
He come in to the door, he couldn't get in
All because of the color of his skin
What do you think about that, my frien'?

Me and my gal, my gal's son
We got met with a tear gas bomb
I don't even know why we come
Goin' back where we come from

Oxford Town in the afternoon
Ev'rybody singin' a sorrowful tune
Two men died 'neath the Mississippi moon
Somebody better investigate soon

Oxford Town, Oxford Town
Ev'rybody's got their heads bowed down
The sun don't shine above the ground
Ain't a-goin' down to Oxford Town

While the lyrics don't mention Meredith by name, they certainly get the point across. Besides, what the hell rhymes with "Meredith"?

Bob Welch

A song called "Talkin' John Birch Blues" was on Freewheelin', *but was pulled by CBS.*

215

United States to enthusiastic crowds who frequently gave him a dozen standing ovations. His anti-Communist message was extremely popular, and he pressed the McCarthyist belief that the U.S. government had been thoroughly infiltrated by its enemies.

In 1962, General Walker appeared before Mississippi U.S. Senator John Stennis' subcommittee investigating "the muzzling of the military" concerning the Communist threat, testifying:

> It is evident that the real control apparatus will not tolerate militant anti-Communist leadership in a division commander. The real control apparatus can be identified by the effects of what it is doing in the Congo, what it did in Korea...

Walker was then asked by Alaskan Senator Bob Bartlett:

> General, are you saying that there exists in this country—in positions of ultimate leadership—a group of sinister men, anti-American, willing and wanting to sell this country out? Is that the correct inference?

Walker replied, "That is correct; yes, sir."

I WILL BE THERE!

On September 26, 1962, just days before the Ole Miss riots, Walker appeared on several radio stations to deliver this message:

> Mississippi: It is time to move. We have talked, listened and been pushed around far too much by the anti-Christ Supreme Court! Rise...to a stand beside Governor Ross Barnett at Jackson, Mississippi! Now is the time to be heard! Thousands strong from every State in the Union! Rally to the cause of freedom! The Battle Cry of the Republic! Barnett yes! Castro no! Bring your flag, your tent and your skillet. It's now or never! The time is when the President of the United States commits or uses any troops, Federal or State, in Mississippi! The last time in such a situation I was on the wrong side. That was in Little Rock, Arkansas in 1957-1958. This time— out of uniform—I am on the right side! I will be there!

216

Three days later, on the 29th, he appeared on television, telling the audience:

> This is Edwin A. Walker. I am in Mississippi beside Governor Ross Barnett. I call for a national protest against the conspiracy from within. Rally to the cause of freedom in righteous indignation, violent vocal protest, and bitter silence under the flag of Mississippi at the use of Federal troops. This today is a disgrace to the nation in 'dire peril,' a disgrace beyond the capacity of anyone except its enemies. This is the conspiracy of the crucifixion by anti-Christ conspirators of the Supreme Court in their denial of prayer and their betrayal of a nation.

After a 15-hour riot in which hundreds were wounded broke out on the Ole Miss campus the next day, Walker was arrested on four federal charges, including sedition and insurrection against the United States. On orders from Robert Kennedy, Walker was temporarily held in a mental institution, and Kennedy demanded that

he undergo a 90-day psychiatric evaluation. Kennedy's decision was promptly challenged by the American Civil Liberties Union and others, and Walker spent only five days in the facility. He was never indicted on any of the accused crimes, and all charges were dropped.

Unlucky Shot

Upon his return home to Dallas, Walker was greeted by a crowd of two hundred supporters. Fellow Dallas resident Lee Harvey Oswald was not among them.

Oswald considered Walker a dangerous fascist, and seven days after Walker made a speech calling on the U.S. military to "liquidate the scourge that has descended upon the island of Cuba," Oswald ordered a Carcano rifle by mail using the alias "A. Hidell." Oswald reportedly began to surveil Walker, taking pictures of his Dallas home, and planning to assassinate him on April 10th.

At about 9 p.m. on that date, Walker was sitting at his desk when ex-Marine Oswald allegedly fired his rifle from less than a hundred feet away. It should have been an easy shot for Oswald, but the bullet struck the window frame and missed Walker.

The bullet police recovered from the scene appeared to be of the same caliber that killed JFK and wounded Governor Connally, but it was too badly damaged for conclusive ballistics testing. Later tests determined that it was extremely unlikely that it was the same ammunition used in the assassination.

Eyewitness accounts reported two men leaving the scene of the crime, and to the end of his life, Walker believed that Oswald had an accomplice, whose identity he spent decades attempting to learn.

TRICK OR TREAT!

Practically a parody unto himself, it will surprise no one to learn that Walker is cited in Mark Lytle's *America's Uncivil Wars: The Sixties Era from Elvis to the Fall of Richard Nixon* as the inspiration for paranoid ultra-nationalist Brigadier General Jack D. Ripper in Stanley Kubrick's 1964 black comedy *Dr. Strangelove*. (Ripper's character was also very likely influenced by Air Force Chief of Staff Curtis "Bombs Away" LeMay, a vocal proponent of the first-strike nuclear strategy.)

It Could Happen

Seven Days in May is a 1964 political thriller directed by John Frankenheimer (director of *The Manchurian Candidate*) starring Burt Lancaster, Kirk Douglas, Fredric March and Ava Gardner.

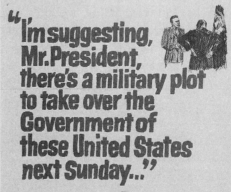

The screenplay was written by Rod Serling and based on a 1962 novel of the same name, said to have been influenced in part by the right-wing anti-Communist activities of General Walker after his resignation from the military. The plot involves a planned coup d'etat by the Joint Chiefs of Staff, and President Kennedy, who read the novel in the summer of '62, reportedly agreed that such a scenario could actually unfold in the United States. Kennedy told friends that he found the plot realistic: "It's possible. It could happen in this country."

(Not) A Conservative Messiah

Founder of the conservative magazine *National Review* and long-time *Firing Line* host William F. Buckley, Jr., (also a CIA agent and a member of the Order of Skull & Bones) at one point considered Walker a potential leader of the conservative movement but eventually gave up on him after his views proved too radical. .

Interestingly, Buckley's final episode of *Firing Line* was taped at the University of Mississippi in 1999. As Michael Kinsley introduced the show, he quipped, "Yes, William F. Buckley is hanging up his tongue, or so he claims. Purveyors of false logic need no longer live in terror."

Buckley had once paid a visit to the *Weekly Standard*'s offices, and among Kent's colleagues at the time was associate editor Jay Nordlinger, whose office was directly across the hall. An avid admirer of Buckley, Nordlinger was excited to meet the conservative icon, who was duly impressed with the junior staffer, and Jay has served as a senior editor at *National Review* for close to a decade.

It will probably not surprise anyone too greatly either to learn that in 1976, at age 66, Walker, who was never married, was arrested for public lewdness in a restroom at a Dallas public park, and accused of fondling an undercover policeman. He was arrested again the very next year, also for public lewdness.

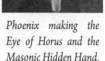

Walker died of lung cancer at his Dallas home on Halloween, October 31st, 1993, the same day as River Phoenix's untimely death outside the West Hollywood nightclub *The Viper Room*. Trick or treat!

Phoenix making the Eye of Horus and the Masonic Hidden Hand.

Postscript: Walker believed, or claimed to, that the Civil Rights movement was a Communist plot. Taking into consideration what we know today about staged terror events and their use to advance the domestic police state agenda, Kent wondered if it might not be valid to ask if the Civil Rights movement was in fact co-opted for this purpose, at least to some degree. Kent also mused: Was General "Jack D. Ripper" Walker really who he appeared to be, or perhaps a CIA creation?

HIS MOST
POWERFUL
WEAPON
IS THE TRUTH

WALKING TALL

Chapter 36

Standing at the Crossroads

K ent liked to think of himself as a poor-man's Robert Langdon, the protagonist of best-selling author Dan Brown's *Da Vinci Code* series. Like Langdon, he, too, was a researcher of occult-based crimes, only without the good looks, athleticism, money, Ivy-League education, great job and adventuresome lifestyle. Other than that, Kent chuckled, they were basically identical.

In the introduction to *The Most Dangerous Book in the World*, Kent wrote:

> As serious a topic as this is, however, don't expect a dry, academic discourse in the pages that follow. The script for the 9/11 Mega-Ritual is dripping with the dark humor of its occult authors, and even if one wanted to, there'd be no way to write about it in a [completely] serious fashion. What ensues might be compared to a combination of *The Da Vinci Code* and an episode of *South Park*; unfortunately, it is neither fiction nor fantasy.

Over the Edge?

Yet, while this light-hearted characterization was accurate on some levels, the book still dealt with heavy, and disturbing, subject matter. During the writing of the book, Kent's wife at the time, Amy, who worked at the North Mississippi State Hospital, the region's largest mental-health facility,* had expressed her concerns to him. She heard this stuff every day, all day: numbers, symbols, brain implants, government conspiracies, etc.

Although Kent showed no real signs of paranoia or delusion, Amy would later admit that the thought of having him committed had crossed her mind more than once. Had she actually taken this step, however, it

---

* A typical day at work for Amy might go something like this: Patient #1, who thinks God is talking to him, approaches the desk to complain about hearing the voice of the Almighty. Patient #2, who thinks he is God, overhears Patient #1 and confronts him, yelling, "You're a goddamn liar, I haven't said a word to you all day!"

would have resulted in Kent ending up at her workplace, which would have likely interfered with the extra-marital affair she was carrying on at the time with a co-worker.

ONE LITTLE RECORD

Although there was no significant history of mental illness in Kent's family, it was not absent altogether. As mentioned in an earlier chapter, Kent was related to historical icons Benjamin Franklin and Davy Crockett on his father's side, but he is also, on his mother's side, related to the only Governor of Arkansas ever to go insane in office (if you don't count Bill Clinton).

John Sebastian Little (1851–1916) served as a member of the United States House of Representatives and was the 21st Governor of the state of Arkansas. Inaugurated in January 1907, Little suffered a nervous breakdown shortly thereafter which left him unable to execute his official duties. Serving only 38 days, he has the unfortunate distinction of holding the record for the shortest term of an elected governor in the state's history. Little never recovered from his breakdown and died in the Arkansas State Hospital for Nervous Disorders in Little Rock some years later.

DANGEROUS CURVES

Amy really couldn't say a whole lot about this distant relative of Kent's, however, because she has some interesting characters in her own family, including her cousin, NASCAR driver Terri Leigh O'Connell, who rose to fame as Winston-Cup winner J.T. Hayes before having gender-reassignment surgery in 1994. Terri's book, *Dangerous Curves*, recounts, among other topics, his/her struggle to continue his/her racing career following the surgery.

Several of Amy's cousins were also featured in a *60 Minutes* segment in the 1980s as part of an investigation into a car insurance fraud scheme: they were secretly filmed donning football helmets before intentionally smashing cars into each other at a rural intersection.

This *was* Corinth, Mississippi, after all, where a local family was once featured on a segment of the 1980s reality-television show, *That's Incredible*, for having a television set in their hog house.

Warrior Princess

Switching genders in the NASCAR world must be difficult enough, Kent figured, but in the U.S. military's special forces community? That would take some real balls (or fake ones), he supposed.

Now known as Kristin Beck, then-Chris Beck was a 20-year veteran of the Navy SEALs, at one point serving as a member of the elite Team 6, which purportedly killed Osama bin Laden several months after Beck's retirement (although as Kent chronicled, that entire episode was riddled with suspicious elements, including the deaths of a number of Team 6 members in Afghanistan months after the operation). A recipient of both the Purple Heart and Bronze Star, Chris underwent thirteen deployments and seven combat deployments.

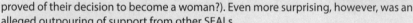

After leaving the military, Beck began undergoing hormonal therapy, and in her biography, *Warrior Princess: A U.S. Navy SEAL's Journey to Coming out Transgender*, she shares her story of transformation. As one reviewer sappily expressed, "It wasn't until Beck retired from the Navy in 2011 that her battle over her true identity could finally be fought."

To Beck's reported surprise, the announcement of her new identity was warmly received by family and friends (then again, would you really tell a former spec ops member that you disapproved of their decision to become a woman?). Even more surprising, however, was an alleged outpouring of support from other SEALs.

After she cut off her burly beard and began wearing women's clothing, she revealed her new look and name to friends on LinkedIn, publishing a photo of herself standing before an American flag. "I am now taking off all my disguises and letting the world know my true identity as a woman," Beck wrote, to which a fellow SEAL replied, "Brother, I am with you ... being a SEAL is hard, this looks harder. Peace."

LITTLE CHICAGO

Corinth is known for a number of things, including having been the "Crossroads of the Western Confederacy" and the site of the largest-ever amassing of troops in the Western hemisphere during the Civil War.

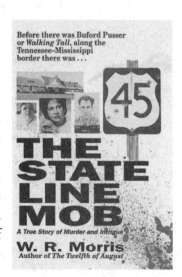

Located in Alcorn County, one of Corinth's nicknames was "Little Chicago," owing to the small town having been a hide-away for several Chicago mob affiliates in the 1940s, 50s and 60s. Corinth was also a center of activity for the infamous "State Line Mob," which gained national exposure as a target of nearby McNairy County's famed Sheriff Buford Pusser, the subject of the *Walking Tall* series of motion pictures.

THE CURSE OF PUSSER'S CURVE

As Pusser's ongoing war against the State Line Mob escalated, the Sheriff and his wife were ambushed one morning in a curve on a winding country road near the Mississippi-Tennessee border. Pusser's wife was mortally wounded in the shooting and hung out the front passenger door of their crashed car. Although he was also seriously injured, Pusser managed to get her back inside and sped off to the hospital.

As it happened, Amy's step-grandfather, Bill Fullwood, lived nearby, heard the gunshots and went to investigate. He came upon the grisly scene just as Pusser had finished loading his wife into the car. Mrs. Pusser had been gravely injured by the gunfire, and there was brain matter and blood on the road.

Mr. Fullwood subsequently returned to his house, retrieved a shovel and a bucket of water, scooped up the brains, buried them in a small hole beside the road, and washed the blood off the asphalt. Apparently not familiar with the criminal offense of tampering with a crime scene, Mr. Fullwood explained to the authorities that he hadn't wanted women and children to see the mess. No charges were ever filed against him.

Decades later, Kent and Amy were on their way to Mr. Fullwood's graveside service when they happened upon the very curve where Mrs. Pusser had been killed. The rest of the funeral procession had not taken that particular route. The couple had been at the rear of the line of cars and fallen behind as they argued over some forgotten subject, falling so far behind in fact that they failed to exit the highway with everyone else. After several miles, they realized their mistake and took the next exit, intending to double back to the cemetery.

As the car came around the infamous curve, the couple, now arguing about how late they were going to be for the burial, took little note of where they were, but within 25 yards after leaving the curve, the right front tire of the vehicle went completely flat in a matter of seconds. Not exactly a blowout, but close.

SIN CITY U.S.A.
AND THE COP WHO SMASHED IT WIDE OPEN!

THE VICE DENS AND HONKY-TONKS.

THE CROOKED GAMBLING JOINTS.

THE CRIME BOSSES' HIT MEN.

THE GANGLAND MURDERS.

WALKING TALL
THE ONLY WAY AN HONEST LAWMAN WALKS!

METRO-GOLDWYN-MAYER Presents "WALKING TALL" Starring JOE DON BAKER
ELIZABETH HARTMAN · ROSEMARY MURPHY · Written by MORT BRISKIN · Music by WALTER SCHARF
Executive Producer CHARLES A. PRATT · Produced by MORT BRISKIN · Directed by PHIL KARLSON · IN COLOR
Title song sung by Johnny Mathis. On Columbia Records
MGM

The bright-blue dye still coloring the white walls on the brand new tires, "goddamn Wal-Mart specials" Kent muttered, only served to agitate him further. It wasn't his car; it belonged to Amy's parents, and her father was notorious for cutting corners on car care.

As Kent stood in the searing summer sun amidst the tall grass beside the road staring at the flat tire, which had partially disintegrated, he felt a sharp pain on his right shin. Then another. And another. He looked down quickly, and saw that his pants legs were covered with fire ants.

He hopped onto the road, bent over, stomping his feet and swiping at the dozens of ants on his britches, realizing that some were underneath his pants on his bare legs and headed north. Following a brief vision of what might ensue were the bugs to get past his knees, he did the only logical thing he could think of: bent over in the middle of the old country road, he jerked his pants down around his ankles.

As he frantically swatted and flicked the stinging creatures from his flesh, and began to dislodge the majority of them from his clothing, he became aware of a faint droning noise, which was rapidly getting louder. It was the sound of tires on asphalt, big mud tires on a four-wheel-drive pickup to be exact, which he saw as he peeked through his bare legs.

Although the tune from *Deliverance* didn't start playing in his head, he quickly stood up, pulled his pants up and jumped to the side of the road. Kent needn't have worried, however, as the driver of the pick-up didn't even bother to slow down as he sped past the stranded vehicle. Given what he'd just observed, who could really blame him?

Finally getting around to opening the trunk, Kent found that the jack was stuck, and somehow sliced his hand attempting to remove it. After bandaging the wound and managing to remove the jack, he found that, not unsurprisingly, it wasn't original to the vehicle and couldn't be made to work.

No one else happened along the old road for quite some time, that is, until many of those friends and family members who had just attended the graveside service began coming down the road on their way home. Kent lost count of how many times he had to explain what their predicament, and eventually gave up trying and just stood there—in his dress shirt and pants, completely soaked with sweat, covered in grease and blood stains, his fire-ant bites still stinging—until someone, he doesn't recall who, came along with a jack that worked.

Kent made a full recovery from the incident physically, although it haunted him psychologically for years to come, and sometimes late at night, even decades later, he found himself pondering whether he'd been the victim of some curse attached to that curve … perhaps it was haunted by the ghost of Sheriff Pusser's wife.

On such occasions, Kent generally ended up attributing his misfortune to his ex-father-in-law's propensity for skimping

Buford!

Of course there's America's other favorite "Sheriff Buford," brilliantly played by Jackie Gleason in *Smokey and the Bandit*—Buford T. Justice, which was reportedly the name of a real Florida Highway Patrolman known to Burt Reynolds' father. Once the Chief of Police of Jupiter, Florida, Reynolds' dad was the inspiration behind Gleason's frequent use of the word "sumbitch" (and various derivatives thereof) in the movie.

"Buford" always struck Kent as a good ole Southern name (like Cleetis, Clive, and Clovis), and during William's younger years it became his favorite nickname for his son. The moniker just seemed to fit somehow, and Kent would occasionally string it together with his other favorites: "Get over here, Buford-Cleetis-Clive-Clovis!"

on car tires and drifted off to sleep, but, still, there was always the possibility…

"I'm gonna barbeque yo' ass in molasses!"

227

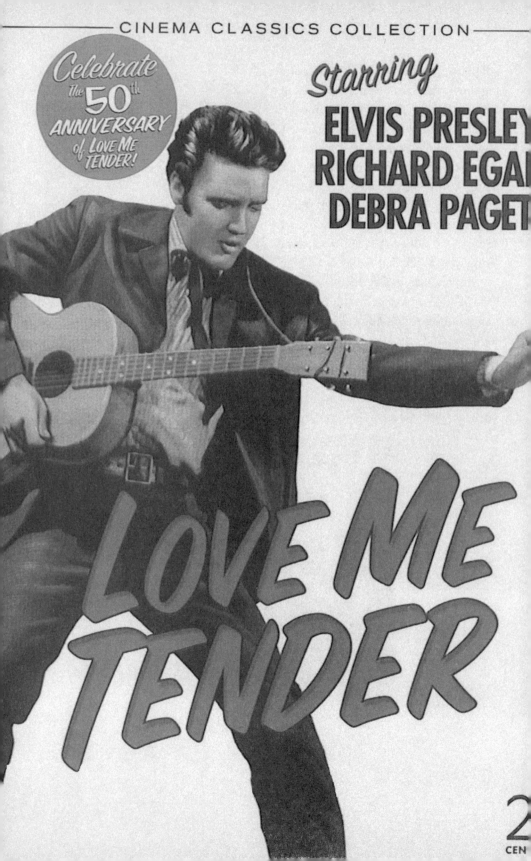

CHAPTER 37

LONG LIVE THE KING

When Kent's son William was about five years old, he took a liking to the music of Elvis Presley. One day as they were talking about the singer, Will asked his father how Elvis had died, and Kent explained in a light-hearted manner that Elvis passed away, so we're told, while sitting on the toilet in his home; a rather ignominious demise, especially for the King of Rock'n'Roll. (Urban legend has it that Elvis spent so much time in the bathroom he had a recliner converted into a toilet.)

With a bit of dry humor, apparently too dry, Kent added that he didn't think they'd let you into heaven if you died on the toilet, and then walked out of the room. What Kent didn't know at the time, and William didn't tell him until years later, was that he hadn't realized that his father was kidding about the last part, and for months afterwards Will had experienced significant anxiety every time he had to go "number two."

ELVIS STORIES

It seems that in Tupelo, Elvis' birthplace, and its environs just about everybody over the age of 50 has an Elvis story of one sort or another. As a child, William's maternal grandfather reportedly once played with Elvis outside a local car repair shop, but one could certainly be forgiven for considering the story somewhat suspect, as, in truth, are many of the Elvis tales one hears in the King's old stomping grounds.

Not quite 50, Kent has no Elvis encounter to tell of, but does have a very tangential story tied to an experience with one of Elvis' relatives—so tangential, in fact, that it probably wouldn't be worth relating if it weren't bizarre in and of itself.

229

While residing in Tupelo during Kent's second-grade year, his family lived directly next door to a Presley family whose father was a first or second cousin of Elvis. One day, Kent and his brother Kevin discovered one of the Presley boys, who was about their age, out back of the house with three small kittens his mother had just gotten him, and he was having great fun  throwing them over the telephone line in their back yard one at a time.

Kent immediately told him to quit, whereupon the boy promptly grabbed another kitten and chunked it over the wire. Kent and Kevin jumped on him, roughed him up, took his kittens and went home. A short while later, Mrs. Presley came around to collect the poor animals.

Beating up a cousin of the King of Rock'n'Roll for abusing kittens isn't much of an Elvis connection by any standards, but it's the best Kent's got, so it'll have to do.

ELVIS IS ALIVE, ETC., ETC.

As Kent reflected on the King's supporting role in the Golden Jubilee festivities, he was fully aware that there are just about as many conspiracy theories concerning Elvis' death as JFK's. The superstar's (supposed) passing was not as violent, or as traumatic for the nation, as President Kennedy's, but it was similarly surrounded by a slew of suspicious facts and circumstances that only served to heighten the public's interest in his death at the time and for decades since.

We know about as little for certain about Elvis' passing as we do JFK's, which is to say, not much. There is of course the Elvis-is-alive crowd and the closely related Elvis-is-dead-but-didn't-die-at-Graceland-in-1977 faction. There's also the Elvis-was-killed-by-the-Mob believers and their counterparts, the Elvis-staged-his-death-to-avoid-being-killed-by-the-Mob. And then there's The-Government-killed-Elvis and their cousins, The-Government-staged-Elvis'-death-to-protect-him-from-the-Mob. There are probably a few folks who believe that Elvis staged his own death to protect himself from the Government, but I don't really care.

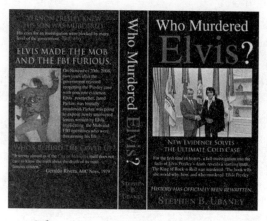

Some researchers even contend that Elvis gave subtle hints that his death would be staged, claiming, for example, that during his last concert tour, he altered the lyrics to his song "Way Down" as follows: "My body's going to be found on the bathroom floor and I'm going to places I've never been before."

Other researchers point out that while the medical examiner's report on Elvis' death states that his body was discovered in rigor mortis in the bathroom, the homicide report states that he was found unconscious in the bedroom.

There are claims that Elvis made inquiries with several creators of wax replicas in the months prior to his alleged death, and eyewitness reports which state that: 1.) the body in the casket sho' nuff looked like a wax replica—of Elvis at 25 years old, no less; 2.) the body in the casket had beads of liquid on its forehead, not sweat for Pete's sake but the wax melting in the summer heat; and, 3.) the casket was inordinately heavy, possibly because it contained a refrigeration device that was unsuccessfully employed to prevent the wax from melting.

There were even reports of an unmarked black helicopter hovering above and/or landing at and/or taking off from Graceland the night of his death (and/or the next day), which, given Kent's personal experience with such aircraft, he didn't doubt one damn bit.

Whether Elvis died, as according to popular mythology, of a drug overdose on the crapper, or was killed in a mob hit or staged his own death or the government staged his death or the government killed him we'll probably never know, and you can be pretty damn sure that, just as with JFK's untimely demise, this is *by design*. It is in part the uncertainty that contributes to the enduring mystique surrounding both their deaths and the odd deaths of other celebrities, politicians and cultural icons.

THE KING AND I

As with the JFK assassination, there are numerous seemingly plausible, yet competing, theories concerning Elvis' death.

Writing in an article entitled, "Why I'm convinced the Mob killed my soulmate Elvis," in the UK's *Daily Mail*, English actress Suzanna Leigh, who starred opposite Elvis in the 1966 film *Paradise, Hawaiian Style*, finds it curious that the singer's post-mortem report won't be released until 2027. "Why would the Federal Bureau of Investigation lock documents away if there was nothing to hide?" she asks.

In 2003, Leigh began working as a VIP tour guide at Graceland, and it was there that she first heard rumors from those working on the estate that Elvis had been murdered. As she began to investigate, she discovered that "many reputable people believed his death—from apparent heart failure, compounded by drug abuse—was not straightforward."

Regarding her investigation into the circumstances surrounding Elvis' death, Leigh writes, "I soon learned Elvis had in fact been part of one of the largest FBI investigations of the Seventies, codenamed Fountain Pen. Apparently, he had been the innocent victim in a Mafia fraud case involving billions of dollars."

While this is true, it is also true that many FBI operations are not what they appear to be on the surface, and thus there's no telling what Elvis was actually mixed up in. Various investigators note that the fraud case involved private airplanes, including one of Elvis', and claim that a CIA drug-running scheme was somehow connected.

"The first person I talked to as I tried to understand more about the mystery was Beecher Smith, who had been Elvis's lawyer," Leigh continued. "He told me that as part of the investigation, Elvis and his father were supposed to appear in front of a federal grand jury on August 16, 1977—the day Elvis died."

Leigh further reported that, "In [former police sergeant and head of Elvis' security team] Dick Grob's opinion, it was organised by the Mob. He told me they did not want Elvis or his father to appear in court because of all the media interest it would create, so they must have got someone inside the house. 'That's what Vernon [Presley] believed all along,' said Dick. 'Someone from inside let the killer into the house.'" (Grob also stated that nothing was properly investigated the night Elvis died due to "pandemonium in the streets, with distraught fans and journalists arriving from all over the world. There were about 200,000 people outside the gate.")

Yet, in the same article, Leigh says, "George Klein had told me that many suspicions were focused on Colonel Parker. Beecher Smith, meanwhile, said Parker had a lot to gain from Elvis's death—only a day after the death, he had persuaded the singer's father to sign over to him 50 per cent of The King's posthumous earnings." Lots of possible suspects and motives; few hard answers. The usual.

Leigh also discovered what happens to people who go poking their noses in places they don't belong. First, a wheel fell off her truck while she was driving, and although she was unhurt, a mechanic told her afterwards that the nuts on the other wheels were about to come off, as well. Then, one evening as she was walking her dog, an assailant fired five shots at her, all of which thankfully missed. Her car was subsequently broken into, and someone attempted to break into her home, stabbing one of her dogs in the process. She eventually left Memphis with precious few answers to her questions concerning the death of her 'soul-mate'.

SECRET AGENT MAN

During Elvis' famous meeting with President Richard Nixon on December 21st, 1970, the singer requested a badge from the Bureau of Narcotics and Dangerous Drugs (the predecessor of the DEA). In a hand-written letter that Elvis hand-delivered to the White House prior to the meeting, he wrote:

> Dear Mr. President.
>
> First, I would like to introduce myself. I am Elvis Presley and admire you and have great respect for your office. I talked to Vice President Agnew in Palm Springs three weeks ago and expressed my concern for our country. The drug culture, the hippie elements, the SDS, Black Panthers, etc. do not consider me as their enemy or as they call it the establishment. I call it America and I love it.

Sir, I can and will be of any service that I can to help the country out. I have no concern or motives other than helping the country out.

So I wish not to be given a title or an appointed position. I can and will do more good if I were made a Federal Agent at Large and I will help out by doing it my way through my communications with people of all ages. First and foremost, I am an entertainer, but all I need is the Federal credentials.

I am on this plane with Senator George Murphy and we have been discussing the problems that our country is faced with.

Sir, I am staying at the Washington Hotel, Room 505-506-507. I have two men who work with me by the name of Jerry Schilling and Sonny West. I am registered under the name of Jon Burrows. I will be here for as long as long as it takes to get the credentials of a Federal Agent. I have done an in-depth study of drug abuse and Communist brainwashing techniques and I am right in the middle of the whole thing where I can and will do the most good.

I am Glad to help just so long as it is kept very private. You can have your staff or whomever call me anytime today, tonight, or tomorrow. I was nominated this coming year one of America's Ten Most Outstanding Young Men. That will be in January 18 in my home town of Memphis, Tennessee. I am sending you the short autobiography about myself so you can better understand this approach. I would love to meet you just to say hello if you're not too busy.

Respectfully,

Elvis Presley

P. S. I believe that you, Sir, were one of the Top Ten Outstanding Men of America also. ...

That sounds very patriotic and all, however, when you consider that Elvis had a highly-prized collection of police badges he'd gathered over the years, one might wonder whether or not he had an ulterior motive in seeking to obtain this federal badge.

Actually, we need not wonder whether another motive was involved, and unfortunately it went beyond just adding another badge to his collection. Writing in her memoir, *Elvis and Me*, Priscilla Presley stated, "The narc badge represented some kind of ultimate power to him," continuing, "With the federal narcotics badge, he [believed he] could legally enter any country both wearing guns and carrying any drugs he wished."

I have no concern or motives other than helping the country out...

Elvis' Evil Stepmother

There were also rumors that Elvis had been looking for a way to escape from his increasingly confined existence, to just disappear and lead a halfway normal life. Before his death, Elvis reportedly told long-time friend George Klein that he had rented a house in Hawaii. So perhaps if Elvis didn't stage his death to escape the Mob, he did so to escape the public mob, the ever-present masses that followed his every move and hounded him wherever he went.

Or, maybe he was trying to get as far as he possibly could from his evil stepmother, Dee Presley, who, according to Priscilla, Elvis couldn't stand, and who became notorious after his passing for making outrageous claims about the singer's sexuality and drug abuse.

Dee made her most jaw-dropping claim about Elvis in her 1993 book, *The Intimate Life and Death of Elvis Presley*, in which she alleged that the King had engaged in an incestuous relationship with his beloved mother, Gladys, who died in 1958. Not satisfied to slander Elvis in print, she repeated her allegations on national television, claiming that she was told of the affair by both the family's long-time maid, and Elvis' grandmother Minnie.

As if that allegation weren't enough, Dee also claimed that Elvis had a homosexual affair with Nick Adams, the Oscar-nominated actor and star of ABC's iconic series "The Rebel," who died of a prescription drug overdose in 1968.

One thing is for certain: Elvis' dislike of his stepmother was rivaled only by his love for his true mother, Gladys, after whose death, said family members who knew Elvis well, "He never seemed like Elvis again."

At her funeral, Elvis threw himself over her body as she lay in the coffin, screaming for her to come back to him and gently stroking her hair with his hands. "Just look at Mama, look at those hands of God, those hands toiled to raise me," Elvis lamented. He couldn't stop touching her, kissing her and whispering to her, and, after the funeral, he carried around her nightgown, clutching it tightly even while he slept.

"THE GREATEST LIVING AMERICAN"

Whether Elvis was purely brown-nosing and bullshitting Nixon, or in fact had mixed motives and was, at least in part, sincere, isn't clear; but regardless, the entertainer returned to Washington a little more than a week later to have a go at long-time FBI Director J. Edgar Hoover, perhaps wanting to add an FBI badge to his growing collection. (While there, he also visited the National Sheriffs' Association head office.)

Having oddly decided to just show up on New Year's Eve, Presley was unable to meet with Hoover, but Elvis and his six bodyguards *were* given a tour of FBI headquarters. During his visit, Elvis offered his confidential services to Hoover as an undercover agent, and subsequently received a letter from Hoover acknowledging his offer of assistance.

"Presley's sincerity and good intentions notwithstanding, he is certainly not the type of individual whom the director would wish to meet," an FBI underling recorded in a memo. "It is noted at the present time he is wearing his hair down to his shoulders and indulges in the wearing of all sorts of exotic dress."

The FBI aide, one M.A. Jones, further noted that, "Presley indicated that he ... has read material prepared by the Director including *Masters of Deceit, A Study of Communism* as well as *J. Edgar Hoover on Communism.* Presley noted that in his opinion no one has ever done as much for his country as has Mr. Hoover, and that he, Presley, considers the Director the 'greatest living American.' He also spoke most favorably of the Bureau."

A valiant attempt on the part of the King, but, alas, no FBI badge was forthcoming.

THANK YA' VERY MUCH

One of the earliest pieces of correspondence in Presley's extensive FBI file, hundreds of pages of which remain classified to this day for national security and foreign policy reasons, was a letter from a La Crosse, Wisconsin, man warning Hoover that Elvis was "a definite danger to the security of the United States." His letter stated that Elvis had autographed "the abdomen and thigh" of two high school girls, and that Elvis fan clubs "degenerate into sex orgies." He further asserted that Elvis was both a drug addict and sexual pervert. Hoover responded to the man, thanking him for his letter but informing him that, "the matter is not within the investigative jurisdiction of the FBI."

One newspaper article included in Elvis' file reported that 1,500 bobbysoxers had threatened to riot when Elvis failed to make an appearance at the debut of *Love Me Tender* at the Paramount Theater in New York in November of 1965. The headline from another article by the Associated Press datelined Louisville, Kentucky, read, "Elvis Faces Wiggle Ban," reporting that the local police chief had banned "any lewd, lascivious contortions that would excite a crowd."

Given these examples, and that many at the time considered Elvis himself to be The Devil in Disguise, it is interesting to note that Mr. Jones' memo from Elvis' New Year's Eve drop-in visit also recorded that:

Presley indicated that he is of the opinion that the Beatles laid the groundwork for many of the problems we are having with young people by their filthy unkempt appearances and suggestive music while entertaining in this country during the early and middle 60s. He advised that the Smothers Brothers, Jane Fonda and other persons … of their ilk have a lot to answer for in the hereafter for the way they have poisoned young minds by disparaging the United States in their public statements and unsavory activities.

(Left) Maybe Elvis was on to something after all with his suspicions about the Beatles. Let's see, that's Paul flashing a 666 sign and John with the Devil's horns, and just in case you didn't catch that, they'll amplify and repeat—note the two-handed horns with reversal, nice (center). And, yeah, that's Aleister Crowley on the cover of Sgt. Peppers Lonely Hearts Club Band amongst other of the band's "heroes."

Elvis was no Anton Lavey or Kenneth Anger, but the idea of Elvis the Pelvis complaining to the FBI about the corrupting influence of the Beatles could strike one as, well, just a tad hypocritical.

"Elvis Presley is the greatest cultural force in the twentieth century," observed composer and conductor Leonard Bernstein. "He introduced the beat to everything and he changed everything—music, language, clothes. It's a whole new social revolution—the sixties came from it." It is no overstatement to say that Elvis was the catalyst for a cultural revolution that transformed popular music and popular culture and swept the globe. Rock'n'roll was defined by a rebellious attitude towards all things traditional, and the "harmless" pelvic thrusts of the King helped birth the sexual revolution of the '60's which, decades later, has bequeathed us the twerking

Miley Cyrus and the ultra-moronic Justin Bieber. Thank ya' very much.

Testifying to Elvis' ongoing impact on the nation, Graceland, which opened to the public in 1982, has become the second-most-visited home in the United States, with only the White House receiving more visitors each year.

REBEL, REBEL

Elvis was not simply the vehicle for the transformation of American culture, he was an unwitting (one assumes) weapon in a broader war on traditional values. He was an instrument of cultural rebellion, and has become an enduring symbol of the same. If JFK was a symbol of hope, Elvis was a symbol of libertinism: *Do What Thou Wilt, baby.*

Regardless of whether his death was staged or orchestrated, or by whom—or whether it was just pure fate—the alleged date of Elvis' passing, August 16th, speaks to that which he embodied.

The 16th of August was the day on which legendary bluesman Robert Johnson, the Father of the Blues—the uniquely American musical genre that gave rise to rock'n'roll, which propelled Elvis to international superstardom and made him a one-man engine of cultural revolution—shuffled off his mortal coil and, per his famous midnight pact at a delta crossroads, paid the Devil his due.

Although Elvis never claimed to have made a deal with the Devil, many suspected (with what appeared to be a good deal of evidence based on the enormous level of success the singer attained) that he had in fact done so, and the notion that Elvis—who, were he to have struck a deal with Ole Pip, got a hell of a lot more out of his

---

Robert Johnson

"Hellhound on My Trail" (excerpt)

I got to keep moving, I got to keep moving
Blues falling down like hail, blues falling down like hail
Mmm, blues falling down like hail, blues falling down like hail
And the day keeps on remindin' me, there's a hellhound on my trail
Hellhound on my trail, hellhound on my trail…

"Me and the Devil Blues" (excerpt)

Early this morning
When you knocked upon my door
Early this morning, oooo
When you knocked upon my door
And I said hello Satan
I believe it's time to go

Me and the Devil
Was walkin' side by side
Me and the Devil, woooo
Was walking side by side
And I'm going to beat my woman
'Til I get satisfied …

You may bury my body, woooo
Down by the highway side
So my old evil spirit
Can get a Greyhound bus and ride

arrangement than Robert Johnson did—had to pay up on the same day as Johnson, well, that somehow just has a fair amount of appeal to it, true or not.

Elvis the Pelvis, the original-and-greatest-of-all-time international symbol of rebelliousness, paying the Devil his due on the anniversary of The Father of the Blues' trend-setting payoff (which set the precedent for a lengthy list of performers who openly claim to have made a similar deal, including Snoop Dogg, Jay-Z and Bob Dylan; see sidebar)—if you can't dig that, you got a hole in your soul, man.

(Left) An inspiration for rock legends such as Eric Clapton, Keith Richards and Jimmy Page, Robert Johnson was also the inspiration for the character Tommy Johnson (although there was also reportedly a pioneering bluesman named Tommy Johnston who may or may not have made his own deal with the man in black) in the Cohen brothers' film O' Brother, Where Art Thou? (Right) Dialogue from O' Brother:

Tommy Johnson: I had to be up at that there crossroads last midnight, to sell my soul to the devil. ...
Ulysses Everett McGill: What'd the devil give you for your soul, Tommy?
Tommy Johnson: Well, he taught me to play this here guitar real good.
Delmar O'Donnell: Oh son, for that you sold your everlasting soul?
Tommy Johnson: Well, I wasn't usin' it.

I Sold My Soul for Rock'n'Roll (or Rap, Hip-Hop, Whatever)

Okay, the first two, Snoop Dogg and Jay-Z, don't require much explanation as they're on the record about their deals with Satan, but Bob Dylan? He is, too, and really, if you think about it, considering his level of success relative to his singing ability, supernatural evil is the only explanation that makes any sense.

The following dialogue is from an interview Dylan did with correspondent Ed Bradley of CBS's *60 Minutes*:

"*... I made a bargain with it, you know, long time ago. And I'm holding up my end ...*" says Dylan.

A bargain for what? "*... to get where I am now,*" Dylan replies.

And with whom did he make the bargain? "*With the chief commander,*" laughs Dylan, continuing, "*in this earth and in the world we can't see.*"

Clear enough for you? Thanks, Bob, take it away...

"Talking Devil" by Bob Dylan (excerpt)

Well, he wants you to hate and he wants you to fear,
Wants you to fear something that's not even there.
He'll give you your hate, and he'll give you his lies,
He'll give you the weapons to run out and die.
And you give him your soul.

ELVIS AND THE UNDEAD

As it turns out, August 16th is also the date on which actor Bela Lugosi died in 1956. Lugosi is best remembered for his role as Dracula, the undead, and in addition to perhaps sharing the quality of never quite actually dying, Elvis had a number of other things in common with the Count, including the slicked-back jet-black hair, capes and high collars, and a habit of sleeping all day and staying up all night—and he certainly had the ability to put a spell on the ladies.

Some also draw parallels between the King of Rock and the King of the Jews (who you could argue is the original undead), and actually this cultural meme has become so popular and widespread that one could devote a rather large volume to the subject.

And even though Elvis was supposedly once heard in concert to say, "I am not the King. Jesus Christ is the King. I'm just an entertainer..." (there are several variations of the quote), the list of similarities between the two is striking nonetheless, as you can see for yourself:

1. Jesus was born in humble surroundings. Elvis was born in a shotgun shack.

2. A star appeared when Jesus was born. (Matthew 2:2) Elvis almost appeared in A Star Is Born.

3. Jesus said "Love thy neighbor." Elvis said "Don't be cruel."

4. Jesus was the Lamb of God. Elvis had mutton-chop sideburns.

5. Jesus is the Lord's shepherd. Elvis dated Cybill Shepherd.

6. Jesus was part of the Trinity. Elvis' first band was a trio.

7. Jesus' entourage, the Apostles, had 12 members. Elvis' entourage, the Memphis Mafia, had 12 members.

8. "[Jesus'] countenance was like lightning, and his raiment white as snow." (Matthew 28:3) Elvis wore snow-white jumpsuits with lightning bolts.

9. Jesus' mother Mary conceived via immaculate conception. Elvis' wife Priscilla went to Immaculate Conception High School.

10. Jesus was resurrected. Elvis had his famous 1968 "Comeback" TV special.

11. Jesus said "If a man thirst, let him come to me, and drink." (John 7:37) Elvis said, "Drinks on me" (Jail House Rock, 1957).

12. People called Jesus "a glutton and a drunk." (Luke 7:34) People called Elvis "an overweight druggie."

13. Jesus said "Today, shalt thou be with me in paradise." (Luke 23:43) Elvis said "Welcome to Paradise-Hawaiian style." (*Paradise-Hawaiian Style*, 1966)

14. Jesus said, "Many shall come in my name, saying I am Christ" (Matthew 24:5). There are thousands of Elvis impersonators in the world today.

15. Jesus walked on water. Elvis surfed. (Blue Hawaii, 1965)

16. Jesus said, "Father, into thy hands I commend my spirit" (Luke 23:46). Elvis sang "Return to Sender."

17. Jesus died in the book of John. Elvis died on the john.

18. Jesus taught that His followers should love Him. Elvis said "Love Me Tender."

19. Both Elvis and Jesus are widely known on a first name basis.

20. Jesus preached the Gospel to Peter, Paul and Mary. Elvis was into the band Peter, Paul and Mary.

21. And, finally, both have a huge cult following years after their deaths, and each has been seen walking around after his reported death, Jesus on the road to Emmaus and Elvis in K-Mart.

ELVIS, CONSPIRACY THEORIST

All joking aside, even after all the conspiracy theories and allegations concerning Elvis we've covered in this chapter, we've yet to discuss one of the most outlandish.

By many accounts, Elvis was practically obsessed with the assassinations of both President John F. Kennedy and Robert Kennedy, and, no slouch of a conspiracy theorist himself, was quite well read on both killings. He had a personal copy of the Zapruder film, and watched it again and again, espousing various theories as to who might have killed JFK.

Interestingly, Elvis' death occurred while the U.S. House of Representatives Select Committee on Assassinations, established in 1976, was investigating the shootings of President Kennedy and Martin Luther King, Jr. The Committee completed its work in 1978, issuing a final report the following year in which it concluded that Kennedy's assassination was likely the result of a conspiracy.

Although there's no evidence whatsoever of any connection between the investigation and Elvis' passing, one wonders what the impact on public opinion might have been if the enormously-popular entertainer had started running his mouth to the media concerning his theories on the assassination, and who in positions of authority might have been concerned about that possibility. (Sure, his popularity was in decline in those years, but still.)

MK-ELVIS

Another, perhaps more pertinent, inquiry was taking place in early August 1977, the same month and year of Elvis' death, in the U.S. Senate, which was conducting hearings on the now-famous CIA MK-Ultra mind-control program after a Freedom of Information Act request had uncovered a cache of 20,000 related documents the previous month.

For those unfamiliar with the details of the program, MK-Ultra, begun in the early 1950s, experimented with a wide variety of methods for human behavioral engineering, and with some 149 subprojects, research was undertaken—in many instances using front organizations—at over 80 institutions, including 44 colleges and universities, as well as hospitals, prisons and pharmaceutical companies.

The program engaged in numerous illegal activities, including the use of unwitting U.S. and Canadian citizens as test subjects, and among the methodologies utilized by MK-Ultra to manipulate mental states and alter brain functions was the surreptitious administration of experimental drugs (LSD, in particular), hypnosis, isolation, sensory deprivation, verbal and sexual abuse and various other forms of physical and psychological torture.

As the Supreme Court later noted, MK-Ultra was concerned with "the research and development of chemical, biological, and radiological materials capable of employment in clandestine operations to control human behavior."

The activities of the program were reduced in scope in 1964, scaled back further in 1967 and officially halted in 1973. In 1975, MK-Ultra was brought to public attention by the Church Committee (the United States Senate Select Committee to Study Governmental Operations with Respect to Intelligence Activities, chaired by Senator Frank Church), but investi-

gative efforts were severely hampered as a result of the actions of CIA Director Richard Helms, who had ordered all MK-Ultra files destroyed in 1973.

The true extent of MK-Ultra's activities were never clear, and still aren't, and many in fact believe that the program never went away, but rather morphed

into a variety of even more clandestine operations focused on individual and mass mind-control.

Elvis, WMD

What's the connection between MK-Ultra and Elvis? Assuming that the timing of Elvis' death and the Church Committee's inquiry into the CIA's mind-control program is purely coincidental, which it almost certainly is, what other link might there be? Was Elvis a victim of government mind-control efforts? Did he exhibit signs of having been subjected to MK-Ultra programming?

Elvis had talent, charisma and animal magnetism oozing out of his pores. Combined with the well-oiled and increasingly advanced technological machinery of the burgeoning entertainment industry of the day, designed to churn out hits and stars by the dozen, you don't need to resort to any wild theories to explain his phenomenal success, just as you needn't invoke the power of Satan as a reason for his rise to fame. Whatever "it" is, Elvis had it in spades.

And one need not refer to his eccentric behavior as evidence of some sort of mind-control, either. Although insisting that six cans of biscuits be kept in the house at all times is a little strange, lots of gifted folks are more than a little flaky.

Is there any indisputable evidence that Elvis was a victim of mind-control? Well, no. Consider this, however.

Elvis was undoubtedly an agent of cultural transformation, whether one attributes this transformation to a broader, multi-faceted conspiracy or not. Many quite sane persons in fact believe that a decades-long program of global social engineering not only exists, but is itself just one component of an agenda of full-spectrum dominance administered by the planet's elite, whose (achieved?) objective is total control of all the earth's resources, including its human population, which they view simply as another of the assets at their disposal.

As an instigator of societal revolution and a vital instrument employed to facilitate the breakdown of Judeo-Christian-values-based society, Elvis was the cultural equivalent of a weapon of mass destruction. In context of a well-orchestrated, multi-generational assault on traditional values, Elvis' meteoric rise and global impact could be compared to the advent of the atomic bomb in the decade before he rose to popularity. He blew everything and everyone who'd come before him away, and changed the face of our collective culture forever.

One could argue whether this was by design or by default 'til the cows come home, but assuming for the sake of argument that it *was* by design—

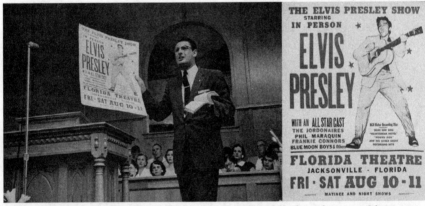

Many pastors preached against the evils of rock'n'roll and lambasted its seminal purveyor, Elvis Presley. In 1956, 30-year-old Bob Gray, pastor of Trinity Baptist Church in Jacksonville, Florida—which eventually became the community's first "mega-church"—stood before his congregation with an Elvis poster in one hand and an open Bible in the other and hammered home his message. In 2006, Gray, then 80 years old, was arrested and charged with four counts of capital sexual battery stemming from incidents in the 1960s and 70s in which he had allegedly French-kissed and fondled six-year-old girls in his office. Eventually over 20 women and one man came forward with allegations, but the statute of limitations had expired in most instances. Gray died before the case went to trial.

244

that the King's Reign of Destruction was part of a coordinated assault not simply on faith and family, but on the individual—one has to ask how much the orchestrators of such a campaign would have left to chance?

If your long-range goal was to create a planet populated with human beings divorced from all moral underpinnings (and largely divorced from each other, maritally speaking) and unsupported by the traditional institutions of family and community—a population that can't think for themselves and that shits its collective pants every time NBC's Brian Williams and his fellow mainstream-media mouthpieces utter the acronym ISIS—a herd of cattle that suckles at the tits of McDonald's and KFC, whose every thought is guided by CNN and whose highest ideals are embodied by members of the NFL and NBA, you could advance your cause through no better means than to produce an endless parade of ever-more-crass entertainers whom the public, with its endless appetite for distraction, would voraciously devour and whose very essences would rot the mindless consumers from the inside out—you'd start with something that looked and behaved just like Elvis and keep right on going through Beyoncé and beyond until your goal was accomplished (and you probably wouldn't stop then).

With so much at stake, how much freedom would *you* grant your living, breathing tools of war? How closely would you seek to control those gifted, often free-spirited individuals who were critical to establishing complete control over the masses? The last thing you need is for one of them to start thinking for themselves. Can't have anybody going off the reservation.

This is not just about entertainment, as much money as there is to be made in the industry: this is about social engineering on a planetary scale. Billions of lives, hundreds of trillions of dollars and complete control of the earth hang in the balance. The carefully, expensively crafted images of Hollywood's best and brightest are valued more than the lives of the celebrities themselves. To those in control, the symbolic value of entertainers far outweighs their worth as human beings.

Girls, Girls, Girls

Elvis of course had relationships with many women during his lifetime, and there were numerous reports of affairs with various Hollywood stars and starlets, including Ann-Margret, Elvis' co-star in the 1964 *Viva Las Vegas*. (Sorry, Suzanna, but Ann-Margret also thought of Elvis as her soulmate.)

Given that Elvis proposed to Ann-Margret, it is questionable whether he ever intended to marry Priscilla, to whom he waited more than seven years before proposing, and it is said that his manager Col. Tom Parker pushed him into the marriage.

Elvis' eventual marriage and plentiful flings with some of the biggest bombshells of the day notwithstanding, the entertainer also, shall we say, enjoyed the company of younger members of the fairer sex, as well. Priscilla Beaulieu was in fact only 14, ten years the singer's junior, when they first met in September 1959, and despite reassurances Elvis' gave her parents at the time, both Elvis and Priscilla would later admit that they were engaged in a full-blown sexual relationship from the outset.

Although their relationship was portrayed as "a sweet and innocent triumph of love across the age divide," it was in reality but one of many of the entertainer's unsettling liaisons with minors following his rise to stardom. Lamar Fike, a former member of Elvis' entourage, claims that, "He was fascinated with the idea of real young teenage girls," continuing, "It scared the hell out of all of us."

Girls as young as fourteen, seemingly a magic age for Elvis, were invited to private pajama parties in Presley's bedroom (so that's where Michael Jackson got the idea...poor Lisa Marie), and the activities involved weren't limited to telling ghost stories and pillow fights.

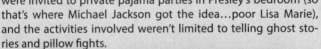

ELVIS, PROTOTYPE

Considering Elvis, then, as an early prototype of what we see so frequently today, we can again ask the question, Was Elvis mind-controlled? The technology and know-how were certainly available, and the enormous stakes would have justified their utilization on him. *Was he*, though?

The larger and more pressing question is, *Are we*? And actually, we should have no real doubt about that fact, it's only a matter of to what extent and how (and those things are fairly clear, as well).

Elvis *could* have been subjected to government mind-control, and he certainly *could* have been used as a tool in part of a broader mind-control operation targeting the masses. Can we know either for certain? No. Does it matter now? Maybe.

That depends on whether or not you think all this somehow stopped with Elvis, and on whether you're discerning enough to connect the dots between the King of Rock and the King of Pop and all the corpses in between and following. It depends on whether you can see the occult-symbol-riddled products of today's filth-laden entertainment industry as the direct legacy of the 1950s, 60s and 70s, because if you can't, nothing really matters all that much anyway.

Whether or not Elvis was a victim of MK-Ultra or was employed as part of an MK-Ultra program targeting the public of that day isn't as important as this: regardless of who has or has not been, is or is not an actual individual victim, celebrity or otherwise, and regardless of exactly how extensive and pervasive you can allow yourself to believe that a mass-mind-control program might be today, evidence suggesting the existence of a worst-case scenario is all around us, whether we like it or not, or want to see it or not. MK-Ultra rules.

The world
will never be the same
once you've
seen it through the eyes of
Forrest Gump.

Tom Hanks is Forrest Gump

WINNER OF 6
ACADEMY AWARDS
—— INCLUDING ——
BEST PICTURE
©A.M.I

"LIFE IS LIKE A BOX OF CHOCOLATES..."

CHAPTER 38

THE FIRSTEST

"… if there is anyone on God's earth who loves the ladies, I believe it is myself."

--Nathan Bedford Forrest

"I have been in the heat of battle when colored men asked me to protect them. I have placed myself between them and the bullets of my men, and told them they should be kept unharmed." If, when asked to identify which famous figure from the Civil War uttered these words, you failed to guess Knights-of-the-Golden-Circle member and Confederate General Nathan Bedford Forrest, you could easily be forgiven.

Though lacking formal education, Forrest was a gifted commander and tactician and the only man on either side to rise from the rank of private to that of general during the four-year conflict. Both Robert E. Lee and William Tecumseh Sherman called him the finest soldier produced by the war, with Sherman confessing to being perpetually flummoxed by Forrest's cunning and exhausted by his relentlessness.

Time and again Forrest defeated larger, better-equipped and better-trained forces, more than once tricking Union commanders into surrendering to his smaller force. By the end of the war, Forrest had been wounded four times and had personally killed 30 Union soldiers, with his horses faring only slightly better—29 were shot from underneath him, sometimes one within minutes of its ill-fated successor.

WIZARD TIMES TWO

Known as "The Wizard of the Saddle," cavalryman Forrest achieved perhaps his greatest military victory at the Battle of Brice's Crossroads near Baldwyn, Mississippi, defeating a much larger Union force through brilliant maneuvering and tactics.

Once when asked what the key to his success on the battlefield was, Forrest replied, "Ma'am, I got there first with the most men." This quote has long been famously mangled, with Forrest being misquoted as saying that his strategy was to "git thar fustest with the mostest" (which is now often recast as "get there firstest with the mostest"). The original misquote first appeared in print in a *New York Tribune* article and was later corrected in the *New York Times* in 1918.

Forrest is probably best known, however, not as "the Wizard of the Saddle," but as the first Grand Wizard of the Ku Klux Klan, and although some researchers question this fact, it is almost assuredly accurate.

William Faulkner's 1943 short story, "My Grandmother Millard and General Bedford Forrest and The Battle of Harrykin Creek," features Forrest as a character, and Faulkner's 1938 novel The Unvanquished *is set against the backdrop of Forrest's engagements with Union General Andrew J. Smith. In the 1994 film* Forrest Gump, *the lead character remarks that he was named after his ancestor, General Nathan Bedford Forrest.*

The Wizard Speaks

There is no question that Forrest was a controversial figure throughout his life, but in his later years, he appeared to have a change in heart on the issue of race.

In 1875, at what would be his last public appearance, addressing the Independent Order of Pole-Bearers Association, a group of black Southerners advocating racial reconciliation, Forrest made what the *New York Times* described as a "friendly speech."

At the event, Forrest was offered a bouquet by an African-American woman, which he accepted, and began his speech thus:

> Ladies and Gentlemen, I accept the flowers as a memento of reconciliation between the white and colored races of the southern states. I accept it more particularly as it comes from a colored lady, for if there is anyone on God's earth who loves the ladies, I believe it is myself. (Immense applause and laughter.)

This day is a day that is proud to me, having occupied the position that I did for the past twelve years, and been misunderstood by your race. This is the first opportunity I have had during that time to say that I am your friend. I am here a representative of the southern people, one more slandered and maligned than any man in the nation.

I will say to you and to the colored race that men who bore arms and followed the flag of the Confederacy are, with very few exceptions, your friends. I have an opportunity of saying what I have always felt— that I am your friend, for my interests are your interests, and your interests are my interests. We were born on the same soil, breathe the same air, and live in the same land. Why, then, can we not live as brothers?

I will say that when the war broke out I felt it my duty to stand by my people. When the time came I did the best I could, and I don't believe I flickered. I came here with the jeers of some white people, who think that I am doing wrong. I believe that I can exert some influence, and do much to assist the people in strengthening fraternal relations, and shall do all in my power to bring about peace. It has always been my motto to elevate every man—to depress none. (Applause.) …

I came to meet you as friends, and welcome you to the white people. I want you to come nearer to us. When I can serve you I will do so. We have but one flag, one country; let us stand together. …

Many things have been said about me which are wrong, and which white and black persons here, who stood by me through the war, can contradict. I have been in the heat of battle when colored men asked me to protect them. I have placed myself between them and the bullets of my men, and told them they should be kept unharmed.

Go to work, be industrious, live honestly and act truly, and when you are oppressed I'll come to your relief. I thank you, ladies and gentlemen, for this opportunity you have afforded me to be with you, and to assure you that I am with you in heart and in hand. (Prolonged applause.)

WOMEN'S HERITAGE FOR MEN

The Mississippi Hills in fact produced a number of noteworthy historical firsts, including the First Lady of Country Music, Tammy Wynette, from Tremont, as well as the first public university for women in the United States, the Mississippi University for Women in Columbus, which the mothers of both William Faulkner and Tennessee Williams attended, along with author Eudora Welty.

The "first" from the Mississippi Hills that most interested Kent, however, dealt with a lesser known aspect of regional women's heritage, one that could not be included in the official promotional literature for the Mississippi Hills National Heritage Area.

Ellen Stratton was born June 9, 1939, in Marietta, Mississippi less than thirty miles from both Tupelo, birthplace of Elvis Presley, and Tremont, hometown of Tammy Wynette. Marietta is also less than 15 miles from the site of N.B. Forrest's famous victory at the Battle of Brice's Crossroads.

Stratton, a legal secretary and model, was *Playboy* magazine's Playmate of the Month for December 1959, and in June 1960, Hugh Hefner named Stratton as the very first Playmate of the Year. (Elvis Presley, Tammy Wynette, Howlin' Wolf, William Faulkner, Tennessee Williams, Ellen Stratton—what the hell was in the water in this place?)

Kent decided that it would probably be best not to suggest to the Board of Directors that the National Heritage Area partner with *Playboy* to celebrate Stratton's legacy. However, he felt that it would certainly be accurate to state that she did "git thar fustest with the mostest."

Roman Polanski's Academy Award® winning thriller.

MIA FARROW

ROSEMARY'S BABY

It's not what you're expecting.

CHAPTER 39

RFK's LAST SUPPER

Although Kent had not really given much thought to the June 5th Snowden revelations coinciding with the date of Robert Kennedy's assassination, he had no doubt whatsoever the death of President Kennedy's brother had been far more than the work of just another lone-nut killer.

On June 5th, 1968, John Frankenheimer, director of the 1962 film version of Richard Condon's novel *The Manchurian Candidate* about a programmed assassin whose target is a U.S. Presidential candidate—the movie was pulled from circulation the next year, some say due to the assassination of President John F. Kennedy—hosts Democratic Presidential candidate Senator Robert F. Kennedy at his home for what would be Kennedy's last supper, then personally drives him to the Ambassador Hotel, where he was killed only hours later by ... a programmed assassin. (Kent wrote briefly about Sirhan Sirhan as an early victim of mind-control programming).

Among the guests attending the small dinner party at Frankenheimer's Malibu home that evening was fellow director Roman Polanski, whose latest film, *Rosemary's Baby*, about a bunch of Satanists facilitating the impregnation of an unsuspecting woman with the Devil's spawn, would premiere a week later on June 12th. (Anton Lavey referred to the film as "the best paid commercial for Satanism since the Inquisition.")

Actress Sharon Tate, Polanski's wife, was also present at the dinner, and only a little over

If you come in five minutes after this picture begins, you won't know what it's all about!

when you've seen it all, you'll swear there's never been anything like it!

Frank Sinatra
Laurence Harvey
Janet Leigh

The Manchurian Candidate

a year later, Tate, eight-and-a-half months pregnant, and her unborn child were brutally murdered by what were essentially a bunch of Satanists, i.e., members of the Manson Family. (Charles Manson borrowed philosophically from the Satan-worshipping Process Church, and, as a Family member told one of the victims that fateful night, "I'm the devil, and I'm here to do the devil's business.")

Manson's killing spree was intended to bring about an apocalyptic race war, which he called "Helter Skelter" after the Beatles' song of the same name on the White Album, *and, in one of those who-the-hell-knows-what-to-make-of-it synchronistic linkages, John Lennon later lived in, and was killed in the lobby of, the Dakota, the Manhattan apartment building where* Rosemary's Baby *was filmed.*

Tate made her film debut in the occult-themed *Eye of the Devil* (1966), in which she played a witch, and also starred in the cult classic, *Valley of the Dolls* (1967), which earned her a Golden Globe Award nomination. The year before they were married, Tate co-starred in *The Fearless Vampire Killers* (1967)—a comedy horror flick that was originally entitled *The Fearless Vampire Killers, or Pardon Me, But Your Teeth Are in My Neck*—with Roman Polanski, who also directed the film. Tate was reportedly inducted into witchcraft on the set of *The Fearless Vampire Killers* by Alex "King of the Witches" Saunders (pictured below), who received instruction as a youth from none other than Aleister Crowley.

HINKEY SQUARED

So, what we're left with is this: Following dinner at his house, the director of the *Manchurian Candidate*, who had been filming RFK throughout his campaign for documentary purposes, chauffeurs Kennedy to his own rendezvous with death, which ostensibly occurred at the hands of a mind-controlled assassin-pat- sy (there is solid evidence of other shooters in the room)—this after RFK's brother was ostensibly assas- sinated by a mind-controlled pat- sy (there is solid evidence of other shooters in Dealey Plaza).

At this same fateful meal are the director of *Rosemary's Baby*—a film about the birth of Satan's child, which would be released in theatres

Photos from "The Tate Gallery" in the March 1967 issue of Playboy *magazine, with several of the images obviously part of the promotion for* The Fearless Vampire Killers.

the very next week—and his stunning blonde wife, who, along with the couple's unborn son, is slaughtered only a little over a year later at the hands of one of the most infamous occultist gangs ever to strike fear into the hearts and imaginations of Americans.

Two famous Hollywood directors, two famous movies, and one really hinkey instance of life-imitates-art *in combination with* what could be viewed as one of the biggest coincidences of the twentieth century, with the director of a hit movie about the birth of Satan's progeny suffering the loss of his al- most-full-term child (Sharon's Baby) *and* his witch wife, who are taken from him by followers of one of the nation's most notorious occult psychopaths, who himself might have been a subject of government mind-control exper- imentation … which is all incredible enough, except that the latter was no coincidence, but rather a *second* really hinkey instance of life-imitates-art.

ROMAN IS GUY

Just as the plot of *The Machu- rian Candidate* foreshadowed the killing of RFK, the plot of *Rosemary's Baby* foreshadowed the brutal death of Sharon Tate.

In the latter movie (for those few who have not seen it), lead male character Guy Woodhouse is a struggling actor who has had to resort to appearing in embarrass- ing TV commercials to make ends

A deceased Sharon Tate. She was stabbed 16 times and her killers wrote the word "pig" on the wall of her house in her blood. Note the prominently displayed inverted five-pointed stars on the flag behind her.

meet. Guy and his wife, Rosemary, move into an apartment at the Bramford Apartments, where Guy soon learns that their eccentric elderly neighbors are Satanists, and he is offered professional success in return for the use of his wife as a living incubator for the Devil's child, an offer he willingly accepts.

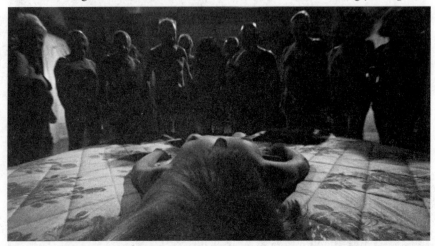

The parallel between the real-life and fictitious careers of Roman Polanski and Guy Woodhouse is obvious, and the parallel between Rosemary's and Sharon's babies disturbing, with each child taken by servants of His Satanic Majesty. The first child was the stated price of success for the father. Was the second also?

Susan Atkins, the Manson family member who murdered Sharon Tate, stated that she'd wanted to cut the baby out of the mother's womb after killing her, but they ran out of time and had to flee the scene. Oh, and the first names of the LaBiancas, the couple who died in the Manson family's continued killing spree the following evening? Leno and *Rosemary*, who just happened to live in a home once owned by Walt Disney.

One night, two Hollywood directors, one dead Presidential candidate and one dead pregnant actress-wife-witch, with both murders being foreshadowed in major Hollywood films directed by the two men sitting around the dinner table on June 5, 1968, along with the very victims of those tragic murders, which are forever engrained in the American psyche.

Demonic twin foreshadowings. You wanna' call the odds on that?

* * *

If you can dream it, you can do it.

--Walt Disney

ROMAN, HIGH PRIEST

Indeed, if everything surrounding RFK's Last Supper sounds rather Satanic to you, there could be a simple explanation for that.

Church of Satan founder Anton Lavey served as a technical adviser on Polanski's *Rosemary's Baby*, and there have been persistent rumors that LaVey played the uncredited role of Satan during the film's disturbing impregnation scene. Many view the movie as an occult manifesto, with Rosemary's baby as Aleister Crowley's "Child of the New Aeon," Horus, the son of Isis.

Roman Polanski is reported to be a Luciferian and to have been part of a powerful star-studded Satanic coven active in Laurel Canyon during the 1960s. (Some investigators even assert that he is a Luciferian High Priest who willingly sacrificed his own wife and unborn child.)

It is theorized that this coven had strong ties to nearby Lookout Mountain (discussed further in the next section) and played a key role in the assassination of RFK and with CIA MK-Ultra mass-murderer Charles Manson and his followers. This group of Aleister Crowley disciples has also been linked to other murders, as well as child pornography, drug trafficking, mind-controlled sex slaves and snuff films.

Rosemary's Baby involved a Satanic coven composed of the elite. Did the film mirror real life in this respect, as well, in that, like Guy Woodhouse, Polanski was also a member of a Satanic coven comprised of the Hollywood elite? Did Polanski know the diabolical script in advance: that Sharon Tate, pregnant with his child, would be murdered by mind-controlled Manson devotees?

THE GRAND CANYON

Laurel Canyon was second only to Haight-Ashbury as a mecca for hippies, who, according to former Governor of California Ronald Reagan, "looked like Tarzan, walked like Jane and smelled like Cheetah."

During the 1950s, Laurel Canyon had been home to many of the hippest young actors, including Marlon Brando, James Dean, James Coburn and Dennis Hopper. However, the Canyon's renewed popularity in the '60s was not some spontaneous, organic expression of Free Love that erupted from the collective unconscious, as there's good evidence that it was a methodically-constructed CIA-military social-engineering experiment, with many children of top intelligence and defense officials taking up residence there as if on cue.

Lookout Mountain Laboratory was a U.S. Air Force military installation located off of what is now Wonderland Park Avenue in Laurel Canyon that produced motion pictures and still-photographs for the Department of Defense and Atomic Energy Commission from 1947 until 1969.

Thought to be the world's only completely self-contained movie studio, Lookout Mountain had 100,000 square feet of floor space and contained sound stages, screening rooms, film-processing labs, editing facilities, an animation depart-

Roman Holiday

In March 1977, Roman Polanski was arrested in Los Angeles and charged with five offenses against 13-year-old Samantha Gailey: rape by use of drugs, furnishing a controlled substance to a minor, perversion, sodomy, and performing a lewd and lascivious act upon a child under 14. Polanski allegedly molested the girl during a photo shoot at the home of Jack Nicholson, who was away at the time. He subsequently fled to France.

Given everything we know and suspect about Polanski, it's no real surprise to find one of today's top "Illuminati" music stars, Nicki Minaj, among whose hit songs is "Roman Holiday," channeling an alter persona named … Roman Zolanski.

"Roman Holiday" (excerpt)

*Take your medication, Roman
Take a short vacation, Roman
You'll be okay
(Stop it mother please)
You need to know your station, Roman
Some alterations on your clothes and your brain
(Get me out of here, mother)
Take a little break, little break
From your silencing
There is so much you can take, you can take
I know how bad you need a Roman holiday
(Roman holiday)
A Roman holiday …
Quack quack to a duck and a chicken too
Put the hyena in a freaking zoo …
Come all ye faithful
Joyful and triumphant
I am Roman Zolanski*

ment and seventeen climate-controlled film vaults. The facility also had underground parking, a helicopter pad and a bomb shelter, and retained as many as 250 producers, directors, technicians, editors and animators, both military and civilian, all with top security clearances.

The studio produced some 19,000 classified motion pictures, and Hollywood luminaries like John Ford, Jimmy Stewart, Howard Hawks, Ronald Reagan, Bing Crosby, Walt Disney and Marilyn Monroe worked there on undisclosed projects.

Among the wave of new residents in the Canyon during the late 60s was The Doors' Jim Morrison, whose father was Navy Admiral George Stephen Morrison, the man who just happened to be in command during the Gulf of Tonkin Incident, or non-incident (some researchers say it never happened, at least not as described in the official account). Morrison was an avid student of the occult, with a particular fascination for the works of Aleister Crowley. (Who's your little buddy, there, Jimmy?)

BETTER LOOKOUT

Now, take a place like Laurel Canyon—just outside Hollywood, with a top secret military/intelligence production facility like Lookout Mountain—throw in a bunch of elite occultists, and you don't have to use a lot of imagination to envision the Canyon as a perfect incubator for exactly the kind of celluloid-turned-reality Satanist kookiness described earlier in this chapter.

Of course I've just scratched the surface here, but we should note a few additional items before we leave just to reinforce that point, including the following: Sharon Tate's father was Colonel Paul Tate of U.S. Army

Robert Kennedy purportedly once demanded of Lyndon Johnson, "Why did you have my brother killed?" RFK found Johnson to be "mean, bitter, vicious—an animal in many ways." "Johnson lies all the time," Robert remarked. "I'm just telling you, he just lies continuously, about everything. In every conversation I have with him, he lies. … he lies even when he doesn't have to." Observers have commented that as much as Johnson disliked JFK, he hated Robert Kennedy. Kinda makes you wonder what Johnson was doing on the night of June 5, 1968.

Intelligence; forensic hypnotist William Jennings Bryan, Jr., a reported MK-Ultra programmer with links to Sirhan Sirhan, served as technical adviser on *The Manchurian Candidate*; and Angela Lansbury, who played the control agent in *The Manchurian Candidate*, gave her daughter

Sinister Forces

Attribution: Much of the original research for this chapter is contained in the seminal *Sinister Forces* trilogy by Peter Levenda, who wrote the foreword for *9/11 as Mass Ritual*. Levenda's writing, like Michael Hoffman's, had a profound influence on Kent's work.

Didi written permission to travel with Charles Manson (damn straight, *Murder, She Wrote*).

That's about as far as I care to take this line of inquiry, and, basically, the only thing I've done here is the disservice of getting you just far enough into this labyrinth to get good and lost. If you care to, you can spend the rest of the decade sorting out all the connections and trying to find your way out with your sanity intact (if you dare, Google "Seven degrees of Charlie Manson").

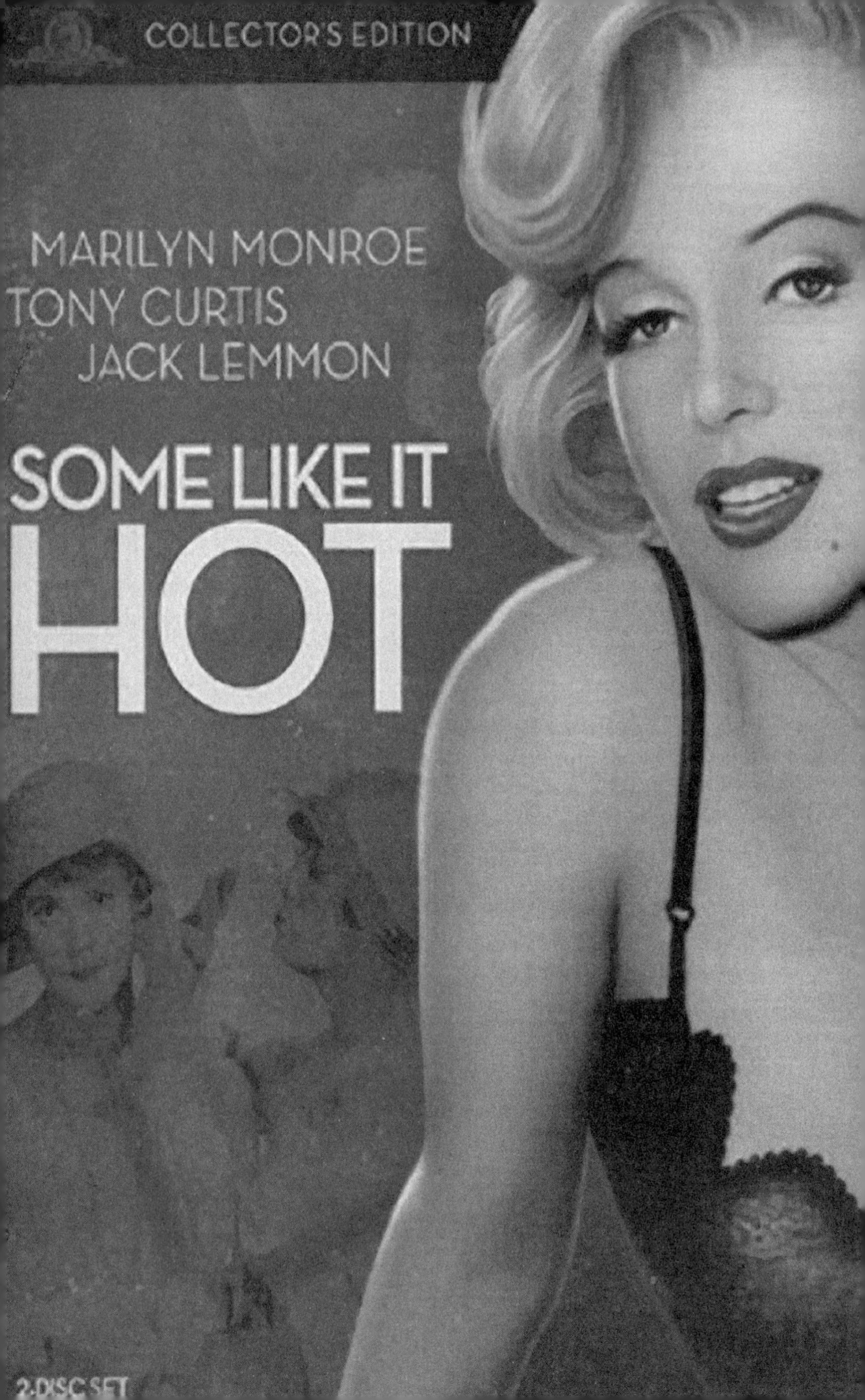
COLLECTOR'S EDITION
MARILYN MONROE
TONY CURTIS
JACK LEMMON
SOME LIKE IT
HOT
2-DISC SET

CHAPTER 40

BOMBSHELLS, BLONDE AND OTHERWISE

John F. Kennedy was friends with a number of the members of the "Rat Pack," including Frank Sinatra and Peter Lawford, Kennedy's brother-in-law, dubbed "Brother-in-Lawford" by Sinatra. When Kennedy visited them in Las Vegas, they referred to themselves as "the Jack Pack."

(Left) JFK and Sinatra. (Right) Fellow Rat Pack member Sammy Davis, Jr., was pals with Church of Satan founder Anton LaVey and Temple of Set founder Michael Aquino.

It was fairly well known at the time that actress Marilyn Monroe was having simultaneous affairs with both Jack and Bobby Kennedy. Decades later, when the FBI released its files on Senator Ted Kennedy following his death, there was one document of particular interest on this subject. It was a one-page memo from Jacqueline Hammond, the ex-wife of Ogden H. Hammond, a former US Ambassador to Spain.

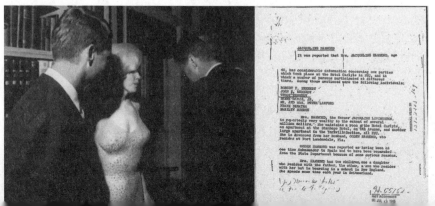

The 1965 memo states that Mrs. Hammond "has considerable information concerning sex parties which took place at the Hotel Carlyle in NYC," where she maintained a room, "and in which a number of persons participated at different times," including John, Robert and Teddy Kennedy, Sammy Davis, Jr., Peter Lawford and Marilyn Monroe. John Kennedy reportedly owned an apartment in the building, as well.

(Left) Marilyn? No, that's Jayne Mansfield and Anton Lavey. (Right) And speaking of Mansfield, an early Playboy Playmate who came to be known as the "Working Man's Monroe," that's her on the cover of Kenneth Anger's book Hollywood Babylon, *which details numerous sordid Hollywood scandals, and about which the* New York Times *wrote upon its second release (it was banned ten days after it was first published in 1965 and not republished until 1975), "If a book such as this can be said to have charm, it lies in the fact that here is a book without one single redeeming merit." Before achieving sex-symbol status, Mansfield won many local beauty pageants, including Miss Fill-er-up, Nylon Sweater Queen, Hot Dog Ambassador, Miss Geiger Counter and Miss Chihuahua Show.*

MK-MARILYN

Before becoming a major celebrity, and the object of affection of at least two of the Kennedy brothers, Marilyn Monroe, it is claimed, had a relationship with Anton LaVey, who, among other peculiar occupations, was a purported MK-Ultra handler.

But regardless of whether Monroe was subjected to mind-control programming by LaVey or anyone else, Kent discovered that it *is* true that she has in the decades since her death become a symbol for sex-kitten programming (i.e., mind-controlled sex slaves) in the entertainment business.

Monroe imitators Scarlett Johansson and Lindsey Lohan.

Britney Spears and Anna Nicole Smith: victims of sex-kitten programming, or just drugged-out morons?

DIED LIKE A DOG

"Shit. My life is shit," Marilyn Monroe once wept. For someone with so much talent, and such enormous popularity, Monroe in fact had remarkably little personal freedom. Whether mind-controlled or just controlled, she was under increasing strain from her isolation.

Did she take her own life, as it was reported she'd attempted on previous occasions? Or, was there something more to her death? She *was* becoming an increasing problem for John F. Kennedy for a variety of reasons, and an indication that perhaps something sinister was at work in her demise is this: as Kent wrote in his book, Marilyn Monroe was found dead on August 5th, a significant date on the occult calendar with deep connections to Sirius, the Dog Star. *Bitch.*

Speaking of sex-kitten programming, here are several scenes from Stanley Kubrick's Eyes Wide Shut. *Kubrick died six days after showing his final cut to Warner Brothers, some say as payback for revealing too much insider knowledge in the film.*

Hmmm, maybe Randy Quaid's "star-whackers" theory isn't so wacky after all.

MK-ULTRA RULES

Actress-comedienne Roseanne Barr recently told her interviewer on a Russia Today network program that "MK-Ultra Mind Control rules in Hollywood."

Well, of course it does, and it has for decades. The genuinely disturbing news is that our Masters now seem to have achieved the same level of control over the real world and its entire population as they have enjoyed in make-believe Hollywood for better than half a century.

Sexy Secret Agent

If '50s sex-goddesses Marilyn Monroe and Jayne Mansfield were targeted by MK-Ultra or other mind-control operations, they apparently weren't the only ones.

Jessica Arline Wilcox (1925–1990), known as Candy Jones, was a leading fashion model and pin-up girl in the 1949s and 50s, as well as a writer and radio talk show hostess. Wilcox was in fact one of the leading pin-up girls of the World War II era, appearing on the covers of 11 different magazines in one month alone in 1943.

In 1972, Jones married her second husband, John Zimmerman, a popular radio show host who went by the name of Long John Nebel, and she became the co-host of his all-night talk show on WMCA in New York City.

The show dealt with a range of engaging and controversial topics, including UFOs, the paranormal and conspiracy theories of all sorts. Author Donald Bain, no relation to Kent, wrote a biography of Zimmerman entitled, *Long John Nebel: Radio Talk King, Master Salesman, Magnificent Charlatan,* for which Jackie Gleason, a fan of Nebel's show and occasional guest, wrote the introduction. On one show, Gleason famously offered $100,000 to anyone able to provide physical proof of alien visitation, an amount he later upped to $1 million. "Why is [Nebel] so strangely entertaining?" Gleason asked rhetorically, "... because the best entertainment is entertainment that opens your mind and tells you the world is bigger than you thought it was."

Soon following his marriage to Jones, Nebel became concerned about her sometimes erratic behavior and began hypnotizing her, supposedly uncovering an alternate personality named "Arlene." Nebel recorded hundreds of hours of these sessions, during which Jones related an elaborate account of her training as part of a CIA mind-control program, much of which allegedly occurred at institutions of higher learning on the west coast.

Among the many experiences Jones recounted was one in which she claimed to have been subjected to a variety of torture methods, ostensibly to test the stability and dependability of her alternate persona. Jones' claims were first made public in 1976, in another book by Donald Bain, entitled, *The Control of Candy Jones,* published by Playboy Press.

The book was initially met with some understandable skepticism, considering that Long John Nebel was a prankster and a hoaxer of long standing, but Jones' story later gained a certain amount of credibility following the public disclosure of MK-Ultra in 1977.

[continued] Dr. Herbert Spiegel, a nationally recognized expert on hypnosis, wrote the forward to Bain's book, in which the author notes that in 1971, in an article published in *Science Digest* written by hypnosis expert George Estabrooks, the successful creation of amnesiac couriers of exactly the sort Jones claimed to have been was openly revealed.

Jones' claims of being a victim of government mind-control continue to intrigue to this day, with her story being featured more recently in an episode of *Dark Matters: Twisted But True* entitled "Sexy Secret Agent."

Jones' alleged experiences are also the subject of a song by Washington, D.C.-based indie rock band Exit Clov, appropriately entitled, "MK ULTRA":

> i remember the days of mkultra
> operation mind control
> my name is candy jones of mkultra
> graduated '74
>
> i survived cause i surrendered to the rules of mkdelta
> a committee artichoke
> feel the power of service, serving the enemy
> It's sexy, infect me!
>
> and in my dreams I see colors of kaleidoscope
> <inbrainwashington>
> and in my head I hear voices on the radio
> <inbrainwashington>
>
> tease me, police me, release me, uh oh!
> tease me, police me, release me, uh oh!
>
> thrill me, fulfill me, then kill me, uh oh!
> thrill me, fulfill me, then kill me, uh oh!

"HELP! I'm kidnapped!"

"HELP! I'm lost on a tropic island!"

"HELP! I'm surrounded by women!"

"HELP! keep our city clean!"

STOP WORRYING!

HELP!

IS ON THE WAY!

The Colorful Adventures of

THE BEATLES

are more Colorful than ever...in COLOR!

ALSO STARRING **LEO McKERN**

HELP YOURSELF TO SEVEN GREAT NEW BEATLE HITS!

ELEANOR BRON   VICTOR SPINETTI   ROY KINNEAR

PRODUCED BY WALTER SHENSON   SCREENPLAY BY MARC BEHM AND CHARLES WOOD   STORY BY MARC BEHM   DIRECTED BY RICHARD LESTER

EASTMANCOLOR   A WALTER SHENSON SUBAFILMS PRODUCTION   A **UNITED ARTISTS** RELEASE

CHAPTER 41

HAPPINESS IS A WARM GUN

Writing in his book, *Aleister Crowley: Magick, Rock and Roll, and the Wickedest Man in the World,* author Gary Lachman notes:

> Twenty years after his death, in the middle of the Swinging Sixties, Crowley was more popular than he ever was in his lifetime. In 1967, the Beatles put him on the cover of *Sgt. Pepper's Lonely Hearts Club Band.* The Rolling Stones became, for a time, serious devotees, their music and image being groomed by one of Crowley's most influential disciples, the avant-garde filmmaker Kenneth Anger. Today, his face is practically as well known as that of Elvis, Marilyn, or Che. His libertarian philosophies informed generations of notable heavy metal groups like Led Zeppelin, Black Sabbath, Metallica, and others, while these same beliefs form the subject of scholarly theses. His image hangs in goth rock bars, occult temples, and college dorm rooms alike, and he's turned up as a character in pop cultural environments from *Batman* comic books to Playstation video games.

In an interview with *Playboy* magazine, John Lennon revealed that the band's whole raison d'être was rooted in Crowley's famous law of Thelema ("Do what thou wilt shall be the whole of the Law. Love is the law, love under will.")

"The whole Beatle idea was to do what you want, right?" said Lennon. "To take your own responsibility. Do what you want and try not to harm other people, right? Do what thou wilst, as long as it doesn't hurt somebody..."

Yeah, well, maybe not so much on that last part there, as many Crowley followers tend to focus exclusively on the "Do what thou wilt" angle, a fact that Lennon, if he wasn't already fully aware of it at the time he made the statement, may have begun to figure out for himself in his later years, as we'll see in a paragraph or two.

(*Left*) *Kent always thought that a better title, at least for this particular limited-distribution version of the album cover, would have been,* Baby Dolls, Meat and Morons. (*Right*) *From the same photo shoot:* Eyes Wide Shut—*see no evil.*

THE NOT-SO-FAB FOUR

Kent knew that, as with so many subjects of a similar nature, you can all too easily find yourself being sucked into a quagmire of Beatles conspiracy theories, never to return.

He realized that the band had played an important role in the earlier years of the grand global social engineering scheme the planet is still being subjected to, but, quite frankly, he disliked their music to such an extent that he couldn't bring himself to do the research necessary to put their influence in proper context.

Kent understood that the Fab Four had been a vital part of the coordinated mass experimentation being conducted by the CIA, Britain's MI6

(*Left, Center*) *Kent could see why some researchers characterize Yoko Ono as a sorceress and master manipulator, perhaps even Lennon's handler, particularly in light of her remix album entitled,* Yes, I'm a Witch. (*Right*) *Yoko Ono, Andy Warhol and John Lennon enjoying each other's company.*

and the Tavistock Institute, utilizing all available tools, from rock music to psychedelic/psychotropic drugs to Satanic cults and everything in between, but even though his publisher encouraged him to explore the subject more fully, and even if trauma-based mind-control techniques had been employed on him, he simply couldn't bring himself to give a shit.

BEATLEMANIACS

In a *Playboy* interview shortly before his death, Lennon remarked, "We must always remember to thank the CIA and the Army for LSD. They invented LSD to control people and what they did was give us freedom."

Lennon seemed to have become aware, at least to a certain degree, of the infiltration, co-opting and corruption of the '60s counterculture—the rock music scene, especially—by government intelligence. What he may not have comprehended, however, was the role these agencies played in *initiating* mass cultural rebellion.

Lennon hinted that the Beatles had themselves been subjected to mind-control experimentation, primarily of the pharmacological variety, and he also intimated an awareness that "Beatlemania" had, to some extent, been simply another component of a wide-scale, multi-pronged, globalist social-manipulation initiative.

Apparently, some of the very same powerful interests who orchestrated this global enterprise viewed Lennon's remarks as talking out of school, and he soon thereafter had his deadly encounter with Manchurian Candidate Mark David Chapman.

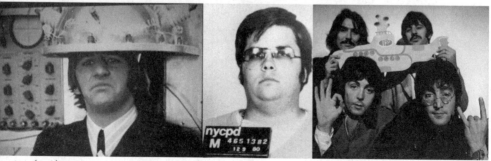

(*Left*) *Ringo Starr in* Help. *In real life, this probably wouldn't have produced any improvement.* (*Center*) *On the other hand, precisely the sort of thing that we see at left may have been what was wrong with Mark David Chapman in the first place. I wonder if he was a fan of* "Happiness is a Warm Gun" *on the* White Album? (*Right*) *The "boys."*

TIME TO GO

Lennon's comments in *Playboy* may not have been his only undoing, though, as his idea for a "revolutionary road show," starring himself and Yoko, very likely antagonized the hell out of the establishment. Envisioned as a combination of rock music and radical politics, the road show was to, as one observer wrote,

> ...barnstorm its way across America in the early summer and end up in a giant protest rally outside the Republican National Convention at San Diego, where President Nixon was almost certain to be nominated for re-election at the presidential elections that November. The aim was a huge "political Woodstock" that would successfully accomplish at San Diego in 1972 what Jerry Rubin and his colleagues had failed to achieve at Chicago in 1968: the disruption of a major party's national convention. An organization originally named the Allamuchy Tribe, and then the Election
>
>
>
> Year Strategy Information Committee, was set up with headquarters in the basement of Lennon and Yoko's apartment in Greenwich Village. No federal law was being broken in this, but it concerned a president of the United States, and was enough to get the FBI and the CIA crucially involved.

Although Lennon later backed down from the plan under threat of deportation from the United States, his actions apparently contributed to someone deciding he'd overstayed his welcome on planet Earth.

THE OTHER PAUL

In the fourth grade, one of Kent's friends suggested that he and two other pals should join him in masquerading as the Beatles. No, not form a Beatles tribute band, as none of them knew how to play any musical instruments or even remotely resembled any of the band members, just walk around telling classmates that they were the Fab Four.

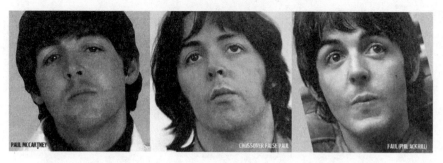

After ceremoniously announcing to the entire classroom that they were, in fact, the Beatles, they offered to sign autographs. One of the young girls in the class actually asked Kent, aka Paul McCartney, to sign her notebook, which he gladly did.

What little crowd had gathered then quickly dispersed, as that was basically the end of the show, and the entire charade didn't quite make it through two class periods, owing in no small part to the fact that very few of the kids knew who the Beatles were, including Kent, who'd never heard of the band, or Paul McCartney, before agreeing to pose as the musician. (This was rural northeast Mississippi in the late '70s, after all.)

Following his short-lived career as a Paul McCartney impersonator, Kent went back to his usual routine, which included attempting to devise ways to attract the attention of one of the young girls in his class; not the one who'd asked for his autograph, unfortunately.

His unsuccessful methods included, but were not entirely limited to, trying to break his leg, but he didn't put much more effort into that than he did his stint as Paul, primarily restricting his attempts at maiming himself to intentionally falling down on his knees on the playground, which didn't quite yield the intended result.

Kent had, again unsuccessfully, employed this same tactic the year before in the third grade—as part of a slightly Hinkley-esque strategy—in hopes of somehow (he never quite had it all worked out, but it would have involved media coverage of his injury) attracting the attention of actress Jessica Lange, with whom he had become mightily smitten after seeing her in the 1976 version of *King Kong* on the big screen. But since he never broke his leg, or even scraped his knee, his plan didn't go very far.

From the Writer-Director of "Gods and Monsters"

Liam Neeson   Laura Linney

KINSEY

Let's talk about sex

FOX SEARCHLIGHT PICTURES AND QWERTY FILMS PRESENT IN ASSOCIATION WITH MYRIAD PICTURES A N1 EUROPEAN FILM PRODUKTIONS/AMERICAN ZOETROPE/
PRETTY PICTURES PRODUCTION A BILL CONDON FILM LIAM NEESON LAURA LINNEY "KINSEY" CHRIS O'DONNELL PETER SARSGAARD TIMOTHY HUTTON JOHN L
TIM CURRY OLIVER PLATT DYLAN BAKER MUSIC BY CARTER BURWELL CO-PRODUCER RICHARD GUAY COSTUME DESIGNER BRUCE FINLAYSON FILM EDITOR VIRGINIA KATZ PRODUCTION DESIGNER RICHARD SHERMA
DIRECTOR OF PHOTOGRAPHY FREDERICK ELMES A.S.C. EXECUTIVE PRODUCERS MICHAEL KUHN FRANCIS FORD COPPOLA BOBBY ROCK KIRK D'AMICO PRODUCED BY GAIL MUTRUX WRITTEN AND DIRECTED BY BILL CONDON

www.otn-film.no

CHAPTER 42

PAGING DR. KINKEY

Pulitzer Prize-winning playwright Thomas Lanier "Tennessee" Williams was born in Columbus, Mississippi, one of the larger communities within the Mississippi Hills National Heritage Area.

In interpreting Williams' creative legacy, the heritage area's website of course makes no reference to his homosexuality, depression, or prescription drug and alcohol abuse, or to his friendship with Kenneth Anger.

Omitted as well is the fact that Williams, Anger and numerous of his friends contributed to celebrated sexologist Alfred Kinsey's groundbreaking survey on human sexuality. Kinsey's 1948 publication, "Sexual Behavior in the Human Male" (the first of the Kinsey Reports), was ostensibly one of the first attempts to scientifically investigate human sexual behavior, although both his methods and findings have been called into serious question in recent years.

Anger met Kinsey when he attended a Los Angeles screening of one of Anger's early films, which Kinsey purchased a copy of for $100 to place in his archives. It was Anger's first film sale and the beginning of a lifelong friendship, with Anger subsequently introducing the Father of the Sexual Revolution to LA's gay underworld.

* * *

The only unnatural sex act is that which you cannot perform.

--Dr. Alfred Kinsey

ALFRED AND KENNETH'S EXCELLENT ADVENTURE

Kinsey (left) and Anger in Thelema Abbey.

Not surprisingly, Kenneth Anger had plans to make a film about Aleister Crowley, the most-appropriate title for which would have been *The Wickedest Man in the World*, but this project never quite got off the ground. In 1955, however, Anger and his pal Alfred Kinsey traveled to the derelict Abbey of Thelema in Cefalù, Sicily in order to film a short documentary about the structure, which Aleister Crowley had used for his commune during the 1920s. Anger restored a number of the erotic wall paintings that Crowley and his disciples had left in the abbey, and performed certain Crowleyan rituals, as well.

(Left) Remaining visible frescoes of the so-called Hell or La Nature Malade. An excerpt of Crowley's poem Leah Sublime, written in honor of his Scarlet Woman, can be seen: "Stab your demoniac smile to my brain! Soak me in cognac, cunt and cocaine..." (Right) Detail of Earth: "Blonde Lady and Her Negro Lover: ease and delight are obtained by blending opposites."

(Left) Detail of the right side of the Mural of Heaven: "The Serpent may find itself utterly neglected by all creation, unable to communicate the Knowledge which would make man as Gods." (Right) Detail of Heaven: "Aiwass gave Will as a Law to Mankind through the mind of The Beast 666."

Turn The Page

"I feel Aleister Crowley is a misunderstood genius of the 20th century," Led Zeppelin guitarist Jimmy Page once said, and this wasn't merely some spur-of-the-moment, off-the-cuff comment, considering that in the early '70s Page owned an occult bookshop and publishing house, The Equinox Booksellers and Publishers, in Kensington High Street, London.

Page was initially commissioned by fellow Crowley enthusiast Kenneth Anger to write the soundtrack for *Lucifer Rising*, but the two had a falling out, with Anger accusing the musician of being too strung out on drugs to complete the project, and Page eventually released the music he wrote for the film via his website in 2012.

In 1970, Jimmy Page purchased Boleskine House, Aleister Crowley's old home on the shores of the famous Loch Ness in Scotland (Aleister Crowley: the *real* Loch Ness monster?), and Page also possessed, in Led Zeppelin biographer Steven Davis' words, "a priceless collection of Crowley artefacts: books, first editions, manuscripts, hats, canes, paintings, even the robes in which Crowley had conducted rituals."

It is also worth noting that Kenneth Anger early on took a deep interest in the careers of the members of *The Rolling Stones*, and it isn't difficult to recognize his influence.

AIDING AND ABETTING

During the course of his research, Kinsey ended up collecting over 10,000 sexual histories, one of which belonged to Rex King, "an Arizona pedophile who raped 800 children," wrote Kinsey colleague Wardell Pomeroy in his 1972 book *Dr. Kinsey and the Institute for Sex Research*.

Pomeroy went on to say that King was introduced to heterosexual intercourse by his grandmother and homosexual intercourse by his father, and engaged in sex with countless adults of both sexes, as well as animals.

Far from being a survey of the sexual activities of average Americans, the people in Kinsey's studies were primarily prostitutes and criminals, which were the only individuals willing to be involved in such research in that era. According to one researcher, "Eighty-seven percent of his subjects were sex addicts, homosexuals, criminals, rapists, prostitutes, pedophiles and prisoners."

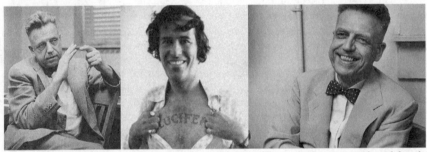

Kenneth Anger chose the Kinsey Institute as the archival home for his own work and for almost daily mailings on the subjects of sex, gender and reproduction. Don't ya know the clerical staff looked forward to opening that envelope.

Another social commentator observed, "The wide dissemination of both 'Sexual Behavior in the Human Male' (1948) and "Sexual Behavior in the Human Female' (1953) ushered in the age of pornography, free love, open marriage, wife-swapping (all of which Kinsey endorsed) and, perhaps the most pervasive social ill of all, the 50 percent divorce rate."

America's most well-known sex researcher, considered the "father of the sexual revolution," "not only relied on serial pedophiles for 'research data' on childhood sexuality, but actually protected and even encouraged those who committed

AGE	NO. OF ORGASMS	TIME INVOLVED	AGE	NO. OF ORGASMS	TIME INVOLVED
5 mon.	3	?	11 yr.	11	1 hr.
11 mon.	10	1 hr.	11 yr.	19	1 hr.
11 mon.	14	38 min.	12 yr.	7	3 hr.
2 yr.	{ 7 / 11	9 min. / 65 min.	12 yr.	{ 3 / 9	3 min. / 2 hr.
2½ yr.	4	2 min.	12 yr.	12	2 hr.
4 yr.	6	5 min.	12 yr.	15	1 hr.
4 yr.	17	10 hr.	13 yr.	7	24 min.
4 yr.	26	24 hr.	13 yr.	8	2½ hr.
7 yr.	7	3 hr.	13 yr.	9	8 hr.
8 yr.	8	2 hr.	13 yr.	3	70 sec.
9 yr.	7	68 min.	13 yr.	{ 11 / 26	8 hr. / 24 hr.
10 yr.	9	52 min.	14 yr.	11	4 hr.
10 yr.	14	24 hr.			

Table 34. Examples of multiple orgasm in pre-adolescent males.

Some instances of higher frequencies.

Table 34 from Sexual Behavior in the Human Male: "Examples of multiple orgasm in pre-adolescent males," with the age category beginning at five months and ending at fourteen years. Excuse me, but how the f*ck did you get that data?

such heinous crimes." Come again? "Kinsey and his colleagues ... refused to report to law enforcement the ongoing child molestation while compiling data."

Perhaps not surprisingly, Kinsey's funding came in part from the Rockefeller Foundation.

IN THE ATTIC

In addition to interviewing subjects, Kinsey filmed various sexual activities in the attic of his Bloomington, Indiana home, a helluva place to conduct legitimate scientific research.

With Mrs. Kinsey downstairs preparing iced tea and persimmon pudding for the volunteers, the camera rolled above on a whole series of sexual acts, including masturbation, a fact that Kenneth Anger personally attested to: "I believed in what they were doing and I wasn't going to refuse."

Filming was somewhat problematic, however, as Kinsey's cameraman only had one arm. As Anger explained, "He was trimming a hedge at home and the hedge-trimmer flipped out of his hand and cut off an arm. It was such a stupid, horrible accident, and for a photographer only to have one arm is kind of unfortunate."

THE FATHER OF LIES

Kinsey's research was not legitimate in any sense of the word, and he perpetrated what has perhaps been one of the biggest hoaxes in the history of the country on the unsuspecting American populace.

Millions have been negatively impacted by the grossly distorted view of human sexuality portrayed by Kinsey and his associates, and the nation's entire hyper-progressive sex-education establishment has been constructed on a foundation of falsehoods.

One of Kinsey's victims was a young girl whose grandfather had become a personal friend of Kinsey while studying at Indiana University. According to the victim, Kinsey enticed her grandfather to participate in his research, and he in turn recruited two of his sons to molest their own young daughters for "data collection purposes."

In 1943, at the age of nine, the girl found a checklist with a variety of sexual acts described on it, which her father was using to keep track of the things he was doing to her. One of the items listed included the phrase "timed orgasm," which the girl was unfamiliar with.

After her father discovered her with the list and grabbed it from her, she asked him what "orgasm" meant. He told her, and she then realized why he had been using a stopwatch. She also recalled that her father filmed some of the sessions and sent the footage to Kinsey.

The girl's father and grandfather were financially compensated by Kinsey, and she personally witnessed Kinsey handing her grandfather a check.

UN-HOLY TRINITY

The Sadistic Father of the Sexual Revolution, Alfred Kinsey, Kenneth Anger and Tennessee Williams: Kent wondered if some might consider the three as an un-Holy Trinity of sorts, but decided that lumping one of America's favorite playwrights in with the other two characters was probably a bit unfair. However, that may have simply been because Williams was a cultural icon from the Mississippi Hills, and as many people are aware, the only thing that oft-conflicted Southerners are more well-known for than rabidly opposing homosexuality in theory is staunchly defending those of their own with an alternative sexual orientation.

Kinsey, Anger and Crowley, however, are most assuredly birds of feather.

Crowley's derelict Abbey of Thelema in Cefalù, Sicily

FULL CIRCLE: FRANCO'S TENNESSEE

Franco and Oz, Franco and Anger, Franco and Faulkner, and now, Franco and Williams. When Kent read that James Franco was planning to take part in a séance to communicate with Tennessee Williams as part of New York City's *Performa 11*, a slight chill ran down his spine.

Franco and video artist Laurel Nakadate joined forces in November 2014 for a three-part production, called "Three Performances in Search of Tennessee," that kicked off with a séance conducted for the purpose of contacting the late playwright to seek his advice on an upcoming production of "The Glass Menagerie."

The second part of the piece consisted of Franco auditioning actresses for the part of Laura in the play, and the third act featured actors auditioning for the role of Tom.

Ironically enough, Franco had recently dropped out of what would have been his Broadway debut in the leading male role in Williams' "Sweet Bird of Youth" opposite Nicole Kidman. The production was postponed until director David Cromer could find a replacement.

Maybe Franco should have asked Tennessee what he thought about that.

Postscript: I *know* that kinky doesn't have an "e" in it, dammit.

PART EIGHT

THE FUN CONTINUES

A FILM BY STEVEN SPIELBERG

DUEL

DENNIS WEAVER

CHAPTER 43

MESSAGE RECEIVED

September 11, 2013: Blue Mountain, Mississippi

It was the first anniversary of his book's publishing, and the 12th anniversary of the September 11, 2001 attacks. The clock on his desk showed 9:00 p.m., and Kent had just finished doing a two-hour live presentation-interview with Conspiracy Culture bookstore in Toronto.

He'd worked with the owner to put together a 20-minute video especially for the occasion, and it had turned out fairly well. The entire event had gone smoothly for the most part, no technical glitches, no jerks in the audience with asinine questions or comments. Oddly enough, however, the store's technical guy, who'd spent hours working with him to help develop the video, had slipped out during the presentation, gotten thoroughly hammered, come back into the rear of the bookstore and was blathering loudly, creating a bit of a disturbance.

Kent appreciated the opportunity, but was glad it was over and began to unwind. The presentation had given him ample occasion to reflect on the first book, and his thoughts now turned to a possible second book.

TAKING HIS TIME

As Kent had watched the events in April unfold around him, and been able to interpret at least some of what was happening in almost real-time, he'd resisted the urge to blog about it. *It's going to take a book to unpack all this stuff*, he'd quickly realized; plus, he'd had an intuition that the fun wasn't over in April, and he also knew that with time and further research new revelations would come to light. He didn't want to tell a partial or inaccurate story. He decided he'd let things continue to unfold and not rush to provide play-by-play coverage.

A couple of weeks after the Twelve Days of Terror, Kent phoned his publisher, Kris Millegan at TrineDay Books, and gave him a quick pitch for a new book based on recent events. Kris was intrigued by the concept and given Kent the thumbs up on the project.

Kent had been making notes and doing other preliminary work, but now, months later, he had yet to begin writing in earnest. He also correctly suspected that the 2013 Mega-Ritual wasn't over yet.

Despite the fact that he was convinced he'd drawn some unwanted attention to himself and some real risk existed, he didn't have any question as to whether he'd write the new book. It was simply a matter of letting events continue to play out and finding time to write.

NIGHT TERRORS

As Kent prepared to get in bed and do some reading, he said goodnight to his son, William, and turned out the light in Will's room. Kent had been reading for about an hour when he heard Will get up and go into the bathroom. There was a loud crash, but Kent figured that the drowsy teenager had just knocked something over. Then, there was another, louder crash. Kent jumped out of bed and ran toward the bathroom.

William was just staggering out of the bathroom door as Kent reached him.

"What happened?" he asked William.

Will looked disoriented as he mumbled something unintelligible.

"What, buddy?" Kent said, his concern heightening.

Will was leaning against the door, staring straight ahead with a blank expression on his face. Suddenly, both his arms jerked outward at the same time.

"Will!" Kent cried, calling his son's name with an increased tone of desperation.

The involuntary movements repeated in sets of three, each lasting four or five seconds. Then Will's body would relax, and soon thereafter the movements would repeat.

Grabbing William by the shoulders, Kent tried to use a calm voice as he instructed his son, "Come on, let's get you back into bed."

The jerking motions continued after Will lay down, but began to decrease in frequency.

The overall effect had been one of watching someone subjected to a series of electric shock treatments. William had no prior history of seizure activity, and no signs that he was susceptible to seizures.

Kent was moments away from putting his son in the car and rushing to the emergency room, when the abnormal activity began to subside. Nonetheless, after Will rested for a few minutes, Kent decided to drive him to his mother's apartment in Tupelo so that they'd be near the North Mississippi Medical Center should another episode occur.

KEEP ON TRUCKIN'

Tupelo was about an hour's drive away, and as Kent made a left-hand turn onto Highway 78 in New Albany, an 18-wheeler turning right onto the same exit ramp ignored the yield sign and cut him off. As the big rig passed uncomfortably close to Kent's front bumper, the driver leered down at him and drove on. *Thanks, asshole, just what I needed tonight,* Kent thought to himself.

Kent's thoughts quickly returned to his son. *What had just happened? Would it recur?*

The dark highway stretched out before him as the familiar trip seemed to take longer than usual, and he had to constantly resist the urge to exceed the 70-m.p.h. speed limit by too much.

They were getting close to the Tupelo city limits when Kent noticed headlights in his rear view mirror on the near-empty stretch of highway, gaining steadily on him as he sped along in the right-hand lane. He didn't think anything of it as they had just passed an on-ramp.

When he glanced in the mirror again, he noted that it was an 18-wheeler, apparently waiting until the last minute to change into the fast lane just for kicks, as there was no vehicle in the left lane as far back as he could see. "Jackass," he muttered to himself.

PEDAL TO THE METAL

As Kent glanced quickly in his rear view mirror again, he saw that the truck was not slowing down, and not changing lanes. It roared up directly onto his bumper, and Kent didn't wait to find out if the driver was going to brake or not. He floored the gas pedal, and the 6-cylinder engine in his Mercury Milan roared to life as he shot away from the truck.

The trucker didn't attempt to match his speed and Kent put a good deal of distance between him and the big rig, keeping a close eye on the rear view. At his exit, he drove far enough up the ramp so that the passing trucker wouldn't have time to turn off and follow him, and then pulled over so he could observe the truck passing on the highway.

It had a white cab and a double trailer, just like the son of a bitch who'd cut him off at the exit in New Albany 20 minutes earlier. *That bastard drove on ahead, pulled off the highway and waited on the on-ramp for me to pass, and then roared up behind me,* Kent concluded. Would the truck have slowed at the last second or would it have rammed him? He had no way of knowing.

BENDING REALITY

Only a few weeks prior, Kent had watched Steven Spielberg's 1971 thriller film *Duel* for the first time. In the movie, a terrified motorist played by Dennis Weaver is stalked over an extended stretch of remote highway, being bullied and almost killed by an anonymous sadistic truck driver.

As he regained his composure and pulled back onto the road, Kent experienced a brief moment of relief, but only temporarily, as several things began to occur to him. His son has just had his first-ever seizure on the anniversary of his book's release, and it had come less than an hour after his special presentation with Conspiracy Culture bookstore in Toronto. Then, as he was attempting to get his son to his mother's apartment in Tupelo, where she'd re-located after her apartment in the Smoky Mountains burned on the day that he signed his book contract, some psychopath re-enacted Spielberg's *Duel*, which Kent had just seen recently for the first time in his life.

Kent wasn't one to go around ascribing everything that happened to the machinations of one conspiracy or another, and he was also familiar with, and had personally experienced, the phenomenon of synchronicity. But he also knew patterns, and he was fully familiar with the *modus operandi* of those who'd orchestrated 9/11 and the Boston Bombings. He knew about microwave and psychotronic weaponry, and also about gang-stalking.

Now, it seemed as though his only son could well have been the target of a brutal form of payback, a form that cloaked itself in a veil of plausible deniability. *What the hell have I done?* he wondered.

The rest of the evening was uneventful, save the loss of a lot of sleep that night and for many nights to come. The next morning, Kent took Will to the doctor, who ordered a series of tests and set up additional tests for later in the week: CAT scans, blood work, EEGs, etc. The doctor's office also made an appointment with a pediatric neurologist at Le Bonheur Children's Hospital in Memphis, although it ended up being close to six weeks away.

A TURN FOR THE WORSE

About a week later, Will had another nocturnal seizure of approximately the same nature and intensity. Again, they headed out to Tupelo to spend the night, just in case further medical treatment was warranted, and in the days that followed Kent continued to work to get an earlier appointment with a specialist.

Thankfully, Will's initial tests had shown no major causes for concern, no brain abnormalities or sign of brain injury. Kent finally succeeded in getting an appointment with a pediatric specialist in Memphis the first week in October, but, as the situation took a very nasty turn, it turned out they wouldn't need it.

The night of September 30, William had a grand mal seizure and was transported by ambulance to Le Bonheur Children's Hospital in Memphis. He underwent further testing and was diagnosed with a form of epilepsy, which of course can have numerous causes, natural and otherwise.

The new book? Well, it'd have to wait. As a matter of fact, Kent began to question seriously whether he should scrap the project altogether. Whether what happened to his son was payback, or a warning to back off, or both, Kent had gotten the message.

CHAPTER 44

HOLY MOSES!

September 16 and October 3, 2013: Washington, D.C.

Mid-September, civilian contractor Aaron Alexis, who claimed to be hearing voices and under assault via some type of extremely-low-frequency (ELF) electromagnetic device, kills 12 employees at the Washington Naval Yard before being killed in a shootout with police.

A little over two weeks later, dental hygienist Miriam Carey, who claims she is hearing the voice of President Barack Obama in her head, is shot to death by law enforcement officers at the U.S. Capitol after attempting to gain vehicular access to the White House.

By the way, if you're a little rusty on your Biblical history, Aaron and Miriam were Moses' siblings: Aaron his older brother and spokesperson, and Miriam senior to them both and a prophetess in her own right.

Both Alexis and Carey were hearing voices, both were African American, both were 34 years old, and they died less than two miles from each other 17 days apart in Washington, DC, in which neither of them lived. Carey lived in Stamford, CT, site of a mass ritual on Christmas Day, 2011, which Kent detailed in a chapter of his book that was removed before publishing. The chapter was subsequently posted on the book's website and entitled, "The Lost Chapter."

THE PROMISED LAND

Aaron and Miriam, along with Moses, led the Children of Israel out of Egypt, through forty years of wandering in the desert and to the Promised Land, although none of the three actually got to enter it. The four biblical books of Exodus, Leviticus, Numbers and Deuteronomy tell the story of their lives.

Contrary to popular belief, it was Aaron's staff, not Moses', which, when cast down before Pharaoh and his magicians, turned into a snake and it was Aaron, not Moses, who held out his staff, thereby triggering the first of three plagues against Egypt. (Aaron Alexis certainly did not share the biblical Aaron's most notable personality trait, that of peacemaker.)

But that's neither here nor there, because we get the Moses joke, and we get the broader point. These two poor souls were yet others in a seemingly endless series of victims who by all appearances were subjected to one or more types of mind-control/behavior-modification techniques (technological, pharmacological, trauma-based programming or any combination thereof).

BETTER OFF THIS WAY

Alexis had filed a police report in Rhode Island on August 2, 2013, in which he claimed to be the victim of electronic harassment and stated that he was hearing voices in his head. A message from Alexis obtained by federal authorities reportedly stated, "Ultra low frequency attack is what I've been subject to for the last 3 months. And to be perfectly honest, that is what has driven me to this." Alexis also carved the phrase "My ELF weapon" on his shotgun before the attack.

The second line reads "My ELF Weapon!" Above that, it appears that Alexis less successfully attempted to inscribe "Better off this way!" which could simply be a straightforward statement, or it could also be a reference to the song of the same name by the metalcore-pop-punk band, A Day to Remember, the lyrics to which include the following lines: "It's all over, I found a better way / To help keep you from me, I'm better off this way." A day to remember, indeed.

Media reports of mental illness with both Alexis and Carey were no surprise, as in practically every instance of this sort the perpetrators *do* suffer from one form of mental imbalance or another. They're either chosen by the controllers *for that very reason* or *made that way* through various means. Lots of classified research has been done on the best methods to drive people nuts, and there's no shortage of practitioners.

The blatant Moses reference and everything else concerning these two related incidents in DC again smacked of the same Revelation of the Method technique Michael Hoffman had written about and that Kent had observed in prior staged events. *Through the structure of the events and the subsequent media coverage, they're telling us what they're doing to us, it's a matter of whether or not we choose to, or have the sense to believe it,* Kent concluded.

294

MEAT PUPPETS

After much research, after everything he'd learned about 9/11, the Boston Bombings and so many other staged events, Kent had come to a most disturbing conclusion. Yes, these things are about demonstrating control over all aspects of existence; yes, they weave together highly creative, sophisticated, insanely funny scripts involving false-flag terrorism, industrial and corporate sabotage, psychological warfare and occult ritual, but the big prize is *us*.

They've demonstrated complete mastery over everything in the material world seven ways from Sunday, but their most cherished act is demonstrating complete mastery of *us*, of human consciousness. We're their little playthings, windup toys, meat puppets. They are the Puppet Masters.

LIGHTS, CAMERA, ...

Indeed, what good is a script without actors? And what fun is it to hire actors? No, the major points in these Hunger Games are awarded for demonstrating absolute control over the unwitting contestants.

The Cryptocracy expends much treasure in concocting their diabolical scripts and setting their elaborate stages—using the real world as their theatre, their coliseum—but the show does not begin until the

---

"Master of Puppets" Excerpt

... Master of Puppets I'm pulling your strings
Twisting your mind and smashing your dreams
Blinded by me, you can't see a thing
Just call my name, 'cause I'll hear you scream ...

Come crawling faster
Obey your Master
Your life burns faster
Obey your Master
Master ...

Master, Master, where's the dreams that I've been after?
Master, Master, you promised only lies
Laughter, Laughter, all I hear or see is laughter
Laughter, Laughter, laughing at my cries
Hell is worth all that, natural habitat
Just a rhyme without a reason
Neverending maze, drift on numbered days
now your life is out of season
I will occupy
I will help you die
I will run through you
Now I rule you too

Come crawling faster
Obey your Master
Your life burns faster
Obey your Master
Master ...

295

hapless pre-programmed characters show up on location, on cue, in exactly the right place at exactly the right time, to kill and/or be killed, many times without having the faintest clue as to what is happening to them or why. (Now that's logistics, baby!)

ALL IN FUN

Some victims do, however, have some idea that something's being done to them against their will. Purported (deceased) Boston Bomber Tamerlan Tzarnaev believed that he was under "majestic mind control." James Eagan Holmes, the alleged sole gunman in the Aurora/*Dark Knight Rises* theatre shooting, reportedly told a cellmate that his former psychotherapist had programmed him to kill.

Also, as Kent noted in his book, Sirhan Sirhan's lawyers have argued in court, with good evidence to back up the claim, that he was the victim of mind-control programming. And who can forget Lee Harvey Oswald's famous statement at Dallas Police Headquarters: "I'm just a patsy." (Some researchers claim that Oswald was in fact a *mind-controlled* patsy, who could possibly have even had a device implanted in his brain during his time in Russia, but who the hell knows?)

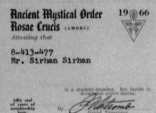

The CIA and Department of Defense, along with untold numbers of private corporations and university research centers, as well as black-project programs we'll never know anything about, have been working feverishly on mind-control techniques and technologies for decades and have made tremendous strides since the 1950's. But that's old news. Haven't you seen *The Bourne Identity*?

No, what we're dealing with here is a practically omniscient, omnipotent global cabal that uses tried-and-true as well as cutting-edge mind-control methods to program the unsuspecting citizenry to unknowingly commit large-scale crimes, participate in grotesque mass rituals and fulfill their roles in diabolical scripts written by the psychopathic controllers of society for their own enrichment and amusement.

No Taking It Back

This is all, or partially at least, about fun and entertainment for the elite. Kent considered naming his second book *Fun House U.S.A.: Carnival of Terror* (he also considered *The Golden Jubilee of the Killing of the King*, but rightly figured that nobody would have any idea what he was talking about), but now it appeared that there wasn't going to be a next book.

These are the most dangerous, ruthless people in the world, and I might have not only managed to get their attention, but to have genuinely antagonized them, Kent reflected. The more he understood about who they were and how they operated, the more he began to wish he'd never even written the first book, but there was no way to take it back now

'THE BIG

BAMBOOZLE

PHILIP MARSHALL

CHAPTER 45

...AND YOUR LITTLE DOG, TOO

O ne particular incident that had occurred earlier in 2013 now began to be of greater concern to Kent. On February 2, the same day that Chris "America's Sniper" Kyle was gunned down, 9/11 researcher and author Philip Marshall was found dead along with his two teenage children in the gated community of Forrest Meadows, California, east of Sacramento.

In what authorities labeled a murder-suicide, Marshall, author of the controversial conspiracy book, *The Big Bamboozle: 9/11 and the War on Terror* (and also *False Flag 911: How Bush, Cheney and the Saudis Created the Post-911 World*), and his children were killed execution style, each with a single gunshot wound to the head. The family dog was also found shot to death.

PERSONAL INSECURITY

A ccording to those who knew him, Marshall had no history of mental illness or depression, was a devoted father and did not have financial problems. He did not appear to have been particularly distraught leading up to the killings, and he had on multiple occasions expressed concerns about his personal safety due to the nature of his published work.

Investigative journalist and conspiracy theorist Wayne Madsen, who, like Kent, attended the University of Mississippi, was a lieutenant in the U.S. Navy until his retirement in 1985. During his time in the service, Madsen claims to have been put on loan to the National Security Agency (NSA) and to have subsequently worked for RCA as a government consultant on contracts for the NSA.

Madsen asserts that during his own investigation into the murders, he discovered that:

1. the crime scene had been illegally scrubbed by professionals prior to the completion of the official investigation;

2. a side door Marshall never used was found wide open;

3. none of Marshall's neighbors heard gunshots yet the 9mm Glock allegedly used in the shootings had no silencer on it; and

4. all of his neighbors believed the killings were a professional hit.

Further, according to Madsen, Marshall had stated that he was in possession of explosive information that would be revealed in his next book. Marshall's computer reportedly disappeared after the murders.

SHUT THE HELL UP

Although Madsen's credibility and research have been called into question on more than one occasion, and the information he claims to have uncovered during his own investigation would have been easy enough to fabricate, serious questions remain.

An article in the *Santa Barbara View* published shortly after the murders reads:

> During the editing and pre-marketing process of Marshall's book, he expressed some degree of paranoia because the nonfiction work accused the George W. Bush administration of being in cahoots with the Saudi intelligence community in training the hijackers who died in the planes used in the attacks.
>
> "Think about this," Marshall said last year in a written statement, "The official version about some ghost (Osama bin Laden) in some cave on the other side of the world defeating our entire military establishment on U.S. soil is absolutely preposterous."
>
> Marshall went on to say: "The true reason the attack was successful is because of an inside military stand-down and a coordinated training operation that prepared the hijackers to fly heavy commercial airliners. We have dozens of FBI documents to prove that this flight training was conducted in California, Florida and Arizona in the 18 months leading up to the attack."
>
> The veteran pilot confided that he was concerned about his 10-year, independent 9/11 study and most recent book since they pointed to the Saudis and the Bush intelligence community as the executioners of the attack that defeated all U.S. military defenses on Sept. 11, 2001. Marshall said he knew his book might cause some people to take issue with him.

"After an exhaustive 10-year study of this lethal attack that used Boeing airliners filled with passengers and fellow crew members as guided missiles, I am 100 percent convinced that a covert team of Saudi intelligence agents was the source of logistical, financial and tactical resources that directed essential flight training to the 9/11 hijackers for 18 months before the attack," Marshall wrote. "This conclusion was determined six years ago and all subsequent evidence has only served to confirm this conclusion."

Marshall made some damning allegations in his book, allegations that could well have caused those involved to do more than "take issue" with him. Kent strongly suspected that if the killings of Marshall and his children had not been a black-ops hit, then the truth might be even more disturbing, although very much in line with what he had uncovered in so many tragedies he'd studied.

As Kent's research indicated, another entirely plausible scenario would have Philip Marshall serving in the role of killer, either through mind-control programming or some form of coercion (i.e., You do it quick, or we'll take our sweet time with your sweet children.)

The murders could have been payback for *The Big Bamboozle*, or, if Madsen were correct concerning Marshall's claim of yet-to-be-revealed "explosive information," an effective way to pre-emptively shut him up. Or both.

A MESSY BUSINESS

Marshall had also been an airline captain for 20 years with major carriers, and before that, a pilot for the CIA and DEA in the years leading up to the Iran-Contra Scandal, during which time he rubbed elbows with some unsavory characters, including Barry Seal.

Lots of people have made a lot of accusations regarding 9/11, and while it's one thing to jump on this bandwagon, it's quite another to threaten to spill the beans on covert activities of the Company (CIA) that you were personally involved with. The latter carries with it an automatic death sentence, and these operators won't hesitate to off a couple of immediate family members as part of the deal just to make the point to others who might be contemplating going public with their own stories.

Kent had made some rather compelling allegations in his own book on 9/11, and although he was no former Company pilot, given recent events involving himself and his family, he had growing concerns that the situation might escalate. That, for example, he, like Philip Marshall, might end up on the floor of his home in a pool of his own blood with dead children and pets strewn about the house.

REMEMBER WHO THE ENEMY IS

THE HUNGER·GAMES:
CATCHING FIRE

LIONSGATE PRESENTS A COLOR FORCE / LIONSGATE PRODUCTION "THE HUNGER GAMES: CATCHING FIRE" JENNIFER LAWRENCE JOSH HUTCHERSON LIAM HEMSWORTH WOODY HARRELSON ELIZABETH BANKS LENNY KRAVITZ
PHILIP SEYMOUR HOFFMAN JEFFREY WRIGHT WITH STANLEY TUCCI AND DONALD SUTHERLAND CASTING DEBRA ZANE C.S.A. MUSIC SUPERVISOR ALEXANDRA PATSAVAS MUSIC BY JAMES NEWTON HOWARD COSTUME DESIGNER TRISH SUMMERVILLE EDITOR ALAN EDWARD BELL A.C.E.
PRODUCTION DESIGNER PHILIP MESSINA DIRECTOR OF PHOTOGRAPHY JO WILLEMS S.B.C. EXECUTIVE PRODUCERS SUZANNE COLLINS LOUISE ROSNER-MEYER JOE DRAKE ALLISON SHEARMUR PRODUCED BY NINA JACOBSON JON KILIK SCREENPLAY BY SIMON BEAUFOY AND MICHAEL deBRUYN
PG-13 DIRECTED BY FRANCIS LAWRENCE NOVEMBER 22 republic #TICKTOCK LIONSGATE
EXPERIENCE IT IN IMAX
THEHUNGERGAMESEXPLORER.COM

Chapter 46

Fifty Years To-The-Day

November 22, 2013: Dallas, Texas

As the first public commemorative service held in Dealey Plaza since JFK's assassination, the ceremony marking the 50th anniversary of the event was relatively modest and tasteful, featuring the tolling of church bells, a moment of silence, readings and remarks by Pulitzer-Prize-winning historian and Presidential biographer David McCullough. The ceremony also featured a performance by the U.S. Naval Academy Men's Glee Club, honoring the former President's service in the Navy.

Two days prior to the 50th anniversary of JFK's assassination, President Obama and the first lady, accompanied by former President Bill Clinton and former Secretary of State Hillary Clinton, laid a wreath at President Kennedy's grave.

The memorial was fittingly conducted at the exact place and time where Kennedy was killed as his motorcade travelled through downtown Dallas in 1963. Earlier that day, at Arlington National Cemetery, U.S. Attorney General Eric Holder visited the graves of both JFK and RFK.

MARKING THE OCCASION

The previous year in November of 2012, a JFK Tribute had been dedicated in downtown Fort Worth, Texas, where, incidentally, Kent was born in 1968. The exhibit features a bronze statue of Kennedy and a granite wall with photographs and quotes from the president. It is located near the site where JFK gave one of this last two public speeches on the morning of November 22, 1963, before he was assassinated two hours later in nearby Dallas.

Yet, while all of the activities on the 50th anniversary of the assassination were quite touching and poignant, pulling at the heart strings of millions of Americans and others watching around the world, those who were responsible for orchestrating the Killing of the King and so many other events since chose to commemorate the occasion in quite a different fashion.

HECKUVA RELEASE DATE

As Kent noted would be the case months in advance on his blog, the major motion picture based on the second book in the *Hunger Games* trilogy, entitled *Catching Fire*, was released on 11/22/13. It had previously become abundantly evident (see next chapter for more) that the Cryptocracy was quite smitten with the premise of the trilogy as a metaphor for their own dark machinations.

And now, they saw fit to use the release of the latest installment in the series to brand the anniversary of their original evil deed with this morbidly humorous stamp. As Adam Weishaupt, founder of the Illuminati, once famously stated, "We shall set all in motion and in flames."

* * *

"We shall set all in motion and in flames."

--Adam Weishaupt

THE HUNGER GAMES:
MOCKINGJAY
PART 1
IF WE BURN YOU BURN WITH US
NOVEMBER 21
EXPERIENCE IT IN IMAX

PHOENIXPX.DEVIANTART.COM

CHAPTER 47

EXTENDED METAPHOR

The Sandy Hook school shooting that took place on December 14, 201, contained an intriguing and obvious *Hunger Games* connection.

Of all the places to live in America, trilogy author Suzanne Collins resides in the little village of Sandy Hook in Newtown, Connecticut, which is the home of an outpost of the Church of Satan (aka, the Church of Tiamat), and whose second-largest employer is Masonicare, the state's leading provider of healthcare and retirement living communities for seniors.

(Left) Suzanne Collins. (Center).Sandy Hook victim Vickie Soto, with the white-haired warlock throwing the horns in the background. (Right) Fellow victim Emilie Parker: sign language for "I love you," or ...

Sandy Hook is also situated just 25 miles from Skull & Bones headquarters in New Haven, Connecticut and, not that this necessarily means anything, but the local Masonic Lodge in Sandy Hook is barely 100 yards from the elementary school where the massacre allegedly occurred.

Strike Zone 1

As Kent noted in a post on his book's website following the tragedy, the *Hunger Games*:

> … revolves around a futuristic storyline dealing with the ritual exploitation and killing of innocent youths for the entertainment of the super-rich/elite ruling class—and its author just happens to live in the same Connecticut small town where a real-life slaughter of innocents takes place just 7 days before the much-ballyhooed Mayan Apocalypse and 11 days before Christmas, not to mention the fact that we immediately start to find all the classic hallmarks of a staged mass terror attack, making this by all appearances a *real-world Hunger Games*.

But there's an additional Sandy Hook connection to another big Hollywood hit which Kent also discussed his blog post:

> In "The Joke's on Us," the chapter in [my book] about the Aurora, CO, theater shooting, I discuss that event in some detail, revealing not only that Aurora was the mother of Lucifer in mythology, but that the date on which the shooting occurred, July 20th, is the Grand Climax on the Satanic calendar. July 20th was also the official release date for *The Dark Knight Rises* (*TDKR*), which was showing in the auditorium that James "I am the Joker" Holmes allegedly launched his assault in.
>
> Many of you are by now probably well aware of the map of Gotham shown in *The Dark Knight Rises*, which quite clearly shows the words, "Sandy Hook," in an area labeled "Strike Zone 1"…

So, *The Dark Knight Rises* predicts "Sandy Hook" as "Strike Zone 1" months in advance, and *Hunger Games* author Suzanne Collins just happens to live there. Damn, what a coincidence.

Oh, but they're not done with the *Hunger Games* trilogy yet—not by a long shot.

DON'T EVEN PRETEND

A ctor Philip Seymour Hoffman, who played head game-maker—and, subsequently, resistance leader—Plutarch Heavensbee in *Catching Fire*, was found dead of an apparent heroin overdose on Big Game Day, Super Bowl Sunday, February 2, 2014, the very same day Chris Kyle was shot to death and Philip Marshall and his kids were found dead the previous year. The takeaway from Hoffman's death:  you even *pretend* like you're going to stand up to us and we'll kill you.

And there's the lone gunman, identified as 22-year-old Elliott Rodger, accused of killing six and wounding seven in a rampage near the University of California Santa Barbara campus in Isla Vista on May 23, 2014, the son of Peter Rodger, an assistant director on *Catching Fire* who is among other things credited with creating the propaganda film used in the movie—Bernays would be so proud.

This is what they do—create a dizzying interplay between fantasy and reality. Recall Oz Pistorius and *Oz the Great and Powerful* on Valentine's Day, and the Luxor hot air balloon tragedy two weeks later. In his book, Kent discussed the use of this predictive programming in the years leading up to 9/11, and the many statistically improbable hidden references that have been discovered since.

Fairly soon, he thought, *we won't be able to tell the difference between fact and fiction.* Exactly as planned.

(Left) Peter Rodger, who rubbed elbows with Hollywood heavyweights such as Steven Spielberg and George Lucas. (Center) Peter and Elliott Rodger at the premiere of Hunger Games *in 2012. (Right) A frame from a video made by self-professed virgin Elliott Rodger explaining why he was going on a killing spree: "College is the time when everyone experiences those things such as sex and fun and pleasure. But in those years I've had to rot in loneliness. It's not fair. You girls have never been attracted to me. I don't know why you girls aren't attracted to me. But I will punish you all for it. I'll take great pleasure in slaughtering all of you."*

All Hunger, No Game

Virgin killer (not virgin-killer) Elliott Rodger had a particularly strong crush on the young woman pictured above, who is lucky to be alive. In his disturbing 141-page manifesto, Rodger claimed that Monette Moio, now a model, "teased and ridiculed him." Referring to Moio as an "evil bitch," Rodger wrote, "To be teased and ridiculed by the girl I had a crush on wounded me deeply."

However, this rejection occurred when Elliott was 12 and Monette was 10 (apparently he wasn't one to move on), and on top of that, she wasn't even aware that he liked her. "The funny part of this," wrote Rodger, "is that I had a secret crush on Monette. She was the first girl I ever had a crush on, and I never admitted it to anyone."

Moio's father, a Hollywood stuntman, told the press, "She was ten years old for God's sake–she can barely remember the guy. He's a sociopath. ... He was weird then and he's weird now." (Actually, he's dead now, but anyway). "He had a secret crush on her, but she was completely unaware of him. She had no idea... If you think about it, he could have killed her, he could have come after her."

Yeah, he sure could have.

TWISTED SISTER

The highest-grossing action heroine of all time, in 2014 Lawrence topped the list of *Forbes'* Most Powerful Actresses as well as *FHM's* 100 Sexiest Women in the World. The *Hollywood Reporter* referred to her as "the ideal screen actress" and *Rolling Stone* called her "the most talented young actress in America." Prior to *The Hunger Games*, not one of the top 200 worldwide box-office hits ever ($350 million and up) had been built around a female action star. Talk about a ground-breaking performance.

Although he'd been fortunate enough to be in close proximity to her on occasion, apparently Elliott Rodger wasn't so delusional as to believe he'd ever have a shot at—uh, change that to "chance with"—Hunger Games' stunning lead actress Jennifer Lawrence.

Lawrence's attractiveness and acting ability are key factors in the tremendous commercial success of the films, which has made them even more potent metaphors for the Cryptocracy. Leave it to them to twist such beauty into something negative.

WITNESS TO CARNAGE

Elliott Rodger's late grandfather, George Rodger, a renowned British war photographer who gained notoriety for his gripping wartime shots, had the unfortunate distinction of having been the first photographer to capture on film the horrors of the Nazi concentration camp at Bergen-Belsen in 1945. The elder Rodger took iconic photos of Jewish survivors and mass graves there and elsewhere in the final weeks of World War II.

Good thing George wasn't around to witness the carnage left behind by his grandson.

PART NINE

A December to Remember

OZZY OSBOURNE

BLIZZARD OF OZZ

"MR. CROWLEY"

Recorded Live On Stage

CHAPTER 48

SPOUTING DEVIL

December 1, 2013: The Bronx, New York City

At 7:22 a.m., as the Metro-North Railroad Hudson Line passenger train headed into the curve 100 yards north of the Spuyten Duyvil station in this borough of the Bronx, it was traveling at 82 m.p.h. in a 30 m.p.h. zone.

In his cab, William Rockefeller, a 15-year Metro-North veteran with 10 years' experience as an engineer, dumped the brakes in an emergency maneuver, but it was too late. The train was already entering the curve. All seven cars and the locomotive left the tracks, the cab coming to rest just short of the Harlem River. Four of the 115 passengers were killed and another 60 or so injured, 11 critically. It was the deadliest train accident in New York City since 1991.

The New York City Fire Department dispatched 125 firefighters to assist in the rescue operation; some EMS workers were delayed in reaching victims as they waited for power to the third rail to be turned off. Survivors were taken to a resource center set up at nearby John F. Kennedy High School.

NTSB investigators soon determined that there had been no problems with the tracks or signals. Rockefeller's blood tests were negative for both drugs and alcohol, and his cellphone records showed that it had not been in use at the time of the accident.

Rockefeller later admitted to investigators that he had drifted into a "daze," likened to "white-line fever" or "highway hypnosis" experienced by truckers, until immediately before entering the curve. Rockefeller had recently switched from the afternoon to the early shift; yet, this may not have played a role in the events of that day. The night before the accident he had reportedly gotten adequate sleep and arrived at work on time, with other employees having observed him in a characteristically alert state.

However, two days after the accident, the head of the Metro-North union said that Rockefeller had "nodded off" before the derailment, and a day later Rockefeller was suspended without pay. Federal investigators would later reveal that the engineer had, since the accident, been diagnosed with severe obstructive sleep apnea, a complication of his obesity. Blood taken after the crash had also been found to contain a small amount of an over-the-counter antihistamine in it.

INHUMAN ERROR

Now, one lacking in curiosity and investigative instincts could easily enough dismiss the possibility of sabotage by concluding, based upon the evidence presented, that the cause of the crash was, plain and simple, a fat-ass engineer who snorked too much cold medicine and fell asleep at the wheel. And if you want to take the easy way out, that's your business. However, there are some things you might want to consider before doing so.

First, December 1st is the date of death of Aleister Crowley, the godfather of modern Satanism, whose memory his followers and admirers frequently commemorate on this day through a variety of means, often involving the death of innocent sacrificial victims, animal and human. Apparently a death-day is just as good as, or even better than, a birthday to these sorts of folks.

As Kent documented in his book, Crowley was the "guest of honor" in the 9/11 Mega-Ritual, with numerous Crowley references woven throughout the structure of the event. There was even a big fat Crowley reference embedded in the JFK assassination that Kent mentioned in *Mass Ritual*.

Second, Spuyten Duyvil is Dutch for "Spouting Devil," which Crowley most certainly was. Third, Spuyten Duyvil is located less than two miles from the Riverdale, New York, home that the Kennedys occupied for a couple of years during JFK's youth, during which time he attended the 5th through the 7th grade at Riverdale Country School, a private school for boys where actor Chevy Chase also studied. Author Tom Wolfe's New York City-based bestseller *The Bonfire of the Vanities* includes many references to Riverdale. (Come on, if you'd somehow forgotten the Golden Jubilee, the above mention of JFK High School should have jogged your memory.)

HOOKED ON CROWLEY

S peaking of Crowley, or speak of the devil, and referring back to the last chapter, in the same blog about Sandy Hook, Kent wrote:

> Given the central diabolical role that the *TDKR* map played in this Ritual [Batman] Trilogy, one might be tempted to think that some black magician had a hand in its creation, and, well, you may just be right: the production designer for the *Dark Knight* trilogy was none other than one Nathan Crowley.
>
> Ooo, ooo, ooo—there's the obligatory Crowley reference, you're thinking excitedly. Apparently, that's not the half of it, as this Crowley is actually related to the Great Beast. In the June 2008 edition of *The Art Newspaper*, he informs us, "Yes, Aleister Crowley is a direct relative, he's my grandfather's cousin..."
>
> And get this: the April 7, 2012, edition of *The Stamford Advocate* (Stamford, CT, is about 40 miles from Newtown, of which Sandy Hook is an affluent village) contains a story reporting the death of one Scott Getzinger, who died in an automobile accident, and the article mentions that Getzinger's injuries were at first considered non-life threatening by police. A motion picture property master, Getzinger was responsible for all props used in a film, and not only had he been prop master on *The Dark Knight Rises*, but he was also a resident of ... Newtown, CT. You just can't make this stuff up.

Indeed, you can't. But they can, and do, all the time.

IT'S BEGINNING TO LOOK A LOT LIKE ...

L astly, some people might try to make something of the fact that the last name of the engineer was Rockefeller, but we'll leave that one alone. We can close this chapter, however, by noting that one of the four killed

in the Spuyten Duyvil crash was James G. Lovell, 58, a veteran audio technician with 20 years of experience on the To-day show. Lovell was on his way to work that December morning to assist in setting up the Christmas tree at Rocke-feller Center Plaza, which prominently features a massive golden statue of Pro-metheus-Lucifer. Tis' the season.

THE CURSE OF SPUYTEN DUYVIL CURVE?

Spuyten Duyvil curve was the scene of another deadly rail accident more than 130 years ago. The disaster was featured in the cover story of *Rail-road Stories*, a pulp magazine for train enthusiasts, more than a half-century later in 1935. In "The Wreck at Spuyten Duyvil," H.R. Edwards wrote:

> A light snow was swirling around the Chicago-New York Express as she double-headed out of Albany at 3:06—twenty-six minutes late—on a gray after-noon of 1882, straightened her "string of varnish" after leaving the yards, and settled down for the 142-mile run to New York City.
>
> It was Friday the 13th. Although there were thir-teen wooden cars in that train, the possibility of a jinx didn't seem to worry the seventy-seven politi-cians who were traveling southward from the New York State capital on free passes given by the New York Central & Hudson River Railroad.

Apparently, the seventy-seven (77) politicians and everybody else should have been worried about a jinx, or something just as bad.

The train had just passed Spuyten Duyvil and travelled about a third of a mile, when one of the airbrakes gave out. Fortunately, the train was brought to a stop about two hundred yards from the notorious curve, which was one of the sharpest on the entire line.

That's when their luck ran out, however. A missed signal and the black of night prevented operators on an approaching train, the Tarry-town Special, from seeing the Express as it sat motionless on the tracks. The Special slammed into the stalled train, igniting a fire that killed a dozen passengers.

One of those killed in the crash was Webster Wagner, five-term State Senator and inventor of the sleeping car, who, according to a headline from the time, was "burned to a crisp in one of his own luxurious cars." Volunteers struggling to put out the fire with snow had about as much success as one might expect, and the scene was all-around a gruesome one.

One news report from the disaster read, "The number `thirteen' seems to run like a theme song through the history of this occurrence. It was Friday the 13th, there were thirteen cars on the express, and the local was running thirteen minutes behind the express."

Three thirteens (and a seventy-seven): Triple bad luck… or something else? Either way, this historical precedent made Spuytin Duyvil a highly-attractive locale for the 2013 sabotage.

IT IS AN IDEAL FOR WHICH I AM PREPARED TO DIE.

IDRIS ELBA
NAOMIE HARRIS

MANDELA
LONG WALK TO FREEDOM

CHAPTER 49

A TIMELY DEATH

December 5, 2013: London, England

The crowds and Press were out in force at London's Odeon Leicester Square for the Royal Premiere of *Mandela: Long Walk to Freedom*, hoping to catch a glimpse of Prince William and Kate, Mandela's daughters Zindzi and Zenani, and the star of the film, British actor Idris Elba.

(Left) The Princess and Prince. (Center) Zindzi and Zenani Mandela. (Right) Prince William exhibiting a curiously disingenuous expression of concern following the announcement of Mandela's passing.

During the premiere (some media reports say immediately preceding), Zindzi and Zenani received word of their father's passing and left the theater, asking that the film play to the end uninterrupted. As the credits were rolling, producer Anant Singh got up on stage and informed the audience of Mandela's death. Gasps, cries of disbelief and sobs were followed by a communal 'Minute of Silence'.

The news had apparently come as a surprise to his daughters, as Zindi had just commented on her father's health earlier that evening on the red carpet, saying that he was "fine," adding, "He's just a typical 95-year-old who is frail."

"It was extremely sad and upsetting news," Prince William told the press afterward. "We were just reminded what an extraordinary and inspiring man Nelson Mandela was." Idris Elba, who portrayed Mandela, echoed William's sentiments, telling reporters, "We have lost one of the greatest human beings to have walked this earth."

What are the odds? A man lives for 95 years, having been both an internationally-admired prisoner for freedom and a global symbol of hope, and midway through the London premiere of a major motion picture about his life—at which his daughters and the Duke and Duchess of Cambridge are in attendance—he shuffles off his mortal coil. Talk about dramatic timing … it was practically Monty-Pythonesque: *Enjoy the film? Good. He's dead.*

AN EMBARRASSING SPECTACLE

Death is something inevitable. When a man has done what he considers to be his duty to his people and his country, he can rest in peace. I believe I have made that effort and that is, therefore, why I will sleep for the eternity.

--Nelson Mandela

Perhaps the only thing as interesting as the timing of Mandela's death was the spectacle that followed on December 10th. To begin with, the stadium was only two-thirds full, and the crowd that was there displayed a distinct lack of class, booing the host of the event, South African President Jacob Zuma, whenever he appeared on the jumbotron. But that wasn't the half of it.

President Barack Obama was in attendance at the memorial, along with former Presidents George W. Bush, Bill Clinton and Jimmy Carter

and numerous other dignitaries and important guests. Obama's remarks that day were poignant:

> To Graça Machel and the Mandela family; to President Zuma and members of the government; to heads of states and government, past and present; distinguished guests—it is a singular honor to be with you today, to celebrate a life like no other. ...
>
> It is hard to eulogize any man—to capture in words not just the facts and the dates that make a life, but the essential truth of a person—their private joys and sorrows; the quiet moments and unique qualities that illuminate someone's soul. How much harder to do so for a giant of history, who moved a nation toward justice, and in the process moved billions around the world.
>
> Born during World War I, far from the corridors of power, a boy raised herding cattle and tutored by the elders of his Thembu tribe, Madiba would emerge as the last great liberator of the 20th century. Like Gandhi, he would lead a resistance movement—a movement that at its start had little prospect for success. Like Dr. King, he would give potent voice to the claims of the oppressed and the moral necessity of racial justice. He would endure a brutal imprisonment that began in the time of Kennedy and Khrushchev, and reached the final days of the Cold War. Emerging from prison, without the force of arms, he would—like Abraham Lincoln—hold his country together when it threatened to break apart. And like America's Founding Fathers, he would erect a constitutional order to preserve freedom for future generations ...

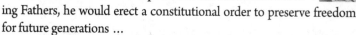

> ... he accepted the consequences of his actions, knowing that standing up to powerful interests and injustice carries a price. "I have fought against white domination and I have fought against black domination. I've cherished the ideal of a democratic and free society in which all persons live together in harmony and [with] equal opportunities. It is an ideal which I hope to live for and to achieve. But if needs be, it is an ideal for which I am prepared to die."

Obama continued,

> ... Mandela understood the ties that bind the human spirit. There is a word in South Africa—Ubuntu—a word that captures Mandela's greatest gift: his recognition that we are all bound together in ways that are invisible to the eye; that there is a oneness to humanity; that

we achieve ourselves by sharing ourselves with others, and caring
for those around us. ...

we achieve ourselves by sharing ourselves with others, and caring
for those around us. ...

We will never see the likes of Nelson Mandela again. ... Over 30
years ago, while still a student, I learned of Nelson Mandela and the
struggles taking place in this beautiful land, and it stirred something
in me. It woke me up to my responsibilities to others and to myself,
and it set me on an improbable journey that finds me here today.
And while I will always fall short of Madiba's example, he makes me
want to be a better man. He speaks to what's best inside us.

After this great liberator is laid to rest, and when we have returned to
our cities and villages and rejoined our daily routines, let us search for his
strength. Let us search for his largeness of spirit somewhere inside of ourselves. And when the night grows dark, when injustice weighs heavy on
our hearts, when our best-laid plans seem beyond our reach, let us think
of Madiba and the words that brought him comfort within the four walls
of his cell: "It matters not how strait the gate, how charged with punish-
ments the scroll, I am the master of my fate: I am the captain of my soul."

What a magnificent soul it was. We will miss him deeply. May
God bless the memory of Nelson Mandela. May God bless the people of South Africa.

Although the words Obama spoke were certainly befitting of the occasion, they may or may not have been his own, although there's nothing
unusual in this, of course. All Presidents have professional speech writers
they depend on to craft effective messages for addresses such as this one.

Whoever authored the speech, one would like to believe that the words
accurately represented the President's personal sentiments; however, his
actions while not at the podium might be cause to question just exactly
how emotionally or intellectually engaged Obama was at this particular
event. And that's putting it mildly.

"HE OWES THE WORLD AN APOLOGY"

Conservative commentators in particular were irritated that Obama
had gone out of his way to seek out and shake the hand of Fidel Castro's brother, Raúl, who has been the President of
the Council of State of Cuba and the President of
the Council of Ministers of Cuba since 2008. Raúl,
a Marxist-Leninist politician and revolutionary, is
also Commander in Chief of the Armed Forces and
has been First Secretary of the Central Committee
of the Communist Party of Cuba since 2011.

Obama's propensity towards glad-handing and/or bowing to noxious characters is certainly not a new phenomenon, however, and Mandela was likewise criticized for his friendship with Fidel Castro, Muammar Gaddafi, Akbar Hashemi Rafsanjani and others, as well as his refusal to criticize their various human rights violations.

No, what received the most attention that day was something far less weighty: a Presidential selfie. Knowing full well that many of the world's leaders were present and that the entire media world, as it always is, was watching his every move, Obama proceeded to engage in what many viewed as highly inappropriate behavior, especially given the solemnity of the occasion and *whose* memory was being observed.

A piece in the *New York Daily News* commented that "normally reserved President Obama and Brit PM David Cameron act[ed] like nerds around a pretty girl, as they yucked it up and posed for selfies with Danish dish Prime Minister Helle Thorning-Schmidt."

A controversial article in the *New York Post*, entitled "Flirty Obama owes us an apology," went even further:

> The president of the United States, leader of the free world, standard-bearer for everything upright, good and wholesome about the nation he leads, lost his morality, his dignity and his mind, using the solemn occasion of Nelson Mandela's memorial service Tuesday to act like a hormone-ravaged frat boy on a road trip to a strip bar.
>
> In front of 91 world leaders, the mourning nation of South Africa and Obama's clearly furious wife, Michelle, the president flirted, giggled, whispered like a recalcitrant child and made a damn fool of himself at first sight of Denmark's voluptuously curvy and married prime minister, Helle Thorning-Schmidt.
>
> Not to be outdone by the president's bad behavior, the Danish hellcat hiked up her skirt to expose long Scandinavian legs covered by nothing more substantial than sheer black stockings.

The piece referred to Thorning-Schmidt as a "Danish cupcake," and went on to say that "The president's cackling head moved inches from the Danish tart's." (Cupcake, tart, same difference.) "Obama then proceeded to absorb body heat from the Dane, which he won't be feeling at home for a long time."

Mandela, opined the article's author, was "a man who Obama compared at the memorial to Abraham Lincoln, Mahatma Gandhi and Dr. Martin Luther King. And here was the president, publicly behaving as if he was plotting his next hookup. ... He owes the world an apology."

Thorning-Schmidt, who subsequently bore a perhaps disproportionate share of the blame,* later attempted to laugh off the whole thing, saying, "It was not inappropriate." And maybe she was correct, at least in this sense: it was not *merely* inappropriate, it was the definition of inappropriate.

The Word of the Year, the Selfie of the Year and the Stink-Eye

And speaking of definitions, just the previous month, the Oxford English Dictionary had named "selfie" the word of the year. Wow. What a coincidence. One month selfie is named word of the year, and the next President Obama is excoriated for including himself in the Selfie of the Year at a

memorial service for a man he himself referred to as "a giant of history" and "the last great liberator of the 20th century," who "makes me want to be a better man."

No wonder Barack was on the receiving end of Michelle's now-famous "stink-eye" (don't bother looking that up because it's not in the dictionary…yet). As noted in *The Atlantic*, "Barack Obama's remarks at a memorial service for Nelson Mandela in Johannesburg were just one of the many notable things about his appearance there. There was that handshake with Raul Castro. The selfie with British Prime Minister David Cameron and Danish Prime Minister Helle Thorning-Schmidt. And then there was the latest instance of Michelle Obama

giving 'le boss de la Maison Blanche' what some French news outlets are inartfully calling 'le regard noir'—literally 'a black look,' or what we call stink-eye." The Presidential Selfie and the Stink-Eye. Beautiful.

---

* Sexual bias given what it is even on the international stage, the *Guardian* newspaper noted, "Although both Obama and Cameron came in for criticism, it was Thorning-Schmidt who bore the brunt of the outrage. Described as a narcissist in the Daily Mail, she was forced to defend her actions at home. 'There were lots of pictures taken that day, and I just thought it was a bit of fun,' she told the Danish newspaper Berlingske. 'Maybe it also shows that when we meet heads of state and government, we too are just people who have fun.'" People who have fun—at a memorial service. Then again, maybe she deserved the extra criticism. This is, after all, the same person who insisted on wearing stilettos—with fatigues, no less—when she traveled to war-torn Libya. When asked about her wardrobe choice, she snarled, "We can't all look like sh-t."

"I SEE ANGELS…"

Certain commentators went so far as to say that the tone of some of the media coverage surrounding the international incident had evoked the image of the "Where the white women at?" scene from Mel Brooks' *Blazing Saddles*.

But you gotta admit, the Preezy of the United Steezy shakin' hands with a commie, snappin' selfies, flirtin' with a white woman, and Michelle givin' him the stink-eye—at a memorial service…for Nelson Mandela. That's good stuff (especially when, as Joan Rivers told us in 2014, everybody knows that Obama is gay and Michelle's a tranny). Could it possibly get any better?

Well, yes. Again, from the *New York Daily News*: "Among the bizarre events that went viral faster than a flu epidemic were those of the phony sign language interpreter/real life criminal Thamsanqa Jantjie, who stood on stage seeming to translate speeches, but in fact was just flapping his hands around like a crazed seal."

Jantjie would later claim that he was hallucinating due to a schizophrenic episode: "What happened that day, I see angels come to the stadium … I start realizing that the problem is here. And the problem, I don't know the attack of this problem, how will it come. Sometimes I get violent on that place. Sometimes I will see things chasing me."

Further, on the day of the memorial service, Jantjie was due for his regular six-month mental-health checkup to determine if his medication was working or needed to be changed, or whether he needed to be admitted to a facility for treatment, the AP reported. According to at least one account, government officials subsequently attempting to track down the company that hired Jantjie for the memorial discovered that the owners "have vanished into thin air."

Jantjie was not your run-of-the-mill mental patient, though. Media reports would quote friends of Jantjie asserting that he had been part of a group that burned two people in 2003. According to *CTV News*:

> Just when it seemed the scandal over the bogus sign language interpreter at Nelson Mandela's memorial had run its course, a cousin and three friends say he was part of a mob that accosted two men found with a stolen television and burned them to death by setting fire to tires placed around their necks.
>
> Thamsanqa Jantjie never went to trial for the 2003 killings when other suspects did because authorities determined he was not mentally fit to stand trial, the four told The Associated Press Monday. They spoke on condition of anonymity because of the sensitivity of the fake signing fiasco, which has deeply embarrassed South Africa's government and prompted a high-level investigation into how it happened. ...
>
> Instead of standing trial in 2006, Jantjie was institutionalized for a period of longer than a year, the four said, and then returned to live in his poor township neighbourhood on the outskirts of Soweto. At some point after that, they said, he started getting jobs doing sign language interpretation at events for the governing African National Congress party.
>
> Jantjie told the AP that he has schizophrenia, hallucinated and believed he saw angels while gesturing incoherently just 3 feet away from President Barack Obama and other world leaders at the memorial on Tuesday. Signing experts said his arm and hand movements were mere gibberish.
>
> In the interview Thursday, Jantjie said he had been violent "a lot" in the past, but declined to provide details. He blamed his behaviour on his schizophrenia, saying he was institutionalized for 19 months, including a period during 2006.

The article continued,

> The 2003 killings, carried out by a grisly method known as "necklacing," occurred a few hundred yards (meters) from Jantjie's tidy

concrete home, according to the cousin and friends, one of whom described himself as Jantjie's best friend.

Necklacing attacks were fairly common during the struggle against apartheid, carried out by blacks on blacks suspected of aiding the white government or belonging to opposing factions. But while people who encounter suspected thieves in South Africa have been known to beat or kill them to mete out punishment, necklacing has been rare in such cases.

An investigation is underway to determine who hired Jantjie for the Mandela memorial service and whether he received security clearance. Government officials have not said how long the investigation will take.

Four government departments involved in organizing the memorial service have distanced themselves from Jantjie, telling the AP they had no contact with him. A fifth government agency, the Department of Public Works, declined to comment and referred all inquiries about Jantjie to the office of South Africa's top government spokeswoman, who has only said a "comprehensive report" will eventually be released.

Jantjie told the AP he was hired by an interpretation company that has used him on a freelance basis for years. ... The owner of the company, South African Interpreters, was identified by the *Sunday Times* as Bantubahle Xozwa, the head of a religious and traditional affairs agency of the ANC.

Xozwa told the newspaper that Jantjie was an administrator in his company but was not an interpreter because he was "was disqualified years ago on the basis of his health."

"He was interpreting at the memorial service in his personal capacity," Xozwa said. The ANC has said it had no role in hiring Jantjie for the memorial, but has acknowledged using him at events in the past. ...

The Deaf Federation of South Africa has said it filed a complaint with the ANC about bogus signing by Jantjie at a previous event where South African President Jacob Zuma was present.

"We will follow up the reported correspondence that has supposedly been sent to us in this regard and where necessary will act on it," the ANC said in a statement last week.

The AP was unable to verify the existence of the school where Jantjie said he studied signing for a year. An online search for the school, which Jantjie said was called Komani and located in Eastern Cape Province, turned up nothing. Advocates for the deaf say they have never heard of the school and there are no known sign language institutes in the province.

Good to see they got that all cleared up. In any case, we're left with a schizophrenic who has a history of violence (of burning people to death, in particular) gesticulating incoherently three feet away from the President of the United States (good job, Secret Service). Rush Limbaugh's dream, perhaps, but certain-

ly damn funny and irresistible fodder for the writers at *Saturday Night Live*.

CERTAIN DEATH

If all of this is starting to strike you as one big charade—from the Royal Premiere to the Selfie of the Year to the Pyro-Schizo—you're on the right track, but what may be the biggest charade of all is this: Mandela may have been dead (or at least brain dead) for months before the dramatic announcement of his passing in London.

Internet rumors circulated that he'd been in a vegetative state since June, kept alive on a ventilator, supposedly due to some inter-family wrangling over his estate. Whether or not this is true, whether his departure was delayed, or hastened, we should have no doubt that the timing of his death (or at least the announcement of it) was coordinated, through whatever means, to coincide with the movie premiere.

It doesn't really matter if we figure out who was involved or who knew what when. Mandela had a chronic respiratory illness, and at the age of 95, no one is going to think a whole lot about how it happened when the time comes for you meet your maker. But you can be sure that Mandela would have died, one way or the other, in 2013.

Birds of a Feather

Kent wrote about the wide array of occult symbolism incorporated into the opening and closing ceremonies of the 2012 London Olympics, especially the flaming phoenix and its burning nest. He found it more than a little interesting that in this context, at this gathering of world leaders, an image strikingly similar to that of the famed resurrection bird presided over the proceedings as part of the South African coat-of-arms. A phoenix look-alike, adorned with a crown of rays, rays of illumination ... here, in this place where Mandela and his legacy were so callously disrespected, just as Kennedy and his memory were disrespected and mocked throughout the entire year.

Following the memorial fiasco, Mandela's body lay in state at the Union buildings in the capitol of Pretoria. Yes, we've come full circle now, and while we're back in Pretoria we might as well say hello to Oscar "Oz" Pistorius. And if you're thinking that this has been one deep rabbit hole (not that it's over just yet), you'll get a kick out of this little bit of royal trivia: while attending the School of Art History at the University of St. Andrews, Princess Kate wrote an honors thesis entitled "Angels from Heaven: Lewis Carroll's Photographic Interpretation of Childhood."

DEADLY CLOCKWORK

The timing of a death can bear tremendous significance, as we know all too well. Recall the passing of Huxley and Lewis on November 22, 1963, or the deaths of Adams and Jefferson on the 50th anniversary of the signing of the Declaration of Independence. All were in poor health, agreed—yet this only made the job easier and less suspicious.

As a global symbol of hope and freedom, Nelson Mandela was indeed a fitting sacrifice** for the Golden Jubilee, the 50th anniversary of the killing of another iconic symbol of hope, JFK. The same psychopathic elite who assassinated John F. Kennedy, Robert Kennedy, Martin Luther King, Jr., and so many others made damn sure that they added Mandela to their list of victims, even if a bullet was not the chosen instrument of death, and even though he may have already been at—or halfway through—death's door.

R.I.P., Mandiba. To quote President Obama, "We will never see the likes of Nelson Mandela again."

** The act may have been all the more fitting if one believes the revelations of author William Blum in "How the CIA Sent Nelson Mandela to Prison for 28 Years," a chapter in his book, *Rogue State: A Guide to the World's Only Superpower*, in which Blum asserts that during the Kennedy administration the CIA was directly responsible for Mandela's arrest and subsequent lengthy imprisonment.

Blum reveals how "a CIA officer, Donald C. Rickard by name, under cover as a consular official in Durban, had tipped off the Special Branch that Mandela would be disguised as a chauffeur in a car headed for Durban. This was information Rickard had obtained through an informant in the ANC...Rickard himself, his tongue perhaps loosened by spirits, stated in the hearing of those present that he had been due to meet Mandela on the fateful night, but tipped off the police instead."

Such is purportedly the real story behind how Mandela, aka The Black Pimpernel, was arrested in Howick, Natal, in 1962. Further emphasizing his point, Blum writes that, "after Mandela's release, the White House was asked if Bush (Sr.) would apologize to the South Africans for the reported US involvement in his arrest at an upcoming meeting between the two men...Spokesman Marlin Fitzwater replied: 'This happened during the Kennedy administration...don't beat me up for what the Kennedy people did.'"

The Dark Side

Excerpt from "Mandela Love Fest Ignores Dark Side of Legacy," published December 6, 2013, on *Infowars.com*:

… Nelson Mandela stands atop a hallowed pedestal in the pantheon of political correctness. His struggle against the scourge of apartheid—government sanctified racism—was fashioned into a human rights struggle by the establishment and its propaganda media. The distorted image of Saint Mandela has been dutifully scrubbed of its dark side. …

Here's what you won't hear. Nelson Mandela was a terrorist. His Umkhonto we Sizwe, the military wing of the African National Congress, targeted civilians.

On May 20, 1983, Umkhonto we Sizwe (aka "Spear of the Nation") set off a car bomb near the Nedbank Square building on Church Street in the South African capital of Pretoria. The bomb was timed to go off at the height of rush hour. The attack killed 19 people and wounded 217. …

MSNBC and CNN and even Fox will not mention this today as they celebrate Mandela's "extraordinary example of moral courage, kindness, and humility," as the White House put it.

Of course, it is hardly surprising the government and its media would praise a terrorist and make him out to be saint. It does this all the time.

From Taliban "freedom fighters"…who would later become convenient enemies to the creation and support of al-Qaeda and its terrorist operations in Afghanistan, Bosnia, Libya, Syria and elsewhere, the U.S. government remains actively in the business of manufacturing terrorists, although most of them are not anointed with sainthood like Nelson Mandela.

But, when you think about it, Mandela is merely a low-level terrorist when stacked up against the sort of psychopaths and knuckle-draggers the U.S. government has supported over the years, including General Augusto Pinochet in Chile and General Suharto in Indonesia, to name but two.

Pinochet, with the help of the CIA, disposed of political enemies by throwing them out of helicopters. He was also behind a terrorist car bombing in Washington, D.C., that killed Chile's ambassador and American citizen Ronni Moffitt. Suharto, a brutal dictator who was installed by the CIA, massacred countless thousands of his fellow Indonesians and arrested and tortured more than 750,000 others.

Other notable examples include Pol Pot in Cambodia. His genocidal Khmer Rouge was favored by the ruling elite as a counter force to Vietnam after it fell to communists outside the bankster sphere of influence. It would take the country a couple decades to transform itself into a globalist slave labor gulag.

It probably will not be mentioned today or in the coming week that in the not too distant past the government Obama now represents (or reads a teleprompter for) supported racists in South Africa and Rhodesia.

Reagan, who liked to fashion himself a libertarian (or his speechwriters did, anyway), supported P.W. Botha's South African government and its "total war" on a black majority. Nixon did likewise when Ian Smith's Rhodesian government engaged in starving to death citizens who wanted to throw out the white minority government ruling with an iron fist.

The list of favored thugs and mass murderers is long and sordid. It includes tenacious bankster support for Adolf Hitler and the Nazis (supporters included members of the Bush crime family).

Finally, while Obama and the establishment lionize Mandela and couple him to the struggle for human rights in Africa, the Pentagon continues its move into the continent under the rubric of AFRICOM, the U.S. military command for Africa. In order to put this into perspective, consider the invasion of Libya that killed more than 30,000 of the north African nation's citizens and installed al-Qaeda and the crazed jihadists.

AFRICOM is designed to pacify the region ahead of normal bankster operations conducted by the World Bank and the IMF. AFRICOM's mission was underscored by Vice Admiral Robert T. Moeller at Fort McNair on February 18, 2008, when he declared the guiding principle of AFRICOM is to protect "the free flow of natural resources from Africa to the global market."

Nelson Mandela is another establishment-generated distraction. His sanitized presence in the manipulated flow of corporate media propaganda and entertainment fluff is designed to bolster the latest tool of domination devised by the ruling elite—color and culturally based political correctness. All who disagree or take issue with the ruling elite and their plan for global domination are dismissed as scurrilous racists and haters.

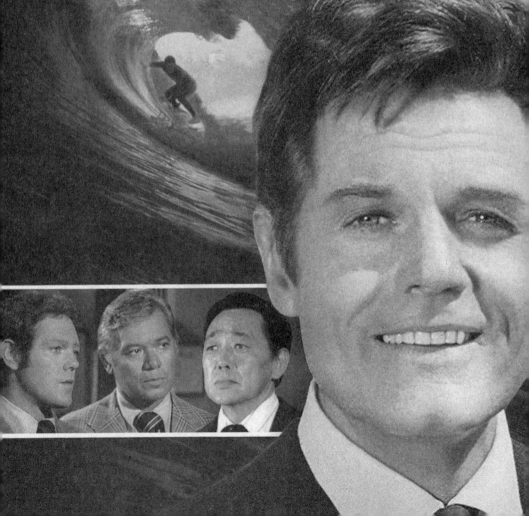

CHAPTER 50

DEATH OF A STATESMAN

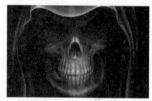

By now, particularly after the last chapter, hopefully you're convinced that it's routine practice for the Cryptocracy to provide the grim reaper a little assistance and give the aged or infirm a little push over to the other side in order to time their crossing to coincide with a specific date—ritual euthanasia, if you will (which is still ritual murder, and, one supposes, beats ritual torture).

WARM-UP ACT

Reflecting on the events of the year to date (thankfully 2013 was almost over), and mindful of the purposeful timing of Mandela's death, or at least the announcement of it, and further recalling the similar auspicious passing of Presidents Adams and Jefferson, as well as Huxley and Lewis, it occurred to Kent that there may have even been a *pre*-Pre-Twelve-Days component of the Golden Jubilee celebrations, a preview of things to come.

December 21, the annual date of the Winter Solstice, in the year 2012: this was to be the exact date, according to many alternative researchers (notice I did not use the word scholars), of the much-ballyhooed Mayan Doomsday.

Everybody from the History Channel to the *Star-Reporter* jumped on the bandwagon, feverishly purveying this particularly noxious formula of post-millennial doom, but, fortunately, like so many hundreds of prophesied end-of-the-worlds before it, the day came and went without incident. Actually, it was a rather slow news day.

SENIOR SENATOR

The day was not without at least one noteworthy incident, however. As Kent noted, "Senator John Kerry was nominated as the next Secretary of State on 12/21/12," and, given Kerry's membership in Yale's Skull and Bones, Kent supposed this meant something, but he didn't care enough to figure out exactly what.

No, what caught Kent's attention, as he went on to discuss in an online piece in early 2013, was this:

> Also on this most auspicious occasion was a funeral service in the National Cathedral for long-time U.S. Senator from Hawaii, Daniel Inouye. Inouye was at the time of his death the second-oldest sitting Senator and third in line for presidential succession. Representing the 50th state, Inouye had served in the Senate from January 3, 1963, until his death on December 17th—just days shy of a full 50 years of service. Our "Hawaiian" President spoke at the funeral in DC, and then attended a second service for Inouye in Hawaii only days later while on vacation in the Aloha State.

President Obama, Vice President Joe Biden and former President Bill Clinton spoke at a funeral service at the National Cathedral on December 21. Biden recalled Inouye's service with the Army's 442nd Infantry Regiment, during which the senator once pried a live grenade from the lifeless hand of his own severed arm and tossed it toward German soldiers before it exploded

THE GENTLEMAN FROM HAWAII

The day before, on December 20th, Inouye's body lay in state at the U.S. Capitol Rotunda. He was only the 31st person, and the first Asian American, so honored. House Speaker John Boehner,

who also spoke at the funeral service the next day, offered a few brief remarks. As the *Washington Post* reported:

> Holding back tears as he often does in such settings, Boehner noted that Inouye attended a similar memorial service in the Rotunda for John F. Kennedy in 1963 and "couldn't have imagined he would spend another five decades passing through this hall."
>
> "He couldn't have fathomed it, and unassuming as he was, he wouldn't have tried," Boehner said. He later added, "While this may be a quiet ceremony for a quiet man, it will endure long after the respects are paid. For when this Rotunda returns to life and the tour guides give their pitch, they will always speak of Daniel Inouye, the gentleman from Hawaii and one of freedom's most gallant champions."

STINKS TO HIGH HEAVEN

"Now, I'm not sure," Kent wrote, "but something smells a little fishy here, like when Obama's grandmother, who lived in Hawaii, died days before his first election." He continued:

> Was Inouye's departure some sort of…ritual/sacrifice-of-the-tribal-elder…on the date of the Mayan Apocalypse intended to ensure the appeasement of the gods? Hell, I don't know, but I do recall that the Queen's 50th Jubilee was in 2012, as well, and I'd say that the odds are better than 50-50 that this was some sort of occult mumbo-jumbo. *Book 'em, Dano.*

At the time, Kent knew something was afoot, he just didn't know quite what. But as 2013 progressed and Kent began to connect the dots that would subsequently reveal the framework of the Golden Jubilee of JFK's assassination, he figured it out: Inouye, from the 50th state, with 50 years of service in the U.S. Senate (which had begun the year JFK died), had been prematurely hastened through death's door ("respiratory complications," my ass), and his funerary rites had been performed on the date of the Mayan Apocalypse—10 days from January 1, 2013, the day that would mark the commencement of the official observance of the 50th anniversary year of President Kennedy's Masonic assassination.

Inouye (who had, by the way, served on the Church/MK-Ultra Committee) had been a living date marker and his funeral had initiated a 10-day countdown to the Golden Jubilee.

Kent felt that the bust of Darth Vader on the exterior of the Washington National Cathedral was a fitting touch to the whole sordid affair.

EIGHTY-EIGHT

As diabolical as all that is, Kent noted an additional aspect of Inouye's passing, one that he felt must have surely been coincidence, but that would have had deep meaning for those who orchestrated the senator's timely death nonetheless. A reward from the dark powers for bad behavior, perhaps.

At the time of his demise, Inouye was 88, which for our occult globalist masters equates to HH (H being the 8th letter of the alphabet), and you can just guess what that stands for—yes, "Heil Hitler!"

DON'T MESS WITH THE SHADOW GOVERNMENT

Kent made one last observation regarding Inouye's death, and it perhaps sheds further light into this apparent "sacrifice of the elder/hero":

> It is also possible that Inouye might have been getting a little payback for making the following statement during the Iran-Contra hearings: "[There exists] a shadowy Government with its own Air Force, its own Navy, its own fundraising mechanism, and the ability to pursue its own ideas of the national interest, free from all checks and balances, and free from the law itself." The moral of the story: if

you dare speak truth to power, you better be prepared for the consequences if they actually listen.

A genuine war hero, a true statesman, an advocate for truth—exactly
the kind of person you'd want for your symbolic sacrificial altar if you were
so inclined.

* * *

*"Never be afraid to raise your voice for honesty and truth and compas-
sion, against injustice and lying and greed. If you … will do this … you
will change the earth; in one generation all the Napoleons and Hitlers and
Caesars and Mussolinis and Stalins and all the other tyrants who want
power and aggrandizement, and the simple politicians and time-servers
who themselves are merely baffled or ignorant or afraid, who have used,
or are using, or hope to use, man's fear and greed for man's enslavement,
will have vanished from the face of it."*

--William Faulkner

*The last word spoken
by Inouye: "Aloha."
Hang loose, Dan'l.*

CHAPTER 51

LOSING HIS HEAD

December 17, 2013: Tucson, Arizona

I n El Presidio Park (formerly JFK Plaza), a bronze bust of President
John F. Kennedy, originally
unveiled on November 22,
1964, is ripped clean off its granite
base and stolen. The 1-foot 8-inch
high bust, together with the base,
stood about 6 feet tall. The park's
live surveillance cameras do not
record, and thus fail to capture
images of the perpetrators in the act.

Was it random vandalism or a simple, but effective, contributing element of the year-long Golden Jubilee festivities? It certainly would have
been an elegant yet low-cost way to zing the old JFK meme one more time.

JFK AT THE J-SIX

There's no way to know for sure; however, as youths, JFK and Joe, Jr., did work on a ranch in nearby Benson, 45 miles east-southeast of Tucson. During the spring and summer of 1936, the brothers rode fence, herded cattle and helped build an adobe office for the owner, who liked to call it "the house that Jack built."

JFK had been attending the London School of Economics but returned home due to ill health. Joe Kennedy, Sr., arranged for his sons to spend a working vacation on the J-Six Ranch, which helped get them both into shape for the fall athletic season at Harvard that year.

Kennedy visited Arizona again on November 3rd, 1960, only days before his election, stepping off the plane at Sky Harbor Airport in Phoenix at 3 o'clock in the morning to make a few remarks to the small crowd of devoted supporters. The one-time Arizona cowboy thanked those present for coming out, then got back on the plane and flew off to become the next president of the United States.

President John F. Kennedy and Senator Carl Hayden sit in a convertible at the Sky Harbor Airport in Phoenix, Arizona, on their way to the Westward Ho Hotel for a 50th anniversary dinner in honor of Senator Hayden. White House Secret Service Agent Toby Chandler (wearing sunglasses) stands behind the President's car. Nov 17, 1961.

Io, Saturnalia!

December 17th was also the date of the first Saturnalia festival in ancient Rome in 497 BC. As Kent had written in *Mass Ritual*:

> While we're on the subject of Saturn, Saturnalia was the ancient Roman festival honoring the deity of the same name, originally held on December 17th and later expanded with unofficial festivities through December 23rd, the poet Catullus calling them "the best of days."
>
> Characterized overall by social role reversals, behavioral license, drunkenness and gluttony, Saturnalia featured a day of gift-giving on December 23rd, often involving gag gifts, of which Julius Caesar Augustus, the first emperor of the Roman Empire, was particularly fond. Such gifts might be expensive or quite cheap, and included items such as toothpicks, spoons and sausages.

Indeed, a bust of the slain King of Camelot would make an *extraordinary* gag gift on the Golden Jubilee of his killing, wouldn't it?

CHAPTER 52

HO, HO, HOMO FOR THE HOLIDAYS

December 21, 2013: Semmes, Alabama

L ike the disappearance of the JFK bust discussed in the last chapter, this story is a situation we just can't be sure about. But it's too good not to tell, whether it was an intentional part of the script for the 2013 Mega-Ritual or not. (As you'll see, it sure has that same familiar feel to it.)

At this point, we're all of course well aware of the Cryptocracy's habit of revisiting the scene of the crime (or visiting it in advance, or both). So recall the twin barge explosions of April 25th, 2013, in Mobile, Alabama that accompanied the White House Correspondents' Dinner, and see what you think about this...

SOLSTICE FESTIVITIES

A bout five miles outside of the Mobile city limits sits the sleepy little town of Semmes. The good people of Semmes decided to have their annual Christmas parade on the Winter Solstice in 2013, with the usual cast of holiday characters, floats, marching bands and the like. A new addition to the lineup that year, however, raised the eyebrows, and ire, of a lot of the locals.

A group of four scantily clad, effeminate African-American males wearing makeup and midriff-baring Santa coats and matching hats, tight-fitting white short-shorts and panty hose with white knee-boots strutted, pranced and prissed their way along the entire parade route. The group's style, known as "J-Setting," is typical of what you might see from an unscrupulous high school dance team or cheerleading squad.

To put it mildly, the performance didn't go over well with town residents. There were plenty of jeers and lots of "Oh my god, what's *that*?," with some parents clutching their children, outraged and appalled, and others shaking their heads, offended at the inappropriateness of the act.

In defense of the fab four, the parade's organizers *had* invited the Mobile-based group to perform. They hadn't just shown up to desecrate the occasion or offend the conservative townsfolk. Yet, given everything that had transpired up to this point in the year, all the disrespectful, denigrating acts of senseless violence and sheer mockery that had been visited upon the unsuspecting American public over the past twelve months, Kent couldn't help but wonder if perhaps someone on the parade planning committee had gotten a call, or been influenced in some way or another to put these fellas in the parade lineup.

RETURN TO MOBILE

The global elite had just spent almost the entire year romping and rampaging across the American countryside, and beyond—stomping on the cherished values and memories of a nation. And they do so like to leave their calling cards, however obscure they might seem to the rest of us, taking credit where credit's due, rubbing our noses in the dirt just one more time.

Kent certainly suspected that could be the case in Semmes. Had this been a "Return to Mobile" or "Mobile, Part II" chapter in the script for the Golden Jubilee? One more good ole thumb in the eye, one more kick in the ribs as they rode through town this last time on their victory lap at year's end?

There was no real way to know for certain, but it sure looked that way to Kent, who'd long ago come to trust his instincts about these sorts of things. Oh, and there was one more item that caught Kent's attention and influenced his opinion on the Winter Solstice Dirty Dancers episode.

Truly, as a signature event for the Cryptocrats, this act had certainly been befitting, and as a *literal* signature, well, our psychopathic friends really couldn't have selected a finer one: the name of the performing group? The Prancing Elites. *Ho, ho, ho.*

CHAPTER 53

RETURN TO TUPELO

December 23, 2013: Tupelo, Mississippi

The call came in over the police band radio: robbery in-progress. Tupelo police officer Gale Stauffer responded to the location at crosstown. Although there were conflicting accounts of the incident in the media, at least one main-stream source stated that traffic was stopped due to a train, and Stauffer noticed a vehicle matching the description of the robbery suspect's car caught in the line of automobiles. Stauffer exited his cruiser and approached the car, weapon drawn.

According to this account, an erroneous description had unfortunately been issued and Stauffer and fellow officer Joseph Maher, who had also arrived on the scene, were approaching the wrong car, yelling instructions at the bewildered driver. In a nearby vehicle, armed robbery suspect Mario Edward Garnett prepared to exit his car and ambush the officers.

Stauffer was subsequently killed and Maher injured. Garnett, who had only days earlier attempted to rob a bank in Atlanta, escaped and a massive national manhunt ensured. Later that week, Garnett was killed while attempting a third bank robbery in Phoenix, Arizona.

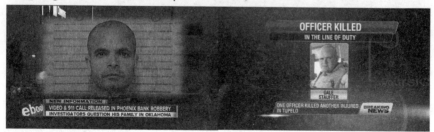

BLUE CHRISTMAS

In any ordinary year, Kent would have chalked the incident in Tupelo up to chance, but this year, with Elvis' hometown having been clearly in the crosshairs of the Cryptocracy, he suspected that there was more to the story than first met the eye.

Several things about the case stood out to Kent. First, policemen are killed in the line of duty with alarming regularity all over the United States, but not in Tupelo: Stauffer's was the first such death in over 30 years. Second, Garnett was former military and had previously been arrested for threatening President Obama. Third, the inconsistent media accounts of the incident, with significant variation on the basic facts, were a hallmark of most, if not all staged events he'd studied in the past—an oft-used tactic in information warfare. Fourth, from Tupelo, Garnett had fled to Phoenix, although he had no ties there, no relatives, nothing.

Regarding the last point, one might respond that criminals don't need a damn itinerary or good reasons for selecting a particular city in which to commit a crime. This was just a violent man on a cross-country bank-robbery spree who, for whatever reasons decided to hit Atlanta, Tupelo and Phoenix.

Maybe; or maybe not. Garnett could also have been another windup toy, another programmed mind-control plaything, set loose to perform his role in this particular installment of the 2013 Mega-Ritual. Could this have been "Return to Tupelo" or "Tupelo, Part II," "Christmas Cop Killer" or, even more fitting, "Blue Christmas"? A Return to Mobile followed days later by a Return to Tupelo—why not? Just another stop on the Victory Tour.

(Left) Tupelo's own. (Right) A candlelight vigil in Tupelo's Fairpark District for the fallen officer.

THE PHOENIX RISES, AGAIN

It had occurred to Kent that if Garnett had been programmed, he could well have had a handler with him. Could this have been the reason for the reported mix-up in the description of the getaway car? If there *had* been a mix-up: he wasn't even sure about this fact. There had also been initial reports of an accomplice, but that aspect of the story faded from sight, as is often the case. There was no way to find out for certain.

But there was one thing that seemed very clear to him, and it was likely another echo of Mobile, part of a pattern (our controllers apparently love a variation on a theme). In that the Prancing Elites could well have been a calling card of sorts, he was even more certain of this: Garnett didn't end up in Arizona by chance. He hadn't blown through Tupelo on a whim, and he hadn't met his fate in Phoenix by coincidence.

The phoenix is *the* signature of the Illuminati (recall the fireboat named Phoenix in Mobile, etc.). Kent had written an entire chapter on this subject, and, presciently, even discussed Phoenix, Arizona, as being the potential target of a mass ritual for this very reason.

So, it would seem that, at his masters' bidding, Mario Edward Garnett had led the Return to Tupelo and then inked the signature on the entire episode by dying in Phoenix. End of story. Merry Christmas.

Three Kings Redux?

It's possible that Garnett, a longtime Oklahoma City resident (we're going to leave that alone), didn't launch his robbery spree in Atlanta on a whim, either. "It's very unusual for a resident of our city to travel to Atlanta, to Tupelo, Miss. and Phoenix, Ariz., and rob or attempt to rob banks in such a short fashion," said Oklahoma City FBI supervisory special agent Gary Johnson. No shit, Sherlock.

We know why Garnett would've been programmed to hit Tupelo, the birthplace of the King of Rock'n'Roll, and the section above explains why he hit Phoenix, Arizona. But why Atlanta?

Because it's the birthplace of yet another king, as in Martin Luther King, Jr., who this same cabal assassinated in Memphis decades earlier. (Yes, yes, there's good evidence that James Earl Ray was subjected to mind-control programming and was the stereotypical patsy/lone-gunman we've come to expect in these situations.)

In fact, the Bank of America branch in Atlanta that Garnett attempted unsuccessfully to rob on December 23rd before heading to Tupelo is only about five miles from the M.L.K. National Historic Site, which includes King's childhood home.

Invoking yet another slain king as part of the Golden Jubilee of the Killing of the King of Camelot—that's pure evil genius. Perhaps, then, this was a Three Kings Redux (J.F.K., E.P. and M.L.K.). No, Siriusly.

(Left) King delivered his famous "I Have a Dream" speech in front of the Lincoln Memorial in Washington, D.C., as the grand finale of the "March on Washington for Jobs and Freedom," on August 28, 1963, only months before J.F.K. was assassinated.

SNOOP DOGG
MALICE N WONDERLA
PARENTAL
ADVISORY
EXPLICIT CONTENT

CHAPTER 54

DISHONORING KENNEDY

December 29, 2013: Washington, D.C.

As a grand finale for the year's odious celebrations, it was, in truth, sheer genius. To most viewers, it was merely the 36th Annual Kennedy Center Honors (KCH). To the Cryptocracy, it was the best of black comedy, in more than one sense. The festivities surrounding the Golden Jubilee of the Killing of the King had featured a heavily African-American cast, and this night would be no different. This night would, in fact, take this aspect of the 2013 Mega-Ritual to a new level altogether.

THE NO-SH*T ZONE

As the choice for presenter to pay tribute to musical genius Herbie Hancock, it was universally thought to be an odd one, to say the least. True, when mixing Washington politicians and political commentators with luminaries from the entertainment industry, some strange combinations are automatically going to occur, but in this instance the result was quite extraordinary.

A slight-yet-audible gasp, accompanied by a look of disbelief on many audience members' faces, was followed by a loud silence. As Fox News commentator Bill O'Reilly stepped to the podium, he smiled and acknowledged the awkwardness of the moment, telling the crowd, "I know, I'm surprised too." The audience laughed and applauded. President Obama and the First Lady chuckled while looking over at Hancock, who was curled up in laughter.

Who they chose to introduce Hancock, however, was only slightly more surprising than the performer they lined up to pay tribute to him— rapper Snoop Dogg (yeah, yeah, yeah, he's Snoop Lion now, but everybody still knows him as Snoop Dogg).

Viewed by many as one of the originators of hip-hop, Hancock is a genuine American music legend, and attempting to pay homage to the breadth and depth of his substantial musical accomplishments through the blunt instrument of rap is akin to using a mop to attempt a reproduction of a Rembrandt masterpiece. There are any number of other incredibly talented musical artists the KCH could have chosen to honor Hancock.

Hey, Hey, Hey!

Herbert Jeffrey "Herbie" Hancock was born in Chicago in 1940. He, like many jazz pianists, began his musical education with classical music, and was considered a child prodigy. At the age of 11, he played the first movement of Mozart's Piano Concerto No. 26 in D Major, K. 537 (*Coronation*) with the Chicago Symphony Orchestra.

Hancock went on to become a keyboardist, bandleader and composer. He helped redefine the role of the jazz rhythm section and was a primary architect of the post-bop sound. In his jazz improvisation, he utilizes a creative blend of jazz, blues and modern classical music.

Hancock was one of the first jazz musicians to embrace synthesizers, and his style incorporates elements of funk and soul while retaining freer stylistic elements from jazz. Many of his songs have crossed over and achieved success in the pop music market.

Perhaps less well known about Hancock is this little fact: in 1969, he composed the theme song for the animated children's television show *Fat Albert and the Cosby Kids*.

HOLLYWOOD FOR UGLY PEOPLE

In addition to being a peculiar pick to introduce Hancock, Bill O'Reilly's mere presence was an insult to another 2013 KCH inductee, Billy Joel, whom O'Reilly once referred to as a "hoodlum." "He used to slick [his hair] back ... would smoke and this and that, and we were more jocks." Whatever, Bill.

Writing in *Variety* about the overall strangeness of the evening, TV columnist Brian Lowry commented:

> "The Kennedy Center Honors" is always a joyous and classy affair ... Yet the 36th edition of this annual celebration of the arts features some truly out-of-the-box choices, with Supreme Court Justice Sonia Sotomayor and Fox News' Bill O'Reilly among the presenters. As usual, there are genuinely heartwarming moments—such as opera singer Martina Arroyo singing along to Billy Joel's "Piano Man"—but this might be the least memorable edition of the Honors in the last several years...

The Kennedy Center draws its strength, in part, from seeing these esteemed artists clearly having a ball, along with the mix of political heavyweights and who's who of celebrities filling the hall. It always looks like a dinner party that would be a blast to attend.

That said, the frequently arbitrary nature of the pre- senters and performers feels especially strained this year, from Snoop Dogg participating in the Herbie Hancock tribute (and trying to get the whole crowd to yell "Ho!") to the introductions by Sotomayor, O'Reil- ly and Tony Bennett for, in sequence, Arroyo, Hancock and Billy Joel.

New Republic reporter Kevin Mahnken had a slightly less favorable impres- sion of the evening's proceedings and the Kennedy Center Honors in general:

> ... the Kennedy Center Honors are a debauched sham and their award a badge of disgrace. The 2013 ceremony, which was held ear- lier this month and aired Sunday night, epitomizes the event's ob- session with schlock and celebrity.
>
> Washington has long been described (accurately) as "Hollywood for ugly people." The Kennedy Center Honors, I suppose, could be seen as the city's version of the Oscars. Rather than evoking in any meaningful way the fun parts of the Academy Awards, however, the Kennedy Center Honors exist as a kind of sad counterfeit, showing the dark turn the show might have taken if the entire thing had grown out of the Lifetime Achievement Award. In fact, they seem to ape the worst flaws of our various national pageants: the unconvincing joviality of the Golden Globes, the irrelevance of the Rock and Roll Hall of Fame induction, the unyielding classicism of the Super Bowl halftime show.

Tell us what you really think, Kevin.

THE HIP-HOP-I-FICATION OF AMERICA

As Mr. Mahnken would likely agree, what's genuinely disturbing is when we as a nation hit an all-time cultural low and nobody even notices. It's not just that rap is a largely crass artistic pursuit (to apply the term very loosely) and Snoop Dogg one of its more vile practitioners, or the fact that a person representing such a stunted musical genre was called on to pay tribute to an American artistic legend.

No, what's far worse is that there registered not a hint, not a smidgen, of dismay or disapproval on any face in the audience that night. If any one of our national political leaders or other distinguished guests had any reservations about anything taking place before them that evening, none dared let it show.

Worse still, not a single soul dared refrain from throwing their arms in the air and swaying back and forth as the entire audience—including, of course, the President and First Lady—enthusiastically joined in a resounding chorus, ably led by Snoop Dogg himself, of "Heeey, ho! Heeey, ho!" (and they didn't just repeat it twice). The painfully-extended and grotesque scene was so surreal that as he watched Kent found himself wondering if somehow the channel had been switched to an episode of *Saturday Night Live* without his realizing it.

(Left) Snoop Dog: "Somebody say 'Ho'!" (Right) First Lady Michelle and President Barack Obama (and everyone else in the Kennedy Center): "Ho!" (Martin Luther King, Jr., would be so proud.)

As he well knew, when the flag of political correctness is raised, failure to salute is a crime punishable by death, political or otherwise, and as Republican and Democrat alike joined together in their heying and hoing, it became painfully clear that the hip-hop-i-fication of America is now complete. The debasement of our national culture is total, our collective capitulation a fact. We officially suck.

THE FIST BUMP HEARD ROUND THE WORLD

So, a rapper with a repertoire so devoid of any redeeming value that the first black president can't even ask him to play at the White House gets center stage at the Kennedy Center Honors. Interesting. Everything turned out great for Snoop in the end, however, because he made it to the White House after all, even if he didn't get to perform there.

Along with the Honorees and members of the Artists Committee who nominated them, as well as the Kennedy Center Board of Trustees, Snoop and his family were invited to Barack and Michelle's crib prior to the gala performance.

While there, Snoop Dogg got a *bona fide* fist bump from Secretary of State John Kerry, the video of which Snoop posted on Instagram, and then Tweeted, "Boss life. me n john kerry at d white house !!! #reincarnated #khc." Kent thought to himself that the only thing more bizarre than the sight of the Dogg-Kerry fist bump was seeing Bill O'Reilly shake Snoop's hand after his performance that night.

In the video, Kerry can be heard saying, "He invented your whole thing," an apparent reference to Herbie Hancock, with which Snoop agrees, replying, "He invented hip-hop." Kerry's Twitter team subsequently re-Tweeted Snoop's post, adding a note from Kerry himself, "Between us we've sold 30 million—JK."

And as if that weren't enough fun for Snoop in Wonderland, he was also videoed standing directly under the official White House portrait of President John F. Kennedy. Interesting.

Pimpin' Ain't EZ

Most Americans who are not themselves fans of Snoop Dogg are likely unaware of exactly what an odious character he is. Born Calvin Cordozar Broadus, Jr., Snoop is a notorious pothead, convicted felon, one-time murder suspect and Rastafarian who claimed in a 2006 *Rolling Stone* interview that, unlike other hip hop artists who adopt a superficial pimp persona, he was actually a professional pimp in 2003-2004.

"That shit was my natural calling and once I got involved with it, it became fun. It was like shootin' layups for me. I was makin' 'em every time." Later in the interview, Snoop slightly redeems himself by revealing that, based on the advice of several fellow pimps, he eventually gave up the profession to "spend more time with his family."

In another setting, apparently lamenting the social limitations his musical style places on him, Snoop commented, "I'm never able to perform in situations where I'd love to because I don't have those kinds of songs...My songs are too hard," adding, "I know Obama wants me to come to the White House but what can I perform?"

Well, let's see. We can rule out "For All My Niggaz& B*tches" from your 1993 album *Doggystyle*, and all of the following from subsequent albums: "Payin' for P*ssy," "B*tch Please," "Fresh Pair of Panties On," "I Wanna F*ck You," "My [continued] F*ckin'House," and "I Don't Need No B*tch." Now, here's a possibility—"I Love My Momma" from *No Limit Top Dogg*. But, if you're talking about the White House, maybe something a little more autobiographical would be appropriate, such as "Pimpin' Ain't EZ" from *Malice N Wonderland*:

"Pimpin Ain't EZ"
(featuring R. Kelly)

[Snoop Dogg]
Well it ain't
All them faces in that laker paint
Casa by the lake
Make a little nigga faint
Balling is what I does
I ain't messing with you can'ts
I'm a can do negro
A real life California hero
About six zeros at the end of the number in my bank account
Nigga ain't ya mad at me
I'm so happy to see that you stopped your life to watch mine
Yeah you see it fool …

[Snoop Dogg]
This ain't a joke a loc made it look easy to you
I been through some shit
I made it easy for ya
Now you ain't got to do much, I pop at everybody
Go unwrap a bottle, share it with them busybodies …

[R. Kelly]
I got pimping in my veins
Pimping in my blood
Pimping in my swag
Pimping in my cup
Walking like a pimp when I walking through the club
Pause like a pimp so the hoes show me love
Pimp by day, pimp by night
Pimp haters make me keep my pimp game tight…

[R. Kelly]
To all my honeys in the club getting money with the thugs
Keep it pimping baby
Keep it pimping baby
Southside, westside, eastside, northside
Keep it pimping baby
Keep it pimping

Keep it pimping, indeed, Calvin.

DISRESPECTING JFK

So, here we have a proud former pimp, convicted felon and obsceni-ty-spewing rapper at the White House,* underneath a portrait of JFK,

---

* Snoop later admitted during an interview with guest Jimmy Kimmel on "Double G News Network," his Internet talk show, that he had smoked weed in the White House that evening. "In the bathroom, in the bathroom," Snoop protested, "Not in the White House,

directly preceding his performance at the Kennedy Center Honors. You couldn't think of a better way to dishonor and disrespect Kennedy's memory and legacy if you wanted to. And that, friends, is the point.

Snoop Dogg *was* the joke in the room, at the White House and later at the KCH. But that's not a racially insensitive thing to say, because Bill O'Reilly, author of the best-selling *Killing Kennedy: The End of Camelot*, was the other joke in the room, just as Conan O'Brien had been at the White House Correspondent's Dinner earlier in the year.

Don't bother trying to figure out how these insulting circumstances were orchestrated. In the grand scheme of things, compared with everything else the Cryptocracy pulled off in 2013, this wouldn't have been too difficult, certainly not much more difficult than, say, getting four fake racially-offensive Asian names broadcast on live TV, and probably not nearly as difficult as slamming a 777 into the tarmac and making it look like an accident.

Whatever the cost, whatever the means required, from their perspective it was well worth the effort, well worth the investment. Everything we hold dear is a joke to them. They take immense pleasure in diminishing our greatest institutions and mocking our greatest leaders. You think they'd really pass up a chance to slap JFK upside the head one last time? Not on your life.

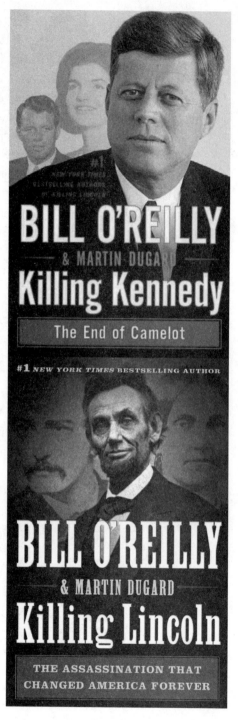

but in the bathroom." Yes, and the bathroom is in the White House. Pot-head. (Elvis, he out-did you, brother.)

THE DOGG STAR

This was indeed mockery at its finest. There is, though, the possibility that it was something more, that little special something extra—which could well be the case, because it would hit a favorite recurring theme, the regular appearance of which we've come to expect.

Although the Kennedy Center Honors ceremony was held on December 8th, it was not broadcast until December 29th, two days before New Year's Eve. This special occasion marks the exact day on which a certain star assumes its position at the precise point of mid-heaven at midnight, and in the days leading up, the star is almost at its zenith, with only a few arc-minutes left to go.

The star? Sirius, of course. Yes, New Year's Eve is, astronomically, all about Sirius. So, the only question left is this: was Snoop's KCH performance an act of disrespect to JFK and simultaneously an oblique tribute to the Dog Star?

DOGGIE STYLE

Before you dismiss entirely the idea that Snoop Dogg might have been a living tribute to the Dog Star, consider this: Kent devoted an entire chapter to Sirius, the Police Dog.

This installment of the 9/11 occult script falls squarely into the you-can't-make-this-stuff-up category…

We've met Sirius, the Dog Star, the shining light of the occultists, whose pernicious presence is ubiquitous throughout the 9/11 Mega-Ritual. Now, meet Sirius, the Police Dog, the only such animal to be killed in the attack on the Twin Towers, who died in his kennel in the basement of Tower Two when it collapsed.

Sirius, a four-and-a-half-year old, ninety pound yellow Labrador Retriever, was an Explosive Detection Dog with the Port Authority of New York and New Jersey Police Department. It just so happens that Sirius' badge number was 17, and the 17th card in the Tarot is…wait for it…The Star, which, according to many occultists, depicts (what else?)—Sirius.

Adding to the occultists' delight is that K is the 11th letter of the alphabet (hooray, another 11), thus K-9 is the reverse of 9/11: K-9, 9/11...oh, who cares.

The intended outcome of the death of this specially named creature was, of course, that through all of the related news coverage, memorials and tributes, the name Sirius would be heavily intermingled with 9/11, spreading like a memetic virus into people's consciousness...

Whassup, Dogg?!

PART TEN

GAME OVER

CHAPTER 55

TOO CLOSE FOR COMFORT

January 22, 2014: Blue Mountain, Mississippi

In the early morning hours, on what turned out to be one of the coldest nights of the year, Kent awakened to bitter cold in his bedroom. As he pulled the covers up around his neck, it also dawned on him that there were no lights on anywhere and it was completely silent. Electricity must be out. If they don't get it back on, that'll make getting ready for work even more of a chore than usual, he thought as he drifted off to sleep again.

Had it been a few weeks earlier, Kent might have suspected that the cause of the power outage was his neighbors a few miles down the road, who have what is most likely the largest collection (over 500) of illuminated Christmas inflatables in the world, including dozens of larger-than-life Santa's, reindeer, cartoon characters and more. As if that weren't enough, they also have 300,000 lights and a computerized musical light show. Chevy Chase's over-the-top decorations in the holiday classic *Christmas Vacation* don't even come close; try to imagine several acres of glowing, distended yuletide glo-

Ho, ho, holy cow—this is just the entrance.

ry. (Lest you think I'm exaggerating, the collection and its owner were featured in an episode of TLC's "My Crazy Obsession.")

Unfortunately for Kent and hundreds of others in the area, power wouldn't be restored until late the following day. What Kent didn't know at the time was that approximately 8 miles from his house, just outside New Albany in neighboring Union County, a massive explosion at a biodiesel plant had blown down the power lines.

The blast obliterated several metal holding tanks and started huge grass fires in nearby fields. New Albany schools and several industries were closed, as well as a stretch of Highway 15 from Blue Mountain to New Albany, the route Kent usually drove to work in Tupelo. A number of families in the vicinity had to be evacuated due to the thick cloud of black, acrid smoke.

The fire, which had occurred around 5:30 a.m., had proved too hot for firefighters to approach and was thus allowed to burn. Around 1:00 p.m., a second massive blast occurred. Kent's father, son William, and daughter Taylor actually witnessed the second blast in person, having driven towards New Albany to observe the damage from the initial explosion from a distance. Schools in Blue Mountain were out that day, as well, due to the power outage.

It's for You

Located only about 20 miles north of Tupelo, New Albany is the birthplace of Nobel Laureate William Faulkner. Talk about *The Sound and the Fury*, Kent thought to himself as he drove into work that morning by an alternate route, arriving a little later than usual.

On his extended drive in, Kent also had time to recall numerous similar incidents from the previous year: the explosions in West, Texas; Mobile, Alabama; Detroit, Michigan; and Lac-Mégantic, Quebec. His imagination began to concoct a hypothetical scenario in which this explosion might not only have been intentional, but intended to send *him* a message.

Yet, even after everything that had already happened to him in 2013, he was reluctant to entertain such a possibility. Shit happens, he told himself, but even as he did, a little voice in the back of his head said, *Yeah, but shit don't usually happen this close to your house, Jack.*

FINGER LICKIN' GOOD

The Mississippi Hills region is known for its colorful characters, and William Faulkner's fiction effectively captures the uniqueness of the region and its people. Yet, Mississippi's general reputation being what it is, Kent couldn't help but find the following aspect of the explosive incident amusing—a bit sad, too, but funny nonetheless.

Biodiesel plants all over the world process many types of materials and substances into fuel, but the one in New Albany primarily used chicken fat. Yes, Mississippians love their fried chicken so much that they have to store the leftover grease in industrial-size vats.

This profound love for the Colonel's finest is no doubt one of the reasons that the state is ranked as the most obese in the nation. But while some might be tempted to observe sarcastically that Mississippi is finally first in something, the situation is actually worse than it appears on the surface. The United States is the fattest country in the world, so Mississippi being the fattest state in the nation also makes it the fattest place on the whole damn planet.

Essentially this had been the biggest chicken-grease fire in history, in the most obese place on the face of the earth. *Now that's finger lickin' good.*

A LETTER OF RESPONSIBILITY?

After Kent arrived at his office, he settled into the daily routine and forgot about the morning's excitement. In between writing emails and performing other joyless administrative tasks, he walked down the hall to check the mail.

As he sorted through the letters, it was mainly the usual fare: junk mail, more junk mail, a bill, an inquiry from a prospective visitor and the like. As he sat down at his desk again, he noted that one of the envelopes had a hand-written address.

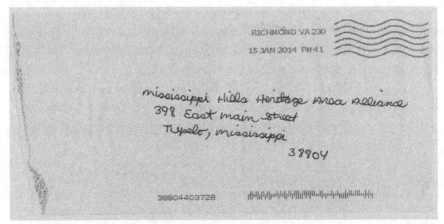

RICHMOND VA 230
15 JAN 2014 PM 4 L

mississippi Hills Heritage Area Alliance
398 East main street
Tupelo, mississippi
38804

38804403728

Upon opening it, he found a collection of what seemed to be random clippings from various publications, mainly travel guides. He thought it a bit odd, but figured that some elderly person with too much time on their hands—and possibly suffering from the early stages of dementia—had arbitrarily stuffed some travel-related items into an envelope and sent them to his office; not an entirely illogical thing to do because the heritage area could generally be considered part of the travel industry.

He set it aside and didn't give it any more thought until later in the day when he picked it up again as he was cleaning off his desk and getting ready to leave. He flipped through the contents again and was about to toss it all in the garbage, when he began to notice some familiar names and places.

He looked at the envelope again—no return address. He'd never received such a letter before, either at the office or at his residence. Ever so briefly, he thought of the letters sent to Wicker, Obama and Holland the previous year.

There were thirteen (hmmm) items in the envelope, and three of the pages were from a travel guide for Outer Banks (whose most famous resident, Andy Griffith, lived on Roanoke Island and was born on the same day as Marilyn Monroe, June 1, 1926).

Kitty Hawk and Kill Devil Hills, Ocracoke Island, Nags Head: these were all places his children had visited with their grandfather only a few years prior on their vacation to the Outer Banks in North Carolina.

There was an advertisement for Rock City/Lookout Mountain (a dual reference encompassing the other Lookout Mountain?), which they'd also visited on that same trip. Included as well were several pages from a visitors' guide for Nashville, Tennessee, where the children had relatives they'd visited several times in the past few years.

Kent's book was all about numbers, symbols, inside jokes and hidden meanings. Now, it looked as if someone were sending him a personal message, on the same day as the explosion in New Albany.

But if the rest of the clippings were completely random, with no buried messages, couldn't this still be a coincidence, some old lady at her kitchen table with a pair of scissors and a bunch of travel guides she ordered through the *Southern Living* travel section, snipping this and that for reasons known only to her, and sending it to him because she'd just happened upon the address for the Mississippi Hills National Heritage Area?

Sure, that might've been the case, but unfortunately, practically every remaining item in the envelope packed a symbolic wallop.

THAT SOUNDS FAMILIAR

Several of the remaining pages were from a tour guide for Charleston, South Carolina, which immediately rang a very loud bell with Kent, given that he'd discussed this city in *Mass Ritual* as the "birthplace of the Freemasonic 'Mother Lodge of the World,' (and the site of the beginning of the Civil War at Fort Sumter in Charleston Harbor, as well as of the Concelebration of the enthroning of Lucifer in the Vatican)." One

of the Charleston pages in particular (pictured above) caught his attention, for obvious reasons. He certainly hoped that it wasn't an overt threat that the sender intended to make good on.

Shepheard's Tavern in Charleston, South Carolina, was the site of many historic and Masonic events and the birthplace of Scottish Rite Freemasonry.

Another of the Charleston pages was plastered with symbols he'd also covered in his book: the five-pointed star, which represents the Blazing Star of the Freemasons, Sirius; and the inverted pentagram, which, as just about everyone on the planet knows, is a key symbol in Satanism.

There were also references to both *The Wizard of Oz* and *Alice in Wonderland*, which, as Kent had included in *Mass Ritual*, are well known for being

utilized in MKULTRA trauma-based mind-control programming (*There's no place like home, there's no place like home...*).

The smallest clipping was from a real estate ad for a home in Georgetown East on Dunbarton Drive (a Dumbarton Oaks/U.N. reference?) in Chesapeake, Virginia, which is only 50 miles or so from Kill Devil Hills. The date stamp on the photo, barely legible, read "11/22/2013"—not just the date of the 50th anniversary of the Kennedy assassination (and Lewis' and Huxley's), and not just the release date of *Catching Fire*, but, on a personal level, the focal point of the new book Kent was considering writing.

ENCORE, ENCORE

A s Kent flipped back through the pages, his sense of dis-ease grew. He knew how to read these sorts of clues, how to construct coherent messages from them, and he didn't like what this one seemed to be saying: *We're watching your kids, we're watching you. Remember Phillip Marshall.*

As plain as the message already was, there was yet another aspect to it he hadn't immediately grasped, but that popped his eyes open a little further when he discovered it.

Kent knew the drill: staged terror attacks (industrial sabotage or what have you) always fall on a date with some significance attached to it, whether astrological or otherwise. January 22nd wasn't a key Satanic or occult holiday, and it wasn't a particularly auspicious occasion astrologically as far as he knew.

It was, however, the date on which, in 1946, the 33rd President of the United States and 33rd degree Freema-

371

son Harry S. Truman (who incidentally, as Kent had noted, "authorized the use of nuclear weapons on civilian populations") issued the Presidential directive that created the Central Intelligence Group, which was the forerunner of the Central Intelligence Agency.

UNCLASSIFIED

ENCLOSURE

THE WHITE HOUSE
WASHINGTON

January 22, 1946

To The Secretary of State,
The Secretary of War, and
The Secretary of the Navy.

1. It is my desire, and I hereby direct, that all Federal foreign intelligence activities be planned, developed and coordinated so as to assure the most effective accomplishment of the intelligence mission related to the national security. I hereby designate you, together with another person to be named by me as my personal representative, as the National Intelligence Authority to accomplish this purpose.

2. Within the limits of available appropriations, you shall

Interestingly, January 22, 1984 was also the date of Super Bowl XVIII, during which Apple introduced the Macintosh with its famous "1984" television commercial, but Kent well knew that, as appropriate a reference as it was, it wasn't the kind of thing you plan an act of false-flag terror around.

However, coming off the year of the Golden Jubilee of the Killing of the King and all the JFK-related lore that had been involved, Kent was still very much attuned to all-things-Kennedy, and sensed that, perhaps, the Cryptocracy wasn't quite finished with this programming theme yet. 2013 was over, but that didn't necessarily mean the commemoration had to end exactly on December 31st, did it? There was still so much to work with.

It was thus with only a slight feeling of surprise that Kent subsequently learned the true significance of the day, and realized that there had been at least one encore performance to the Golden Jubilee. The show might be over, but it wasn't finished…

Recall the Spouting-Devil death-date ceremony for Aleister Crowley and then chew on this: January 22nd, 1973, and January 22nd, 1995, are the dates of death of, respectively, President Lyndon B. Johnson and, wait for it … JFK's mother, Rose Kennedy.

NO WAY OUT

A massive chicken-grease explosion (two, actually, and an all-day fire) just down the road from Kent's house, coinciding with the arrival of an anonymous letter filled with an intimidating, occult-symbol-laden personal message for Kent and his children, received on the anniversary of the passing of both JFK's successor and his mother, *and* the birthday of the CIA?

"Well, shit," Kent muttered to himself upon considering the circumstances. It was about all he could say. He seemed to find himself hopelessly entangled in a frightening web from which he saw no escape. He was apparently squarely in the crosshairs of those whom he'd written about, and they seemed to be turning up the heat, literally (and, if you count the power outage, turning it off, too).

IS THAT YOU?

Knowing full well there was no way for him to find out for sure, Kent still wondered who might have sent the letter. As he contemplated the matter, several things occurred to him.

The sender had included a very limited number of items (specifically, 13), each for very a specific reason: it had been up to him to figure out the significance of each one. What if the person responsible for sending the items had purposely left clues to their identity in the materials, as well? What if some items contained multiple levels of meaning, or represented clues to more than one thing?

And was there anybody in particular who might want to send Kent a cryptically threatening personal message?

As Kent mulled all this over, a series of vague impressions slowly became clearer and more defined, the links connecting the dots becoming more solid.

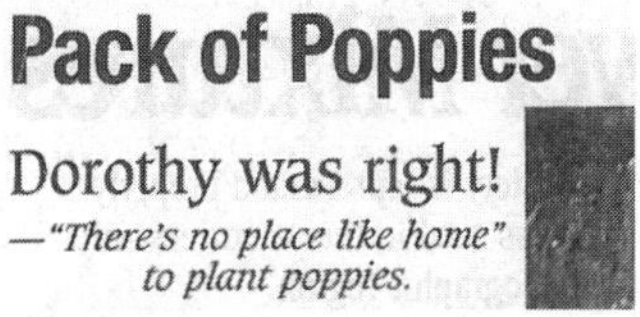

The "Pack of Poppies" ad with the *Wizard of Oz* quote had stood out like a sore thumb from the rest of the items. There had to be any number of places to pull an *Oz* quote from:

Pack of Poppies

Dorothy was right!
—"There's no place like home"
to plant poppies.

why this one? Kent's brain didn't want to go where his instincts were telling him to, and a brief-but-pointless cognitive struggle ensued.

Kent had written some fairly harsh (and offensive) things about the Bushes in *Mass Ritual*, George H.W. Bush, in particular. As Kent well knew, the 41st President of the United States' nickname is "Poppy," and while most people interpret this as a term of endearment, there is a deeper significance to the name, stemming from Bush Sr.'s stint as Director of the Central Intelligence Agency. "Poppy" is an insider reference to the CIA's involvement in the opium trade; opium, of course, being derived from poppies.

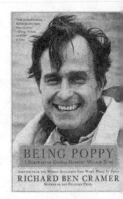

Poppies, Poppy—that's about as clear a signature as you could possibly expect from a former President and CIA hack or someone acting on his behalf.

Kent's mind repeatedly attempted to regurgitate it, to rid itself of this notion: that he had actually attracted the unwanted attention of Poppy Bush or one of his cronies. That cannot be true, repeated his skeptical self over and over like a mind-control recording. But it didn't work. His mother's apartment, his son's seizures, Carol the Elephant getting shot directly across from his office, the letter … Kent couldn't force these out of his head, nor, he decided, should he.

He couldn't ignore everything that had happened, or the possibility, however remote, that word of him and his book might have reached the top (or near to it) of the pyramid. Without question, he'd gotten on *someone's* radar, Poppy or not, and he didn't know how to get off it.

SAY IT AIN'T SO

As Kent considered whether he'd actually managed to antagonize Bush Sr., he thought back to a potentially related event in late 2013. It was the evening of Monday, November 28th, the week of the 50th anniversary of the JFK assassination.

Former First Lady Laura Bush was in Tupelo, giving a speech at the convention center directly across the street from Kent's office. When he'd first heard that she was going to be in town, he'd briefly considered staging something clever. He could recruit a group of people to stand around menacingly at the venue in Guy Fawkes masks and Aleister Crowley t-shirts. Yeah, and he could film it and put it up on YouTube.

"Great idea, dipshit," he murmured to himself as he quickly realized just how little he needed to draw additional attention to himself at this point. A stunt like this could get him fired, put in jail, or worse. After what had happened to William, he didn't figure he should do anything else that might piss someone off.

Still, here it was, the Monday of the Big Week, and there's W.'s woman, in Tupelo, Mississippi, one of the main stages used in the Golden Jubilee, featuring Roger Wicker, Kevin Curtis, Everett Dutschke and Carol the Circus Elephant, in a convention center adjacent to the parking lot where the pachyderm was shot, one month before the "Blue Christmas" shooting of Tupelo police officer Gale Stauffer.

Laura Bush, official representative of the Bush Family Crime Syndicate? Kent had always thought of Laura Bush in a positive light, and wanted to dismiss the entire incident as the one coincidence of the entire year. If it was, however, it was one *hell* of a coincidence.

Maybe, somehow, Kent thought hopefully, this speaking engagement was arranged without her knowing anything about the rest of it. Laura Bush: *unwitting* official representative of the Bush Family Crime Syndicate?

Stubbornly, Kent refused to believe the worst: *Come on, Laura, say it ain't so.*

375

LUCIFER RISING

· A LOVE VISION ·

· BY ·

· KENNETH ANGER ·

666   666

CHAPTER 56

LUCIFER RISING?

*T*he *Most Dangerous Book in the World* had sold relatively well for a niche publication, although this was little consolation to Kent given all the trouble the book had caused him.

When it was released in fall of 2012, Kris Millegan, the publisher, sent out numerous review copies to a wide variety of media, including some of Kent's old colleagues at the *Weekly Standard*, knowing all the while that the conventional outlets wouldn't touch it with a ten-foot pole (and, indeed, they didn't).

In early 2014, Kent struck up an email correspondence with former *Standard* co-worker Tucker Carlson, now editor-in-chief of the *Daily Caller*, after Carlson put in an appearance on the *Alex Jones Show*, hoping that Tucker's recent foray into the alternative media might indicate a broadening of his mind on the subject of 9/11.

Such was apparently not the case, however, and Kent subsequently regretted wasting $20 to FedEx Tucker a book, because he never heard back from him. Interestingly enough, conspiracy-theorist-extraordinaire Alex Jones wouldn't touch the book either.

RECEIVED AND ACKNOWLEDGED

*T*wo years after *Mass Ritual* had first been published, and after all the interviews and reviews, Kent still hadn't connected with the one person whose opinion he would have welcomed most, Michael Hoffman, who, as discussed earlier, is the author of *Secret Societies and Psychological Warfare*.

Kent had attempted to contact him on several occasions during the writing of his book and after it had been released, but had not heard back from him. Kent became quite accustomed to people ignoring him, and given the subject of his book, didn't really blame most of them for doing so.

Then, one fine spring morning in April, 2014, it arrived: a forwarded package from his publisher containing a letter from Hoffman and a copy of the April-May issue of his newsletter, *Revisionist History*, in which Hoffman had reviewed *Mass Ritual* as the cover story in a piece entitled, "The 9/11 Terror Attacks as Alchemical Process."

Given Kent's level of anticipation as he hurriedly began reading the article, one would've thought it was the lead story in the *New York Times Book Review*. Finally, he jokingly thought to himself, the master acknowledges the apprentice.

Kent was indeed pleased to learn that, not only had Hoffman reviewed his book, he had in general given it high marks. The review began:

> Those who aspire to teach can check the effectiveness of their instruction by determining whether or not anyone has come along to extend or elaborate on what was taught. In the case of our book *Secret Societies and Psychological Warfare* ... we are gratified to see that S.K. Bain, a former staff member of the *Oxford American* magazine and the neoconservative *Weekly Standard* ... has indeed, in many respects, taken our own research to another level.

This brief moment of reward was a much-needed bright spot on an increasingly gloomy horizon. Unfortunately, after all he'd been through, Kent's spirits were sinking, and there wasn't a life preserver in sight.

THE DARK SIDE

Kent wasn't sure, but he thought that he might be suffering from a form of the Stockholm Syndrome, whereby captives begin to identify favorably with their captors.

Even though he was quite certain that he was one of their innumerable faceless victims, after everything he'd learned about his occult oppressors, about their capabilities, their power and prowess, their wicked sense of humor, somewhere, deep down, ashamedly, he felt a sense of awe, of twisted admiration even.

Struggle though he might, he could not suppress the thought: compared to them, are we not all, in fact, as they assert, a bunch of damn useless eaters? As strongly as he rejected this notion, Kent knew the next step in this progression, in this deranged devolvement in one's sense of self-worth, and it was worse than admiration: worship.

Despite all he had suffered at their hands, would he eventually find himself worshipping his oppressors, the oppressors of all humanity? Had they already won? Had he subconsciously given himself over to the Dark Side?

So this is how they maintain their positions of ultimate authority, he thought: even those who dare oppose them sooner or later come to worship at their feet. Are they indeed gods among men?

(Left) Illustration by Gustave Doré in Paradise Lost, *book IX, 179–187: "… he [Satan] held on / His midnight search, where soonest he might finde / The Serpent: him fast sleeping soon he found."*

As he'd studied their evil deeds and immersed himself in the dark subjects necessary to understand their motives and actions, had he unwittingly undergone some black process of transformation, the negredo phase of alchemical transmutation?

In seeking to expose acts of darkness, he had exposed himself to a power he hadn't understood nearly well enough. Had he been led down the path of illumination, only to discover that the light at the end of the tunnel is indeed the Light-Bearer himself?

JESUS HATES ME, THIS I KNOW…

As he slipped further into psycho-spiritual oblivion, Kent found himself trawling the Web late at night, visiting with increasing frequency one forbidden website after another. He knew that he shouldn't be looking at things like that, but he couldn't help himself. He knew that he was consciously corrupting his mind, but he didn't care. Somehow the images fed a deep, unmet need, and as ashamed as he was over it, he didn't *want* to stop.

The stress of everything was getting to him, compounding, multiplying—eroding deep channels into his subconscious, only to reemerge in unexpected ways. He wasn't quite coming unraveled, but he sensed that he needed relief, and his new almost-addiction was the only way he knew how to get it.

In the broader scheme of things, it really wasn't all that bad, he told himself—a few naughty images here and there. For Christ's sake, he thought, he hadn't turned to Satanism, or Luciferianism, and he wasn't beating his kids or gambling away his paycheck. He wasn't purchasing illegal drugs or drinking heavily, visiting strip clubs, so what was the harm in a little guilty pleasure?

He knew all too well what the harm might be, that he might lose control and develop an uncontrollable habit, but he still couldn't seem to stop himself. Kent lived half a block from the church he was baptized in as a child and about the same distance from the small Southern Baptist College where his father had taught in the Bible Division for almost 40 years, but that didn't make any difference. The images were always there, waiting for him, calling him, and he couldn't help but look. It was blasphemy, plain and simple.

No, literally. For reasons known only to himself, Kent had discovered profound relief from the mounting anxieties in his life by viewing online blasphemy—and not just your run-of-the-mill blasphemic imagery, but the good stuff, the high-quality stuff.

Kent had discovered "creative blasphemy as a psychotherapeutic tool," and even ever so briefly contemplated writing a book on the subject. While his deep immersion in occult research hadn't transformed him into a God-hater, it had initiated a process of inner evolution, of spiritual exploration and growth, and whatever else all that meant in terms of personal transformation, it also resulted in his deriving a perhaps above-normal (although not necessarily unhealthy) amount of pleasure from viewing religiously-inappropriate materials.

(Left) Jesus F-Bomb Christ. (Right) "Christ on a cracker."

(Left) Zombie Jesuses (Jesus, the original undead). (Center) Selfie Jesus, from Saturday Night Live. (Right) Barack "The Savior" Hussein Obama.

Blasphemy for kids. (Left) Lego Jesus: Crucifixion Scene. (Right) Mr. Potato Head Jesus.

(Left) Barbie and Baby Jesus. (Right) Ken on the Cross.

More than just pictures: www.jesusdressup.com (Lady Gaga module shown, others include Batman and Star Wars) and www.mohammeddressup.com. From Normal Bob Smith.

Not a parody: After a judge ruled that religious pamphlets could be distributed in the Orange County, Florida school district, the Satanic Temple announced that it would be handing out its own literature: "The Satanic Children's Big Book of Activities." "I am quite certain that all of the children in these Florida schools are already aware of the Christian religion and its Bible," a Temple spokesperson told the press. "And this might be the first exposure these children have to the actual practice of Satanism." He concluded, "We think many students will be very curious to see what we offer."

Kent didn't view it as an expression of ill will toward the Creator, but rather an extreme form of comic relief to counteract the overwhelming pressures of life, which, if kept to oneself and not announced all over the countryside, shouldn't really be considered all that bad in and of itself—especially when compared to the many other problematic behaviors in which he could engage in an attempt to gain relief from the stress of being targeted by global psychopaths.

CHAPTER 57

THE YEAR FROM HELL

K ent was descending into his own personal hell. He wasn't sure how far down he'd go or even where the bottom was.

The year 2013 had been bad, and 2014 wasn't shaping up to be much better. Plus, there was still something nagging him about the Golden Jubilee, a distinct pattern he'd noticed, but not known what to make of it. A certain number had appeared with a statistically-improbable frequency. After all that he'd been through, he simply wanted to quit thinking about it all and chalk it up to coincidence, but he somehow couldn't manage to. The dots were there, staring at him, just waiting for him to connect them…

Play had been suspended at the New Orleans' Blackout Bowl for 34 minutes, and the game had been won with 34 points. Aaron Alexis and Miriam Carey were both 34 years old at the time of their untimely deaths. Cop-killer Mario Edward Garnett had reportedly lived in an apartment in Oklahoma City on NW 34th Street, and died outside the Compass Bank at 34th and Thomas in Phoenix.

Perhaps the December 23rd shooting in Tupelo had been a satanic inversion of the Christmas classic *Miracle on 34th Street*, perhaps not. In any case, the whole thing seemed to Kent to be some kind of puzzle, or maybe something more along the lines of Albrecht Dürer's magic square—the sum of which, no matter how you slice it, is 34—that played a significant role in the 2009 novel *The Lost Symbol* by Dan Brown.

Speaking of whom, Brown's *Inferno*, released in May 2013 and built on clues connected to the first cantica of Dante's three-part *Divine Comedy* with the same name, was the best-selling book of that year, which was quite fitting if you think about it, given "The Train from Hell" in July, the release of *Catching Fire* in November, and the fireworks in West, Texas; Mobile, Alabama; Detroit, Michigan and elsewhere.

In light of that fact, it is certainly of interest that in Dante's classic poem we find Satan trapped in the inner-most Circle of Hell, half-entombed in ice, the account of which is contained in Canto *XXXIV*. Also, if you're interested, a full description of the Ninth Circle of Hell is found in Cantos 31-34, which, by the way, was the final score of Super Bowl 47. (On a related note, for those poor souls trapped in the Superdome after Hurricane Katrina, it was indeed the Ninth Circle of Hell.)

Inferno, 34, the abode of Satan…after all, Kent reflected, it was certainly the year from hell. And, no, it wasn't just chance that Brown's book, the title of which flatly stated the theme of the year, came out in 2013. *We shall set all in motion and in flames.*

No Exceptions

"If it exists, there IS porn of it." (Alternatively, "There is pornography of it. No exceptions.")

Speaking of the number 34, Rule 34 is an 'internet rule' that states that pornography or sexually-explicit material exists for every conceivable subject. (I personally wouldn't recommend performing a Google image search in order to verify this, however.)

Not quite Rule 34 material, but close enough.

PARANORMAL ACTIVITY

WHAT HAPPENS WHEN YOU SLEEP?

3:08:26 A

"One of the SCARIEST AT-HOME VIEWING EXPERIENCES ever!"
– Harry Knowles, AIN'T IT COOL NEWS

CHAPTER 58

LIVING UP TO ITS NAME

K ent began to fear that perhaps he was in more danger than he had dared realize, not simply of the physical sort, but of a far worse and permanent fate. What, indeed, had he gotten himself into?

The truth was, he hadn't been privy to any insider information working at the *Weekly Standard*. In fact, he hadn't paid much attention at all to 9/11 for years after it occurred, and when he had become interested in the subject, he was highly skeptical of the claims of conspiracy.

He had originally launched into a deeper study of the attacks of September 11, 2001, to disprove to his own satisfaction some of the more outlandish claims he'd encountered concerning the incident—and, somehow, several years later, had ironically ended up producing a book detailing what was essentially the Mother of All 9/11 Conspiracy Theories.

He hadn't personally betrayed any neo-conservative cabal, or surreptitiously listened in on any New-Pearl-Harbor planning sessions at the Project for the New American Century, nor did he believe there had been any such sessions.

No, if he, or William, had indeed become a target, as it certainly appeared, it was strictly because of the damn book. It seemed like an open-and-shut case at this point, with the evidence appearing to support the conclusion that he'd attracted more attention than he'd bargained for with *Mass Ritual*, and that he was being warned to back off any further investigation or new book.

MOST UNUSUAL

There was, however, another, previously undisclosed incident which occurred several weeks after William's grand mal seizure, one that again seemed to indicate the use of some sort of electromagnetic weaponry.

Around 9:00 p.m., William and Kent were taking a walk in their neighborhood, engaged in discussion about Will's epileptic condition. As they rounded a corner by the old bank building downtown and headed up Main Street, Kent began to notice a car alarm in the distance.

It was not going off in a normal fashion, but intermittently, and it slowly occurred to him that the closer they got to the vehicle, the greater the frequency of the alarm—until, at last, as they were parallel with the car on the sidewalk across the street from the parking lot in which the automobile sat, the alarm was going off with full intensity, lights flashing and horn blaring. Then he noticed something else peculiar: the flood light on the building behind the vehicle was flashing on and off in unison with the car lights.

Will had noticed the commotion, too, and, especially given that they could no longer hear each other because of the noise, stopped talking. As they stood and stared, Will shouted, "What the hell is all that about?"

"I don't know," his father replied, and, after a few moments they continued on, if for no other reason than to escape the blaring horn and blinding lights. As they moved past that spot, the car alarm began to decrease in frequency, and the flood-light shut off.

They were just rounding the corner of the street their house was on, with the light and racket finally subsiding behind them. Will was about to ask again what had just happened, when the alarm on the vehicle directly beside them went off—again, not at full strength or frequency, and, like before, as they moved away from the vehicle, the alarm dissipated.

Kent was growing understandably concerned, halfway expecting something—hopefully not one or both of *them*—to burst into flames at any moment. Fortunately, they were now directly in front of their home and hurried inside.

SHADOW OF A DOUBT

Upon reflection, Kent had significant difficulty disputing the conclusion that had immediately come to mind regarding the incident: that this was further proof of the deployment of sophisticated electronic equipment against his son.

Not that Kent had much doubt about Will's seizures having been the result of a prior assault with such a device, but there was one fact that prevented him from drawing a definitive conclusion to this effect. The Saturday before William's first seizure on Wednesday, September 11th, he had been inadvertently elbowed in the temple during his jujitsu class.

Although Will had shown no significant sign of injury following the incident, and exhibited no symptoms (other than localized tenderness in the area of the accidental strike) in the days afterward, and though a battery of initial tests following his first seizure had indicated no sign of brain injury, Kent knew that head trauma can cause seizures days, weeks and even months after the injury.

Yes, but the car alarms and flood-light? That was indisputable proof of the use of some sort of electromagnetic gadgetry, right? Well, again, perhaps, but Kent was aware of an alternative explanation, one that was not necessarily any less disconcerting, but perhaps a little easier to live with.

THE COSMOS SPEAKS

It is not uncommon in paranormal literature to find accounts involving adolescents in which they by all appearances are subconsciously-psychically manipulating objects in their environment. This often happens during periods of turmoil, and episodes appear to be brought on by the heightened emotional state of the teenager. (There is a difference between this phenomenon and those cases in which an adolescent somehow triggers the manifestation of, or induces an increase in the activity of, a poltergeist.)

On their walk that evening, William had been expressing concerns brought about by having had a brush with death, expressing understandable fears, asking ultimate questions. Kent had done his best to provide some meaningful insights; not conclusive answers necessarily, but perspectives that would put his son's mind at ease.

William was not wailing or bitchin' and moanin', but he was in metaphysical distress, a youth experiencing existential angst, and Kent wished he could find some way to ease his pain. The longer they walked and talked, the more intense William's distress became, despite (or perhaps because of) what little eternal wisdom Kent had managed to scratch together to share with him.

It had been at that very point in their conversation that the progressively intense light-and-sound show had commenced, and, Kent noted, as they got closer to its source, the more intense it had become. Had this been the cosmos' way of responding to Will's need, or hisWilliam's 'higher self' reaching out to its suffering earth-bound fragment, or, perhaps, God speaking to him through mysterious means?

Those sure seemed more palatable explanations to Kent than the thought of their having been harassed by some jackasses in an unmarked van using some kind of wave-gun to set off car alarms and security lights, but the truth was that there was no way to know for sure.

Postscript: The day after this chapter was completed, Kent was standing at his toilet early that morning, having just gotten out of bed, when, POW!, he was showered with glass and the bathroom went completely dark (the door was shut and there were no windows). The 100-watt light bulb in the ceiling fixture had blown out, exploded. There had been no power surge and nothing else in the house was affected. He'd had no previous problems with that light fixture in the past. This was exactly one week prior to September 11, 2014, and Kent decided then and there that he was going to

Closing with an Introduction

Kent had, some time in 2013, drafted an introduction for *Funhouse U.S.A.*, and, with the project officially dead, the material—which is as relevant as ever—somehow seems a fitting bit of material to include as we conclude our journey:

You believe that the government works for us. You trust what you hear on the nightly news and read in the newspapers. You watch the news stories about one tragedy after another and accept the official explanations. The idea of looking for deeper connections in national and world events doesn't even cross your mind. You're too sophisticated, too intelligent for conspiracy theories.

You are the government's dream: you pay your taxes and ask no questions. You have been raised in a system that discourages individual thought, demands compliance, breeds conformity and generates complacency. You are exactly what they have sought to create through their decades-long comprehensive social engineering: another one of the cattle.

Don't think, don't ask, if you see something, say something—cattle that tattle, bitches'n'snitches. You'll be genuinely surprised when you find yourself at the end of the chute, next in line for the bullet in the head. Sweet dreams…the American dream has become a nightmare.

I can show you the evidence, and you will refuse to believe it. Most Americans are complacent in their captivity—they don't know they're in bondage, and thus have no thought of resistance––exactly as planned.

I'll show you the deeper scripted events, the connections, the machinations. You can still choose to see the world according to the nightly news reports and ignore the ever-more-abundant evidence that things are not as they seem, as we're told they are.

[continued] If you don't want to see the monsters, just don't look under the bed—but your fear of looking doesn't mean they're not there.

You're an adult. You're too serious, too mature for this kind of nonsense. You have bills to pay. You have Facebook requests to respond to, Tweets to read. *American Idol* is on tonight, and you have two NFL games Tivo'd. You're too smart to be manipulated.

You, a socially-programmed autobot? Never. A rat in a maze? Never. You, lorded over by elitist techno-fascist psychopaths who've created a full-spectrum-dominance scientific cattle-control grid you can't even recognize even though you're stuck in it with tens of millions of your fellow consumers? Complete nonsense.

Conspiracy theories? They are such an affront to your intellect as to be patently offensive—not worth your time to even consider. Never mind that many of them make more sense of this mad existence than the accepted models of the way the world works and official versions of history.

You're just too damn smart, too damn attractive, too damn well-educated to be duped. That you could be controlled like a wind-up toy and manipulated by methods visible to the naked eye and in plain sight—impossible, and more impossible still, the notion that unseen oppressors mock you to your faces while leading you around by your pretty little noses.

That's *pure fantasy*. You're too sophisticated for that. End of story.

Thus, you never even bother to look for the curtain, much less to pull it back and see what's on the other side. Oh, they're there, all right, pulling the levers and making the grand pronouncements you accept as fact. But they're invisible—to you—because you don't believe they exist. Hell, they don't even *need* the curtain, and frequently step out from behind it, because they can stand before you in broad daylight in all of their hideous, cruel glory and you won't even see them.

You're a citizen of the twenty-first century. Your iPhone is your charm against superstitious nonsense. Occult masters who rule the world? What a joke.

And you, my friend, are their perfect creation. A being of such arrogance and self-assuredness that you simply cannot fathom that you might not be at the top of the food chain. The perfect prey, bred with cruel scientific precision over centuries.

You live in the Land of Oz, the Matrix, Wonderland. You're not simply a flesh-and-blood commodity, to be manipulated and exploited, you are a contestant in the Hunger Games. The world is their Coliseum, and you are the entertainment.

Gladiators. Lions. That's child's play. Try mass school shootings, bombings, industrial sabotage, mind-controlled assassins playing their roles in wildly dark comedic scripts, scripts under development for years, if not decades. There are no traps doors, no props. The real world is their stage.

You live in a world they've created for you, lit by the bright lights of television cameras, HDTVs and electronic billboards. You can ignore the shadows, and those lurking in them. It's safe in the light…isn't it?

Your world is illusion. The predators' eyes are adapted to the dark. You don't see them, but they see you, scurrying around in the light of the campfire, thinking it will keep you safe. Your false sense of security serves its purpose, keeps the livestock rounded up and calm…and supremely vulnerable.

In truth, you are in such jeopardy, you can't fathom it. You are helpless, yet you believe yourself invincible. Your oppressors place no value on individual human life—except as sacrifices. You are objects of exploitation, and ridicule. To them, you are another species altogether: *homo sapiens inferioris*.

Good show, old boy, you might be thinking, nice Introduction, way to pull us in and get our attention.

Friend, I'm not exaggerating for effect—I know what's in the chapters ahead. I'm not trying to lure you in, I'm trying to prepare you. We'll all in deep trouble, and the sooner we realize it, the better.

Amen, brother. Amen.

dig a hole and hide in it on the day of the 9/11 anniversary the following week.,

That's It

Too much had happened; there were too many unanswered and unanswerable questions, too many disturbing possibilities; too much was at stake. There would be no second book, Kent decided once and for all. *Funhouse U.S.A.: Carnival of Terror* was stillborn.

No matter how hard he tried, Kent simply couldn't escape the growing suspicion that, purely though his own doing, he and Will had been targeted as contestants in the *real* Hunger Games. And although the title of his first book had essentially (but not entirely) been a sales hook, the book itself had indeed proven to be, at least for him and his son, The Most Dangerous Book in the World.

THE FUTURE'S SO BRIGHT ...

O f course, the game is *never* over...
CNN's Richard Quest with Fariq Abdul Hamid (below), the co-pilot of doomed Malaysian Air- lines Flight 370, just weeks before the aircraft's tragic disappearance. The missing plane was the 404th Boeing 777 produced, which is quite interesting considering that error message 404 is one of the most widely-encountered and recognizable errors confronted by internet us- ers worldwide: "404 Not Found."

404 File Not found

It's all a conspiracy.
We're hiding everything from you...
or maybe the file doesn't actually exist.
hmmm....

Incidentally, in 2008 Quest was busted in New York's Central Park at 3:40 a.m. with illegal drugs in his pocket, a rope around his neck that was for whatever reason tied to his genitals, and a sex toy in his  boot. Quest would have been merely escorted out of the park for being there after hours had he not volunteered to police, "I have meth in my pocket." 404-Brain not found.

Say, Richard, whatcha doin' with your tie there in the photo with Fariq? Wouldn't have anything to do with the old Masonic cable tow, now, would it? (A rope around his neck …)

Then of course there's this (Katy Perry's Satanic "Dark Horse" 2014 Grammy performance).

Preparation in Entered Apprentice Degree.

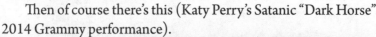

And this.

And this, this and this.

And this.

And this.

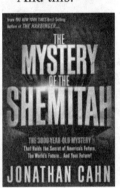

And this.

Not to mention this.

But that's a story for another time.

In Memoriam

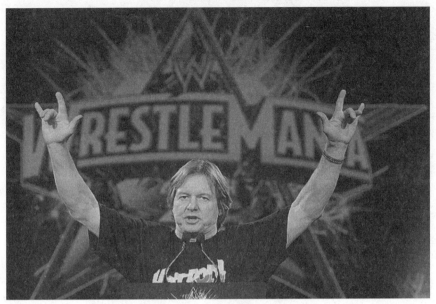

Roderick George "Roddy" Toombs
(April 17, 1954 – July 31, 2015)

"Rowdy" Roddy Piper

R.I.P., brother...